PERGAMON INTERNATIONAL LIBRARY
of Science, Technology, Engineering and Social Studies

The 1000-volume original paperback library in aid of education,
industrial training and the enjoyment of leisure

Publisher: Robert Maxwell, M.C.

Educating For Peace

THE ATHENE SERIES
An International Collection of Feminist Books
General Editors: Gloria Bowles and Renate Duelli-Klein
Consulting Editor: Dale Spender

The ATHENE SERIES assumes that all those who are concerned with for-
mulating explanations of the way the world works need to know and appreciate
the significance of basic feminist principles.

The growth of feminist research has challenged almost all aspects of social
organization in our culture. The ATHENE SERIES focuses on the construction
of knowledge and the exclusion of women from the process — both as theorists
and subjects of study—and offers innovative studies that challenge established
theories and research.

ON ATHENE — When Metis, goddess of wisdom who presided over all
knowledge was pregnant with ATHENE, she was swallowed up by Zeus who
then gave birth to ATHENE from his head. The original ATHENE is thus the
parthenogenetic daughter of a strong mother and as the feminist myth goes, at
the "third birth" of ATHENE she stops being Zeus' obedient mouthpiece and
returns to her real source: the science and wisdom of womankind

Volumes in the Series

MEN'S STUDIES MODIFIED The Impact of Feminism
on the Academic Disciplines
edited by Dale Spender

MACHINA EX DEA Feminist Perspectives on Technology
edited by Joan Rothschild

WOMEN'S NATURE Rationalizations of Inequality
edited by Marian Lowe and Ruth Hubbard

SCIENCE AND GENDER A Critique of Biology and Its Theories on Women
Ruth Bleier

WOMAN IN THE MUSLIM UNCONSCIOUS
Fatna A. Sabbah

MEN'S IDEAS/WOMEN'S REALITIES *Popular Science,* 1870-1915
edited by Louise Michele Newman

BLACK FEMINIST CRITICISM Perspectives on Black Women Writers
Barbara Christian

THE SISTER BOND A Feminist View of a Timeless Connection
edited by Toni A.H. McNaron

EDUCATING FOR PEACE A Feminist Perspective
Birgit Brock-Utne

NOTICE TO READERS

May we suggest that your library places a standing/continuation order to receive
all future volumes in the Athene Series immediately on publication?
Your order can be cancelled at any time.

Also of Interest
WOMEN'S STUDIES INTERNATIONAL FORUM*
Editor: Dale Spender
*Free sample copy available on request

Educating For Peace

A Feminist Perspective

Birgit Brock-Utne
University of Oslo

Pergamon Press

New York • Oxford • Toronto • Sydney • Paris • Frankfurt

Pergamon Press Offices:

U.S.A.	Pergamon Press Inc., Maxwell House, Fairview Park, Elmsford, New York 10523, U.S.A.
U.K.	Pergamon Press Ltd., Headington Hill Hall, Oxford OX3 0BW, England
CANADA	Pergamon Press Canada Ltd., Suite 104, 150 Consumers Road, Willowdale, Ontario M2J 1P9, Canada
AUSTRALIA	Pergamon Press (Aust.) Pty. Ltd., P.O. Box 544, Potts Point, NSW 2011, Australia
FRANCE	Pergamon Press SARL, 24 rue des Ecoles, 75240 Paris, Cedex 05, France
FEDERAL REPUBLIC OF GERMANY	Pergamon Press GmbH, Hammerweg 6, D-6242 Kronberg-Taunus, Federal Republic of Germany

Library of Congress Cataloging in Publication Data

Brock-Utne, Birgit, 1938-
    Educating for peace.

    (The Athene series)
    Bibliography: p.
    Includes index.
    1. Women and peace. 2. Peace--Study and teaching.
I. Title. II. Series.
JX1965.B76   1985   327.1′72′088042   84-26523
ISBN 0-08-032370-7
ISBN 0-08-032369-3 (pbk.)

Printed in Great Britain by A. Wheaton & Co. Ltd., Exeter

This book is dedicated to:

- my eldest son, Karsten Brock-Utne (21), who is demonstrating his reverence for life by refusing to do military service.
- my daughter, Siri Gaarder Brock-Utne (16), the young Socialist and Peace Activist.
- my youngest son, Gunnar Garbo Brock-Utne (7), who states that "if everybody gives talks about peace, we shall have no war."
- my lover, life companion, and husband, Gunnar Garbo, who shows me daily that it is possible to have an equal partnership with a man, to share power, responsibility, and love.

This dedication was written on the 14th of June, 1983. Two months later, on the 20th of August, Karsten was killed in a car accident. The book is written in his memory. It is also dedicated to:

- my stepdaughter, Tora Garbo, who helped me during difficult days.
- Karsten's good, good friends, Frank Rognsaa, Dag Olav Jensen, Bjørn Haugan, Otto Bjarte Johnsen, Guttorm Johnsen and Halvor Losnedahl, who have written to me, visited me, called me and comforted me in every possible way.

The biological imperative alone is not enough to defeat militarism. Rather than assuming that women as women will end war, I suggest that it is the relationship between feminism and disarmament that provides hope for change. I would like to propose in this paper that contemporary feminism, whose ideology includes the replacing of aggression, authoritarianism, discrimination with reason, democracy, tolerance and an acceptance of all possibilities in life for women and men provides the best starting point for a popular and effective disarmament movement.

Senator Susan Ryan,
Australian Minister for Education
July, 1982

Contents

Introduction

This book began as a 50-page paper that I was asked to write for a UNESCO conference while I was working at the International Peace Research Institute of Oslo. The topic was: the role of women as mothers and members of society in the education of the young for peace, mutual understanding, and the respect for human rights. It was to be presented at a UNESCO conference about the role of women in peace education held in New Delhi in December 1981.

My knowledge base for writing such a paper was the study of education, psychology, sociology, feminist research, and peace studies. I began my research by going through literature on mothers, on the education mothers give, and on literature about aggression and violence. I discovered, first of all, that one could not treat "the young" as one big sexless group. There were vast differences in the socialization of girls and boys, in the way they were treated by their mothers and also by their fathers. It became clear that fathers had a greater responsibility for making boys into "real" men than mothers had. They were even more instrumental than mothers in making girls into "real" women. It thus seemed rather unjust to blame the mothers for the socialization patterns. It was not difficult to see that girls were becoming much more educated than boys for peace. But training girls in the values of caring, sharing, and love for humankind does not help the world very much as long as girls and women remain universally oppressed. So I decided that the oppression of women would naturally have to be an essential part of my paper.

However, the resulting feminist approach, which in my view was the only possible scholarly approach to write the commissioned paper, did not meet with approval from the male researchers present when the paper was discussed in a meeting at the Institute. For me this discussion was a good and sobering illustration of the necessity of bringing feminist perspectives to peace research and also of the difficulties faced by feminists who try to do so. It is all too obvious that our perspective will not be welcomed with enthusiasm. We shall have to fight our way.

I want to thank four women who were present at that meeting. They are: Cheryl Payer, Margaret Chapman, Julianne Traylor (all from the U.S.) and Kari Fasting from Norway.

I also want to thank the Norwegian researcher Brita Brantzæg and the Indian researcher Govind Kelkar for reading the paper and giving me valuable

ix

comments on it before I left for India. Govind read the paper in Norway and asked me to conduct a seminar on it at the Women's Center for Development Studies in New Delhi when I was there for the conference. I thank her for distributing the paper, for her warm hospitality and for arranging an extremely interesting seminar at the Center.

The UNESCO conference itself was a disappointment. All the more controversial bits of my paper had been deleted—about Marx, Reagan, Lyndon B. Johnson—supposedly because they might offend someone. (They are back in this book!) I was introduced as a "militant feminist"—one that had to be watched out for! And the paper was officially discussed as little as possible. But it was discussed unofficially a great deal in the evening. And some women at the conference gave me great encouragement and urged me to make it available to a wider audience. I especially want to thank Fulada Stanakovitch from Yugoslavia, Carole Hahn from the United States, Helena Kekkonen from Finland, and last but not least my good, good friend Iftikar Hassan from Pakistan. We met again in London in the summer of 1982 and continued our discussions on women and violence.

Back in Norway I was extremely happy that the Norwegian National Commission to UNESCO found the paper so interesting that they arranged a one-day seminar on it. Professionals well trained in feminist research, history, social and political science, as well as education and psychology contributed to a stimulating discussion. I especially want to thank Torild Skard, the chairwoman of the UNESCO commission in Norway, and Sissel Volan, the head of the School section of the United Nations Agency in Norway, for having arranged the seminar and for their valuable comments. They urged me to expand the paper and also to translate it into Norwegian.

But the comments that came from Renate Duelli Klein in London and from the Australian feminist researcher, my good, good friend Dale Spender, were the ones that made me decide that the paper deserved an expansion and a wider distribution. Dale asked me to expand it into a book. I did not find this difficult, since so much had been going on in women's peace movements lately, and I had got new information and collected more literature. But it was difficult to find the time. In the summer of 1982 when I had got the encouragement and felt compelled to start expanding the paper, I was back at the Institute for Educational Research at the University of Oslo, acting as the Administrative Head of the Section for Social Education and the Deputy Director of the Institute. Such jobs do not give time for writing books, especially when one also gives talks for Women for Peace, No to Nuclear Arms, and participates in peace marches, council meetings, and serves on a county committee on defense and security questions within the Labor Party. So I was not able to start on the book before my Christmas holiday 1982/1983, spent on the Canary islands, when I was greatly assisted by my daily companion, Gunnar Garbo. I thank him for taking care of the children and thus making it possible for me to write. I also appreciate his many valuable comments on the book as it has been proceeding.

One other inspiration to expand part of the India paper was given me by the German peace activist Christa Randzio-Plath, who visited the International Peace Research Institute together with a group of women from the women's section of the Socialist International while I was at the Institute. She was editing a book on women and peace and asked me to expand parts of my India paper and make it into a chapter for her book. So I did. My chapter was called: "Gewaltfrei denken. Zur Rolle der Frauen in der Friedensforschung" (Non-violent thinking. On the role of women in peace research) published in Christa Randzio-Plath's *Was geht uns Frauen der Krieg an*? (How does war concern women?). I thank my mother, Gertrud Brock-Utne, for the German translation. And I thank Christa for the inspiration to expand the point on women and peace research in my original paper.

I also want to extend my thanks to some of the members of the women's network group within the International Peace Research Association. We first met at the IPRA meeting in Toronto, Canada, in June 1981; then some of us met again in New York in the summer of 1982 and in Gyor, Hungary in August 1983. I especially want to thank Corinne Kumar d'Souza from India, Celina García from Costa Rica, and Robin Burns from Australia, who also visited me a couple of times in Norway while she was working in Sweden. It is good to meet feminists around the world whose thinking is so alike. Last but not least from this network, I must mention the feminist peace activist and researcher Betty Reardon from the United States. Her writings and our exchange of ideas have been a great source of inspiration for this work. Two men who have been helping the network gain money and approval should also be named. One of them is Robert Aspeslagh from the Netherlands, the chairman of the Peace Education Commission of the International Peace Research Association; the other is Stephen Marks from the United States, who was working for UNESCO in Paris. I believe that we do need men to back us up, as long as they are doing it on our terms.

The staff of the International Peace Research Institute of Oslo also supported us morally and financially by granting the women's group money to hold a seminar on women and militarism in November 1982. That seminar also served as a great inspiration for me as I worked on the extension of the original paper into a book. I especially want to thank Ellen Elster, Ingrid Eide, Helga Stene, and Beth Romstad for valuable contributions.

One other good friend who has been especially stimulating to exchange ideas with about the topic of the book must be mentioned in this list of thanks and acknowledgments. It is the social psychologist and great peace activist and feminist Berit Ås, whom I would like to thank for giving comments on the paper, for our many discussions, exchange of papers, and her great encouragement to feminists. I have also felt sympathy and encouragement for my work on peace education from my friend and close colleague Eva Nordland, one of the most active women in the Norwegian Women for Peace. My thanks also go to the many Women for Peace groups in Norway that I have had the pleasure to meet and talk with during the last couple of years. A special thanks to the group in Tromsø with the wonderful Margot Lorentsen, the seventy-year old socialist, feminist, and great peace activist, who has visited the Soviet Union more than twenty times. A special thanks also to the Sandefjord group with Tulle Elster and all her inventive ideas for spreading the gospel of peace. And thanks to the Drammen group and the Sarpsborg group, who made beautiful bags with the peace dove holding the feminist symbol which they sold to get money for the Peace March to Moscow. Keep on working, Women for Peace. You are so good at it.

Another group I want to thank for their inspiration is the Finnish Women for Peace, who liked the India paper so much that they translated it into Finnish, furnished it with some beautiful drawings, and published it as a nice book to be sold by the Women for Peace groups in Finland. I did not know about this until the book was produced, and I was asked to come to Finland in the beginning of December 1982 for a press conference. I was so happy that they found the paper worthwhile to translate. The press conference, the meeting with the Finnish Women for Peace, and the responses to my lectures at the University of Helsinki and at the Swedish Workers' Institute were all inspiration to continue to write. We need to know more about women's actions for peace, they said. Do go on writing. Of these women I must thank Tatjana Sundgren for the arrangements and my good friend Helena Allahwerdi for her hospitality and valuable comments on the paper and on the direction of the expansion of it.

But on August 20, 1983 my beloved son, Karsten, was killed in a car accident in the Canary Islands. For 21 and a half years Karsten had been my closest friend. One of my girlfriends wrote me: "I often had the feeling that he was your ideal of a man." Yes, he was. I had created him myself, borne him, fed him from my body, had him in my bed till he was quite grown up. We had been alone when I divorced his father. He had taken my name when I took it back. He had been with me on political campaigns, in marches, heard me give peace talks many times. He was a pacifist. I was so proud of him. Nothing worse could have happened to me than to lose him. At first I did not want to live any more. He, whom I had created, who could have been a living example of a good peace education, was dead. I had invested so much love, time, energy in him. Now it was all wasted. When I described him in the speech I gave at his funeral, one of my good friends, a feminist and peace activist, said to me afterwards: "What a loss for the world, for the work for a new and peaceful society where women are liberated. There are so many fine women and so few fine men. We would have needed him in our fight for a changed society." Certainly, we would have needed him. The question was: Would I be able to live without him, to go on working for peace and the liberation of women without having him at my side? "You must work even harder now," said my good husband, Gunnar. "You must work for him too now." But I felt empty, numb.

In the time between the day he was killed and the funeral I went to Hungary with my daughter Siri. There I led a meeting of the women's network group within the International Peace Research Association. I led the meetings very well, they told me. And I gave a paper on the relationship of feminism to peace and peace education. I don't remember much of the meeting, except that Siri and I shared the same room and that I cried all night and she had nightmares in which she experienced the car accident that had killed Karsten. And I remember the warmth and sympathy from all the 25 women researchers present. They cried with me between meetings and went with Siri and me to the hot springs of Gyor. My thoughts go to Judit Balazs from Hungary who put beautiful flowers in Siri's and my room. They go to Carolyn Stephenson from the United States who had lost a son herself and knew what I was going through. They go to my good friends Govind Kelkar and Corinne Kumar d'Souza, both from India, who shared my grief and to Hilkka Pietilä from Finland, who also cried with me. Last, but not least, I must mention my good friends Ines Vargas from Chile, Julianne Traylor from the United States, and Solveig Aas and Vigdis Mathiesen, both from Norway, who convinced me that it was right for me to go to the conference despite the desperate state I was in. And they were right. These wonderful women helped me as best they could. They encouraged me to go on working and gave me valuable ideas for the UN paper. Though I do not remember much from the conference, I took notes and I got some fine papers that I have been able to use in this book.

It was difficult to go on working with the UN paper after the funeral. I wrote some pages, cried for an hour, and wrote some more. But I liked working on the paper, and I was fairly satisfied with the end result. But the organizers of the Vienna conference were not satisfied. They could not see that rapes and personal violence against women were one form of breaking the peace. They did not see that the oppression of women had to be a central theme in an essay on women and peace. In short, they found my paper too feminist. They also did not like my broad definition of peace, though I could afterwards show them that it was the same definition used in UN and UNESCO documents.

Right after, however, I got an enthusiastic letter from Renate Duelli Klein from the Athene Series of Pergamon Press. She had read that same Vienna paper and liked it. Would it not be a good idea to use thoughts from that paper as a base and start writing a book on women and peace from a feminist perspective? I could use part of what I had already written in my previous manuscript and add my new insights. She also gave quite concrete advice on how to do this. Even though I felt tired and was on the point of giving up on the whole theme as a topic for a book, her letter was such a great encouragement that I started anew in the late fall 1983. So without Renate's good advice, there would not have been a book. Renate also commented on my chapters as I proceeded, as did Nigel Young from Bradford School of Peace Studies. My various drafts of the manuscript and the final version have been neatly typed and retyped by Betty Nicolaisen, Edel Sandbugt and Ine Vangsal, at the Institute for Educational Research at the University of Oslo where I work, and I would like to thank them.

I have been able to get feedback on the ideas for the manuscript from the many women's peace groups I have lectured to and met with in Norway, Sweden, and Finland. Two invitations I had to Swedish peace activities in Umeå in September 1983 and March 1984 while I was working on the book meant much to me personally and for the progress of the book. I lectured at the seminar in women's studies at the University of Umeå, at the Institute for Educational Research at the University, at a high school, to the Women for Peace, and to the physicians against nuclear arms. I especially want to thank Ingegerd Lundström from the women's studies group and her husband, Bo Lundström from the physicians against nuclear weapons, for their hospitality. The women from the Swedish Women for Peace seminar in Lövånger were wonderful. Thanks to them all, especially Katty Alatalo. They decided to apply for money to get this book translated into Swedish.

I also want to extend my thanks to the Norwegian psychologist Hanne Haavind, who gave me some recent and valuable articles on parent-child interactions when I was working at a rewriting of Chapter 3. My thanks also go to the sociologist Runa Haukaa, who gave me valuable information on the connection between the feminist movement and feminist research in Norway.

After the final draft of the book I had to re-do some of the calculations used after valuable criticism from mathematician Bjørn Kirkerud. Thank you for that much needed help.

I would also like to thank Pergamon Press for valuable assistance and cooperation.

It is my hope that this book will be used as a textbook both in courses in women's studies and in peace studies and that it will become a basic text for seminars around the world. I hope it will be used both in universities and in peace groups, especially for women in peace groups and that it will be read widely and internationally and provoke actions. Above all, I hope that it will contribute to the making of a more peaceful future.

1 What is Peace?

How we define peace influences what we have to say about it. Peace may simply mean the absence of war, of direct, impersonal, often collective violence. It may describe the relationship *between* states and not the internal conditions of particular states. But a broad definition of peace encompasses far more than the concept of an absence of direct confrontation between states: It includes such factors as the distribution of wealth within states.

When dealing with the concept of violence, peace researchers generally make a distinction between direct violence (such as war) and indirect or structural violence. To put it quite simply, while both forms of violence can kill, indirect violence takes longer than direct violence. *Indirect violence* is the term often used to describe the relationship between industrialized countries and the developing countries: It is also a term that can be used to describe the state within a specific country where society is structured so that a few people make big profits from the work of many, who are exploited to the point of starvation. When it comes to individuals or countries, existing structures ensure that the rich get richer and the poor get poorer. This is a form of violence. But not all violence within a particular country is of the indirect kind: There is direct violence in many so-called peaceful countries. Battered women and children are the victims of direct violence and are found in peaceful nations.

So how do we define peace? To me, a fruitful definition of peace has to include both the absence of direct violence and the absence of indirect or structural violence. Yet this is a rather negative way to define peace, and several peace researchers and peace educators have attempted to arrive at more positive definitions of the term. Garcia (1981) holds that one of the most attractive definitions of peace and peace education for a broader and more realistic scope is the following one given by Mario Borelli:

> By *peace* we mean the results in any given society of equality of rights, by which every member of that society participates equally in decisional power which regulates it, and the distribution of the resources which sustain it. (Garcia, 1981, p. 165)

Looking at the first part of this definition, I see great potential in Borelli's positive peace concept. It inspires endless action, a constant search and research of the past, the present, and the future; a continuous questioning of values. But the concept still leaves something out. It may define a society in which there is no indirect or structural violence, but what about direct violence, acts of aggression, and war? A peaceful society where equality of rights persists could be invaded by an enemy. An otherwise egalitarian society could still use violence to resolve internal conflicts. (The rather brutal yet rather egalitarian society of ancient Sparta is a case in point.) Therefore I should like to add the concept of nonviolence to Borelli's definition:

> By *peace* we mean the absence of violence in any given society, both internal and external, direct and indirect. We further mean the nonviolent results of equality of rights, by which every member of that society, through nonviolent means, participates equally in decisional power which regulates it, and the distribution of the resources which sustain it.

This definition corresponds well with definitions of peace agreed upon in the United Nations system, in resolutions from the United Nations and UNESCO. UNESCO's Medium-Term Plan for 1977–1982, agreed upon by all member nations, states:

> . . . . No international settlement secured at the cost of the freedom and dignity of peoples and respect for individuals can claim to be a truly peaceful settlement, either in its spirit or in terms of its durability. In the resolutions which it has adopted respecting this problem, particularly those adopted at its most recent sessions, the General Conference has associated the struggle for peace with a condemnation of all forms of oppression, discrimination and exploitation of one nation by another, not only because they inevitably generate violence but also because they themselves constitute a form of violence and partake of the spirit of war. (*Thinking Ahead*, UNESCO, 1977, p. 62)

In the same UNESCO publication we read that the General Conference "condemns all violations of human rights as a threat and contrary to its very spirit." The struggle for peace and action to promote human rights are recognized as being inseparable: their linking together in the same program "constitutes a coherent conceptual framework." UNESCO stresses that the *past three decades* have seen a notable change in the way in which the problem of peace is conceived (*Thinking Ahead*, 1977, p. 62). This change has occurred as a result of the growing awareness of the factors involved. There is little doubt that peace researchers have contributed toward improving the understanding of the peace concept and broadening its scope.

The more up-to-date definitions of peace within the UN system do not define peace only as the absence of war and violence, but as the presence of justice. Peace is defined in more positive terms. This view was well expressed at the General Conference of UNESCO at its eighteenth session (Resolution

11.1): "Peace cannot consist solely in the absence of armed conflict but implies principally a process of progress, justice and mutual respect among the peoples designed to secure the building of an international society in which everyone can find his true place and enjoy his share of the world's intellectual and material resources."

The same broadened view can be found in the Declaration on the Preparation of Societies for Life in Peace adopted by the United Nations General Assembly at its thirty-third session, in the autumn of 1978 (Resolution 33/73). The resolution was put forward by Poland on behalf of several East European and nonaligned countries. The General Assembly adopted the resolution with 138 votes in favor, none against, and 2 abstentions. The declaration states as its first principle that "every nation and every human being, regardless of race, conscience, language or sex has the inherent right to a life in peace."

Chapter 12 of UNESCO's Second Medium-Term Plan (1984–1989) adopted at the General Conference in Paris in 1982 states:

> There can be no genuine peace when the most elementary human rights are violated, or while situations of injustice continue to exist; conversely, human rights for all cannot take root and achieve full growth while latent or open conflicts are rife. This is the principle which is basic to UNESCO's action and which has been confirmed and illustrated by a great many studies and exchanges of views. (Second Medium-Term Plan, 1984–1989, 4 XC/4 Approved, Unesco 1983, p. 259)

The plan goes on to state:

> Peace is incompatible with malnutrition, extreme poverty and the refusal of the rights of peoples to self-determination. Disregard for the rights of individuals and peoples, the persistence of inequitable international economic structures, interference in the internal affairs of other states, foreign occupation and apartheid are always real or potential sources of armed conflict and international crisis. The only lasting peace is a just peace based on respect for human rights. Furthermore, a just peace calls for the establishment of an equitable international order which will preserve future generations from the scourge of war.

When the concept of peace implies that every human being regardless of sex has the right to a life in peace (the UN declaration of 1978) and peace is defined as justice, the right to fulfillment of basic needs, to self-determination, most feminist research can be called research on women and peace.

Such feminist research may include time studies showing the longer average working hours per day of women as well as statistics on the income distribution of women and men. Analysis of prostitution, rape, and battered women also belong under the same heading as do reports on the health conditions of women as a result of indirect violence. Since most feminist research has focused on unveiling the exploitation and oppression of women all over the world, this research is highly relevant to any analysis of research on women and peace. Researchers, most of them men, for instance, have looked into the relationship between disarmament and development, between unemployment and the accelerating arms race: They have found (contrary to conventional wisdom) that disarmament would create more job opportunities while rearmament makes for unemployment. But feminist researchers have taken this one step further: They have looked at which sex loses most jobs. I shall come back to this point.

WOMEN AS VICTIMS OF STRUCTURAL VIOLENCE

Mortality

The single most basic element of good health for most people is an *adequate diet*. Considerable evidence shows that women and girls feel the pinch of food scarcity earlier and more frequently than their husbands and brothers (Carloni, 1981). Where difficult choices have to be made about which child to feed, a boy is more likely to be fed than a girl. Field studies by the Indian Council of Medical Research showed that in 1971 girls outnumbered boys four to three among children with kwashiorkor, a disease of severe malnutrition (Newland, 1979). Even more discouraging was the subsequent observation that among children who were hospitalized for kwashiorkor, there were more boys than girls. Though girls were more likely to be suffering from the disease, boys were more likely to be taken to the hospital for treatment.

Giele and Smock (1977) report a mortality rate in Bangladesh for girls under age five that is 30 to 50 percent higher than that for boys in the same age group. The same researchers attributed higher death rates among girls admitted to a large university hospital in Africa to the girls' inferior nutritional state. More girls than boys died from routine infectious diseases like measles, which seldom kills unless a child is weakened by malnutrition.

Sex Ratio

All over the world, more boys are born than girls. But in the developed countries, so many more baby boys than baby girls die that the life expectancy at birth is higher among females. This is not so in the developing countries. In India, for instance, the male population grew at a faster rate than the female population from 1901 through 1974. According to official estimates, quoted in the *Report of the Committee on the Status of Women in India* (1974), the total population of India in 1974 was 301 million males and 280 million females. There were 21 million fewer females. Statistics in this report show that the gap in life expectancy between men and women has just been widened, in this century up to 1974 to the detriment of women. But according to the 1981 census, there were 354 million males and 331 million females, a difference of 23 million. This means that the percentage of females in the

Indian population was 51.9 in 1974 and 51.7 in 1981. There now is a slight tendency towards a reduction of the gap between the life expectancies of men and women.

The Committee on the Status of Women in India, which delivered its extensive report in 1974, claims here that the decline in sex ratio ever since 1901 is a disturbing phenomenon in the status of women (p. 11). Demographers suggest various hypotheses to explain this. Among these are: the higher mortality rate of females, the marked cultural preference for sons and the consequent neglect of female infants, the lower status of women and the general neglect of women at all ages, the adverse impact of frequent and excessive childbearing on the health of women, and the higher incidence of certain diseases in women. But the explanation that seems to have received general acceptance is that due to improvement of health services in the last few decades, the reduction in mortality has been greater for males than for females. The differential improvement in health conditions must have contributed to the decline in sex ratio.

As can be seen in Table 1.1 there are more males than females in all groups in India except the age group 20-29 years. It is worth noting that even in 1891, the census reported 1,071 females per 1,000 males in the age group 20-24. Though the phenomenon of excess females over males in the age group 20-24 has persisted, the number of females in this group declined to 1,008 in 1971. It seems strange that one has this excess of females in this age group. Several explanations for this phenomenon can be found. Neglect of female infants and later dowry deaths are explanations. But I think we also have to consider the possibility that girls and mature women count very little and have become invisible in the statistics.

These studies show that demographic data, provided they are split on sex, can give valuable information on the conditions of women. But in such research and in census taking, the original questionnaires are mostly made up by men and reveal male-dominant thinking.

Head of Household

According to the census, a woman is counted as the head of the household only when she is not permanently living with a male breadwinner. A woman may become head of household as a result of four causes: death of the husband, divorce or abandonment, migration of men or women in disproportionate numbers, or childbearing outside of any stable union with a man. Though these phenomena have multiple causes, they yield a uniform result: poverty. These households are the poorest of families.

In families where both male and female are breadwinners there may be some disagreement between the spouses as to who is the head of family. Willis (1978) reports that when surveying Soviet families in 1976, the Soviet sociologist

Table 1.1. Sex ratio by age groups, India, 1971*
Females per 1,000 males

Age groups	Total	Rural	Urban
All ages	931	951	857
0-4	969	972	953
5-9	935	935	931
10-14	887	885	895
15-19	883	896	839
20-24	1,008	1,074	830
25-29	1,027	1,078	863
30-34	990	1,045	811
35-39	916	949	802
40-44	882	922	737
45-49	839	876	705
50-54	848	868	761
55-59	867	882	801
60-64	923	926	908
65-69	916	921	895
70-	961	957	978
Age not stated	1,050	1,068	972

*Figures are provisional, estimated from 1 percent sample data.

E. K. Vasilyeva found that between 15 and 30 percent of the women interviewed described themselves as the head of a household, but only 2 to 4 percent of their husbands agreed. Official statistics grant the man the last word. A woman is not regarded as the head of the household if she is living permanently with a man who is employed, though she may be earning more than he and most likely is working much longer hours than he is for the good of the family: The energy *she* has left when her paid workday is finished goes into unpaid work for her family.

Working Hours

It is a fact that women all over the world have longer working hours than men. A woman has less leisure time than her husband, less time for sports, politics, games. A recent study (Bergom-Larsson, 1979) from Sweden reveals that the leisure time for men, in families with children in which both spouses are gainfully employed, is two to three hours longer a day than for women. I shall return to this point.

All over the world, women are required to undertake unpaid housework, usually in the name of love. Norwegian statistics show that full-time housewives in Norway spend 5.4 hours each day on unpaid housework, while wives who are full-time career women spend 3.8 hours per day on the same amount of work. This means that women are forced into a double shift. The Norwegian researcher Berit Ås (1981) names this double workload system the "double ghetto in which modern women are exploited both by employers and husbands." The same statistics already referred to (Studies of the use of time, from the Norwegian Central Bureau of Statistics, 1972) show that husbands spend exactly the same amount of time—0.7 hours per day—on unpaid housework whether their wives are full-time housewives or full-time career women. The work that men do has been organized into paid labor, while women's work has been kept invisible and unpaid. Indeed, unpaid work has been kept so invisible that full-time housewives raising children and taking care of a big house without any help answer when they are asked if they are working: "No, I am not working. I am only at home." Yet they usually work longer hours than their husbands; they have less leisure time, they have no vacation, no sick leave, no pension, and no salary. And they are brought up to do all this "for love." In Burkina Faso (Upper Volta), for instance, the working hours of a sample of rural women exceed those of men by about 27 percent, while men, on the average, have two more hours of leisure per day. The same is found in Botswana, where rural women appear to work 20 percent longer than men and have 20 percent less leisure (Buvinic, 1981). These studies show that as women in poor households enter the labor market, it is their leisure time rather than time spent in work at home that is reduced.

An interesting Indian study, reported in the Indian feminist magazine *Manushi*, also showed that women, whether they were agricultural laborers or belonged to the landowning class, worked much longer hours than men (Horowitz and Kishwar, 1982). This study also makes it clear that the traditional male-constructed economic indicators such as average household income, per capita income, and per capita food consumption, all fail to tell us who actually gets how much of what. They fail to look into:

1. how economic resources are distributed within the family and with what consequences
2. which family members have acquired greater decision-making powers over others
3. how much each family member contributes to family income
4. what the labor contribution of each family member is
5. what the contributions of the family members are commensurate with the benefits he or she derives from membership in it.

Distribution of Resources

Looking into the internal distribution of money, food, and decision-making power within families, one finds a steady pattern of discrimination of women that varies little from one class to another. The previously mentioned Indian study showed that those who decided whether the woman in the family would be available for paid work outside of the family were men; mostly the husband, sometimes the sons or a father-in-law. This fact did not vary according to whether the woman belonged to a landowning family or to a landless agricultural family. The same study shows that even when the women worked for wages, very few seemed to have much say in how the bulk of the family's income would be spent; nor were they allowed to participate in other important areas of family decision-making. Some women reported being subjected to severe physical violence in the family. The lives of the women were limited by crippling restrictions. This was especially true for women from landholding families. They were even more restricted and powerless than the women in the landless families. The study also points to a discrimination in the allocation of food within the family. In both types of families women got less to eat than men and had to eat last in the family. By way of summing up, the researchers conclude:

> The women from both these groups put in 15 to 16 hours of arduous work a day. But they receive less than adequate nourishment and care. This seems to have a rather disastrous effect on their health, especially during periods of pregnancy and breast-feeding. It is ironic that their much-glorified role as producers of sons does not even get them some minimal measure of work relief and extra diet and care during their childbearing period. Consequently, most of them seemed in poor health, some of them even seriously sick. Yet their need for medical care goes largely unattended. (Horowitz and Kishwar, 1982, p. 18)

It is important to uncover the factors that result in the loss of millions of Indian women, and the extent to which the family's neglect of its female members contributes to this appalling situation.

Like many other European and American studies (see especially Eichler, 1980),the Indian study shows, that the lives and living conditions of women cannot be properly described by the social class or ethnic group of their husbands. The outward economy of a family may seem good, yet the wife may have to beg the husband for every penny or repay him with sexual favors as would a prostitute.

Since women are oppressed in all societies and classes, though in different ways and to different degrees, we may look at this total absence of resources as the most fundamental oppression there is. Some women who are eager not to alienate men as potential supporters claim that there ought to be an alliance of all "outsiders": not just women, but also children, unemployed, blacks, working classes, and so on (see, for instance, Eglin, 1982). This position overlooks the fact that all of the other groups mentioned also include women—girls, unemployed women, black women, working class women— and in each of these categories women are worse off than the men. They are exploited and oppressed by those they are asked to form an alliance with. The Australian researcher Robin Burns (1982) puts it this way:

Women not only have to overcome the structural barriers that other marginalised or oppressed groups face, including the language, consciousness and sense of identity, which they have accepted from the wider society in exchange for alternative rewards, but to face the consequences of male frustration, especially oppressed men whose only way to maintain some sense of worth is through keeping women out or even lower.

Refugees

Of the millions of refugees and displaced persons who come under the mandate of the United Nations High Commissioner for Refugees (UNHCR), women constitute a majority caseload in the adult refugee population. In some countries the breakdown on the basis of sex reveals that women and children refugees comprise as much as 90 percent (UN High Commissioner for Refugees, 1980). The UNHCR reports studies that show that even after adequate supplies of basic and supplementary food (earmarked for vulnerable groups) were available, women and children *continued* to suffer from malnutrition. It was observed that in such situations the patterns of distribution, both within the refugee camps and within the refugee family, reflected the discriminatory socioeconomic relations prevailing in the refugee groups. The UNHCR deplores the fact that the final stage of food distribution within the family is difficult to observe or control. He notes that the widespread cultural practice of men eating first may result in major health problems for the other members of the family when food is scarce. To quote the High Commissioner's report: "Relief workers have become familiar with the sight of well-fed men alongside under-fed and sickly women and children" (p. 7). He tells how in camps in Bangladesh for Burmese refugees the distribution of supplementary food had to be completely reorganized to give direct benefit to gaunt women and malnourished children. The High Commissioner also condemns the fact that there are hardly any women involved in the administration of the refugee centers, though so much of the organization of the center and the delivery systems for services has special significance for women.

In order to facilitate the integration of urban refugees, counseling services have been established in many places. But even though the majority of the refugees may be women, the majority of the refugees using the counseling services are men. Men push themselves forward and make themselves noticed. Women lack this type of socialization. In the Sudan, which has the largest urban refugee population in Africa, UNHCR provides a counseling service in Khartoum which serves a clientele that is 70 percent male.

Both in the initial flight and asylum phases and in the integration process, refugee women tend to suffer more than men from the loss of their roots and the radical change in their way of life. In situations often characterized by physical insecurity, the breakdown of law and order, or the absence of social constraints, women and teenage girls become especially vulnerable to various forms of sexual intimidation and exploitation. It is recognized that in the search for asylum, women face special hazards during their flight and in many instances in their intended country of asylum. For example, both on the high seas and in the territorial waters of various states in Southeast Asia, a large number of women have been victims of attack by pirates. In the course of these attacks women asylum seekers, including minor girls, have been victims of physical violence and acts of rape resulting in physical injury and frequently in loss of life. Eve Burton (1983), who has looked into the situation for Vietnamese refugee women on Vietnamese boats, concludes: "Despite two internationally-funded programs to combat piracy in Thai waters, the rate of attacks on Vietnamese refugee boats has changed little. Women on the boats often reach Thailand physically battered, and when they arrive in the United States still bear psychological scars." From June through October 1980, approximately 75 percent of the Vietnamese boats arriving on the shores of southern Thailand reported attacks by pirates, and 48 percent reported attacks involving rape. Reports of a single victim being raped twenty times were not uncommon. Eve Burton describes cases where Vietnamese women have been raped repeatedly by Thai pirates. Their vaginal bleeding has been severe. They have been unable to walk for days. And the psychological damages of rape, in many cases, can never be healed.

In the case of rapes committed on innocent refugees, the traditional distinction between structural and direct violence becomes blurred and useless. Women may have become refugees as the result of structural violence in their own country, which has led to lack of food and grave poverty. In their status as refugees they may, as do the Vietnamese refugee women, suffer direct and personal violence.

Military Spending and Unemployment

Structural violence within states as well as insufficiently peaceful relationships among states have specific effects on women's conditions. One of these is in the area of unemployment. Although it is now a well-documented fact that the arms race creates unemployment (see, for instance, United Nations, Studies Series 5, 1982), there is limited research showing which sex loses the most when money is used in the military instead of the civilian sector.

Some years ago one often heard the argument that military spending is good for the economy and creates jobs. Such a false myth might easily have arisen from the following facts: In the 1930s the United States and great parts of western Europe experienced a great economic depression, the worst in modern history. Millions were unemployed. Then, with the onset of World War II, many of the unemployed got jobs in military plants or joined the armed forces, thereby leaving behind civilian jobs that the unemployed took over. And so economic depression ended. An oversimplified conclusion was drawn from this experience, namely that World War II ended the Depression, and, therefore, military spending creates jobs and is good for the economy. But it was not the war that ended the Depression; it was high government spending. Any vast influx of investment and consumption into the economy would have terminated the Depression. Marion Anderson (1982b) points out that if the U.S. government had spent $80 billion on any other number of things in 1941 instead of the military, it would have ended the Depression. The federal government could have carried out a vast scheme of replacing worn-out housing, run-down schools, and decrepit hospitals, and it would have had the same effect of creating jobs and ending depression. But most Americans simply observed that the war began, the Depression ended, and therefore assumed that military spending was good for the economy.

It is a truism that armaments and the arms race—apart from their inherent political harmfulness as agents of international tension, violence, and war—represent a socioeconomic burden on society in general, since arms production is by its very nature a socially unproductive pursuit (see Thee, 1983). Although it is usually included in the gross national product, it does not provide socially useful goods or services, nor does it have any capacity to raise levels of consumption.

An important feature of the arms industry is the fact that it is exceptionally capital-intensive. Investment costs per workplace are far higher in the arms industry than in the civilian sector of the economy. It is certainly true that the higher the investment in armaments, the lower the growth rate and the efficiency of the civilian sector. This is perceptible in both East and West (Dumas, 1981). A recent study from the United Nations (Study Series 5, 1982) on the relationship between disarmament and development notes: "The job-creating differential between spending $1 billion on the military sector and the same amount on public service employment has been estimated to be roughly about 51,000 jobs in a major industrialized country like the United States."

Recent years have brought a whole series of so-called conversion studies showing what other workplaces could be created had money now being used in the military sector been used elsewhere. Some of the studies have been commissioned by the United Nations or United Nations agencies like the UN Center for Disarmament. Some of the studies have been undertaken by independent researchers, such as Mary Kaldor from Britain and Nils Petter Gleditsch from the International Peace Research Institute of Oslo. All of these studies show that the myth that the arms race creates employment is false. Of course, military spending creates some job opportunities, but the point is that less jobs are created when money is spent in the military sector than in almost any other sector of the economy.

The number of jobs directly or indirectly created by the investment of $1 billion in various sectors of the United States economy, as given by the Bureau of Labor Statistics are as follows: military production: 76,000; machinery production: 86,000; administration: 87,000; transport: 92,000; construction: 100,000; health: 139,000; education: 187,000. This means that if $1 billion is spent to create jobs in the educational instead of the military sector, there will be 111,000 more jobs created. Marion Anderson (1982a) documents in her publication, *The Empty Pork Barrel*, that military spending at a rate of $135 billion a year is responsible for the annual net loss of 1,422,000 jobs. This analysis was carried out by first determining how many fewer jobs there were in various sectors of the economy when $135 billion of tax money was going to the Pentagon. Second, the number of jobs generated by military contracts and by stationing military personnel in each state was calculated. Finally, the difference between these two sets of numbers was calculated on a state-by-state basis showing the net job loss or gain at a given level of military spending.

Table 1.2 shows that spending money on either military industry or military personnel increased the country's unemployment. If $1 billion were transferred from the military industry to the civilian industry, 9,000 more jobs would be created. If $1 billion were used by state and local governments to hire teachers, clerks, and firefighters, 35,000 more jobs would be created than if the same billion dollars were used to hire military personnel. Either way, the economy gains and unemployment goes down. This means that, contrary to popular belief, continuation of the arms race creates unemployment, while disarmament and reallocation of money into the civilian sector would create more jobs and cut down on unemployment.

Both men and women suffer a net loss of jobs when military spending is high. The substantial job gains men have as military personnel is more than counterbalanced by their loss of industrial and governmental jobs. From the analysis done by Anderson (1982b), it clearly seems that women in relation to men are losing more jobs. Workers in services and in state and local government

Table 1.2. Jobs created per billion dollars of expenditure (1978 dollars)

Jobs created by:	If spent to create jobs in industry	If spent to create jobs in government
$1 billion spent in civilian sector	27,000 jobs	72,000 jobs
$1 billion spent in military sector	18,000 jobs	37,000 jobs
Jobs foregone by spending on the military	9,000 jobs	35,000 jobs

The figures are calculated from Burea of Labor Statistics data and 1978 Statistical Abstract of the United States.

suffer the most in lost job opportunities when military spending is high. Women comprise 54 percent of service employees, including hotel and restaurant employees and clerks. Women comprise 51 percent of state and local government employees, including teachers, librarians, office workers, and social workers. American women's jobs are heavily concentrated in manufacturing, services, and local governments. These are the hardest hit categories of the economy when military spending is high.

In her analysis Marion Anderson determined on a state-by-state basis how many fewer jobs for women there were when military spending was at the 1980 level of $135 billion. She found that there were over 1,895,000 fewer jobs for women in civilian industry, services, and state and local government because of the military budget. "These are the civilian jobs lost or never created (foregone) when people are heavily taxed to pay for the military and are unable to spend the money upon their own needs or upon the services provided by their state and local government" (p. 4). During this period 232,000 women were engaged in work on military contracts. This is one-half of 1 percent of the female workforce. When the 232,000 jobs generated from military contracts and the 382,000 jobs held by women in the armed forces in the United States were subtracted from the 1,895,000 jobs lost, the total net loss for women turned out to be 1,281,000 jobs. This means that every time the Pentagon's budget goes up $1 billion, 9,500 jobs disappear for American women.

Anderson's study shows how women lose job opportunities when money is spent in the military instead of the civilian sector of the same country. The 1,281,000 net job loss to women she claims to be a conservative estimate, since it does not account for additional jobs when the laid-off teachers, office workers, and production workers buy less because they are out of work. It has been estimated that for each person laid off, at least one other job is affected. Most of the women who lose their jobs because of increased military budgets have entered the workforce out of economic necessity, many of them the sole supporter of their families.

Military Spending and Social Welfare

Money used in the military sector could also have been used for food. In a pamphlet distributed to announce the first National Women's Conference to Prevent Nuclear War[1] (Capitol Hill, Washington DC, September 12, 1984) Marian Wright Edelman, who is the President of the Children's Defense

---

[1]This conference has been organized by women, for women, as a project of the Center for Defense Information in Washington. The advisory board includes among many others: Geraldine Ferraro, Helen Caldicott, Betty Goetz Lall, Marion Anderson, Eleanor Smeal, Marian Wright Edelman and Gloria Steinem.

Fund, tells that the United States plans to build about 226 missiles at about $110 million each: "For each missile we cancel, we could eliminate poverty in 101,000 female-headed families for a year" (p. 1). She further states that if the United States cancelled the whole program, poverty for all children in the United States could be eliminated, and there would still be enough left to send all female heads of low-income families to college for a year.

Military spending, which is highest in the industrialized countries in the northern half of the globe, could also have been used to overcome hunger and illness in developing countries. In the 1978 Special Session of the United Nations devoted to disarmament, the Swedish disarmament expert and Under-Secretary of State, Inga Thorsson, used the annual yearbook on the World's Military and Social Expenditures by Ruth Leger Sivard to show what a redistribution of 5 percent of the world's military expenditures to meet the needs of children in developing countries could mean (Thorsson, 1978). For this sum, which would amount to $17.5 billion, one could save the lives of millions of children and prevent thousands of children from becoming blind by giving them and their pregnant mothers vitamins and a proper diet.

Five million children in developing countries die each year from six contagious diseases for which they could have been vaccinated (95 percent of the children born in developing countries each year are not vaccinated). Thorsson suggests that part of the $17.5 billion saved be used to vaccinate all children in developing countries against these six common diseases. Such a vaccination program would cost $600 million. Half of the children in developing countries are malnourished or undernourished. In the Far East more than a hundred thousand children become blind each year because of lack of vitamin A. Inga Thorsson suggests a food and vitamin program to secure the physical and mental health of these undernourished and malnourished children. Such a program would cost $4 billion.

More than a billion people living in rural areas and 200 million people living in cities in the developing countries lack fresh water supplies. More than 25,000 people in these areas die daily as the consequence of bad water supply. Illness through diarrhea, which is connected to lack of a fresh water supply, is the most frequent cause of death of children under five years of age. Thorsson maintains that to supply all human beings with fresh water by 1990 would cost $3 billion.

In the introduction to the 1981 edition of *World Military and Social Expenditures*, Sivard (1981) comments: "No evidence more directly and starkly measures the impact of military expenditures on the social condition than the fact that the 550 billion dollars now spent in one year for arms and armies equals the entire income of 2 billion people living in the poorest countries. This is the bottom line on the world's military-social balance." Wherever there is hunger and deprivation, women and their children, especially daughters, suffer the most, which means that women pay for the male priorities of this world with their lives. They pay even when there is no war by virtue of the fact that money that could have been used for food, vitamins, and medicines is being used on arms and armies.

The industrialized countries are increasingly selling weapons to the developing countries, which in return, provide important raw materials. By this means, developing countries are trading away the bread of the hungry masses, of the starving children, in exchange for bombs, instruments of murder. Some people in the industrialized countries make big profits on these weapons sales, but they are not women. And as we have seen, not average men either: They also lose their jobs and their money in the arms race.

In periods of war, women are not only tortured and slaughtered like men, but are commonly raped. There are reports of gang rapes of Vietnamese women by American soldiers during the Vietnam War. Brownmiller (1975) mentions an example where the last soldier "making love" to the woman shot her afterwards. But usually rape is reported only when it is committed by the other side. Such selective reporting stimulates and justifies retaliation in kind by "this side" (Daly, 1979, p. 362). News of sexual abuses and rape caused by "this side" is not usually reported. Brownmiller (1975) shows that selective reporting of rape has provided an ideological excuse for men to rape women "belonging" to other men. She also shows that since rape has frequently been a prelude to murder, it has conveniently been minimized in reporting of the allegedly more serious act. As Brownmiller (1975) indicated, rape has been perpetrated everywhere, on all sides, in patriarchal wars. She states: "From prehistoric times to the present, I believe rape has played a critical function. It is nothing more or less than a conscious process of intimidation by which all men keep all women in a state of fear" (p. 114). Rape is to male-female relations what conquering troops are to occupied territories.

The American peace researcher Betty Reardon (1982, p. 45) comments on the fact the the male-dominated media are rather unwilling to report that women who were murdered have also been raped. She refers to the rape and later murder of four American churchwomen in El Salvador in December 1980. She claims that there was a virtual failure of most media to report that they were also raped before they were murdered. One who did report it was Mary Bader Papa in the *National Catholic Reporter* (here taken from Reardon, 1982), who wrote: "A special message was sent us by the rapists and murderers of the four American women. They wanted to make it clear that women who step out of their place will find no special protection behind the labels of 'nun or churchworker'. Or even American." Reardon comments: "Rape is, indeed, a deliberate device to keep women in line."

WOMEN AS VICTIMS OF DIRECT VIOLENCE

As already mentioned, structural violence often leads to personal and direct violence against women. Periods of national economic crises not only affect women's employment opportunities, they can also affect women in other ways. Some studies (Bard, 1974; Steinmetz and Strauss, 1974), show, for example, that the shortage of resources in a family group increases the incidence of violence in the family, thus verbal and physical attacks on women and children are one of the symptoms of such a problem. According to Elise Boulding (1978) women receive more beatings in periods of high unemployment. In the same study, Boulding finds that women feel especially menaced when the level of general violence increases, because of the strong psychological nexus between violence and rape.

In periods of political violence, war, or revolution, women, even if they have not been involved themselves in the struggle, are imprisoned and tortured only because they are wives, mothers, daughters, or sisters of the combatants. The Chilean researcher Ines Vargas (1983) points to the fact that the torture of women has taken on sexual-pathological properties, with rape and violence directed toward sexual organs as very common. The female physiological functions are used as torture tools in very sophisticated ways. Many different elements of social, psychological, and cultural order contribute to making these sexual abuses, including rape, into tools for dissolving and destroying the personality of the victims. One aspect of this problem is that the women who suffer such torture find it difficult to denounce these men, are ashamed, and feel a sense of guilt. According to Vargas, religious and cultural factors limit the denunciation of rapists and sexual abuses because the victim and her family prefer not to disclose such atrocities. This may be part of the reason why this phenomenon is not studied as much as it should be.

Even in states that are not at war with each other, women are being beaten, mutilated, burned, sexually abused and raped daily. These atrocities may take on different forms in various societies, but there are some common characteristics. In a majority of cases the violence against the women is committed by men she is well acquainted with, her husband, father, brother, or father-in-law. Another common denominator is that male society is reluctant to report and research such "private," personal violence against women. The official apparatus has been unwilling to explore and condemn acts of violence, especially of a sexual nature, against women. In this area feminist research, feminist writers, and feminist organizations have made the invisible violence visible, have unveiled the abuses against their sisters, and have taken action to have it stopped.

Ine Megens and Mary Wings (1981) report that "rape is twice as frequent in the U.S. military as in civilian life. Sexual harassment and regular 'witch hunts' for lesbians are all commonplace" (p. 47). This is rape of American women serving in the U.S. military in peacetime and rape by their American "comrades" serving in the same regiments. The U.S. military does not like to have this fact revealed. It contradicts the message in a pamphlet used to recruit women into the U.S. Army: "Since the men and women work together as a team, you'll have a lot of help to get through rough times."

The abuse of women physically and sexually is done by men all over the world, not only in the military, but also in civilian life. Feminists in Europe and the United States are building centers for raped and battered women. In Africa women have started fighting against genital mutilation of young girls. And in India feminists are fighting against the increased incidences of dowry deaths.

The first center for battered women in London was built in 1971, the Chiswick's Women's Aid. A group of feminists had been working long and hard to have the center erected. One of the leading organizers behind this initiative was Erin Pizzey (Janssen-Jurreit, 1979, p. 233). Her book reporting the difficulties the women endured who sought refuge in Chiswick's Women's Aid is now a well-known classic in the history of the centers for battered women (Pizzey, 1974). She was also one of the leading women to press the British government to appoint a committee in 1975 to look into the question of wife beatings. At that time the committee members were faced by the fact that of the 6,680,000 wives in Britain more than 5,000 per year were known to have been severely injured and molested by their husbands. After 23 hearings the committee concluded that the 5,000 wives only constituted the tip of the iceberg; the actual number was much higher. The committee also reported on the prejudices by which their work had been met (House of Commons, 1976), admitting that there were many men, especially in leading positions, who did not want to acknowledge that the fact that women are beaten by their husbands constitutes a problem warranting official recognition and action. They had met with phrases like "nobody should inquire into the privacy of the home" and "if a man beats his wife, she has probably deserved it." Reardon (1982) describes such attitudes this way:

> A society which deems wifebeating to be a private matter between spouses, not subject to civil interference, is not likely to perceive excessive exploitation of female labor as a significant problem of economic equity. . . . The degree to which violence operates in the relations between men and women is becoming more apparent as feminist research begins to reveal how many experiences formerly deemed "seduction" were in fact consummated through various forms of intimidation if not force, and to expose how many women have been attacked by men with whom they are acquainted. It is also reinforced by the "blaming the victim syndrome", which insists that the victim provoked the attack, much as the aggression of one state against another has been rationalized by the aggressor as the consequence of "provocation". Social scientists and lawyers have had equally difficult and similar problems in defining both rape and armed aggression. (p. 47)

In other parts of the world women are mutilated in other ways, though they may also be beaten. In some places women live in lifelong physical pain or are tortured to death as a result of barbaric rituals. This is the case with ritual genital mutilations—excision and infibulation—still inflicted upon women throughout Africa today and practiced in many parts of the world in the past. Immediate medical results of excision and infibulation include: hemorrhage, infections, shock, retention of urine, damage to adjacent tissues, coital difficulties, and infertility caused by chronic pelvic infections, in addition to the psychological maiming caused by this torture.

The World Health Organization has refused for many years to concern itself with the problem. When it was asked in 1958 to study the problem, it took the position that such operations were based on "social and cultural backgrounds" and were outside its competence. Mary Daly (1978) comments: "This basic attitude has not changed. There has been a conspiracy of silence" (p. 157). As many feminists have pointed out, hatred of the clitoris is almost universal, for this organ is strictly female, for women's pleasure. Thus it is by nature "impure," and the logical conclusion, acted out by tribes that practice excision and infibulation, is to "purify" women of the capacity for sexual pleasure by removing the clitoris.

In India, feminists are fighting against the increased incidences of "dowry deaths." According to official figures, 332 cases of "accidental burning" were reported in New Delhi in 1982 as against 305 in 1981 (Kelkar, 1983). But according to various women's organizations an equal number of accidental burning cases go unreported. Many times this is because of the refusal of the police to register the cases. The dowry witch-hunt has taken its heaviest toll in the middle-class urban areas, but the burning of women for money and domestic goods in the form of dowry is quite widespread in the slums and rural areas. Indian feminist researchers see the dowry witch-hunts in India as stemming from women's subordination in the structure of material production, the organization of marriage and family, and the sexual division of labor (Kelkar, 1983). For the past few years in Delhi and other major cities in the country, women's organizations and housewives have had sporadic demonstrations against the husbands, in-laws, lawyers, and police officers involved in the cases of women-burning or killing by other means. In early August 1982, 30 women's groups in Delhi jointly organized a protest march against the dowry, and they were joined by several hundred ordinary women and bystanders. According to the Indian researcher Govind Kelkar (1983) from the Center for Women's Development Studies, New Delhi, these demonstrations have acted as checks on the husbands and in-laws by exposing the real nature of violence or crime (i.e., protracted harassment and battering of the woman followed by killing and/or burning her) and thereby disallowing an easy exit through a facade of suicide or accidental deaths, called "kitchen accidents." The demonstrations have also pressed for effective implementation of laws, tightening of the loopholes in the legal procedures, and giving due consideration to women's unspoken experiences of harassment, torture and molestation through proposals for reorganization of arrangements for police inquiries. "The women's protest through their studies and demonstrations has made this violent crime of women burning visible as a serious social problem. It has opened a whole new vista by calling attention to the oppression, conflict and violence hidden behind the portrait of love, support and nurturance in the family" (Kelkar, 1983, p. 7). Indian feminist researchers are critical of the family research most prevalent in Indian social science. This research deals mostly with the nuclearization or non-nuclearization of joint-family structures. But research has not questioned the complex power relations between gender, caste, and generation that underlie the family, the ideology and structure of dependence and sexual division of labor that strengthen the patterns of inequality, and the oppression of women and children. These are aspects that feminist researchers are now exploring.

WOMEN AND WARS OF MASS DESTRUCTION

In earlier wars, men went onto battlefields to kill other men. They left homes, wives, and children to kill the husbands and sons of wives in a neighboring country. Women lost their husbands, lovers, sons, and fathers. Usually women were not killed themselves, but the incidences of rape and prostitution were high. In modern warfare military men are not fighting other military men primarily. They are primarily killing us: women and children, the so-called civilian population. The battlefield is not in the mountains somewhere. The battlefield is our own homes. In Vietnam, even without the use of nuclear bombs, 90 percent of those killed belonged to the civilian population.

At the end of the Second World War, two nuclear bombs were dropped on Japanese towns. The ordinary people, not the military, became the butt of the war. Innocent children were dying in the most terrible pain or saw their parents die before their eyes. Nuclear bombs do not deserve the label 'weapon,' since they cannot be used for defense. They destroy what they should defend. It is the thinking of lunatic minds that anyone should feel secure because their country is in possession of nuclear bombs and able to destroy our sisters and brothers, the children of another population.

In 1982 the United States had 23,838 nuclear warheads and the Soviet Union had 13,552 (World nuclear stockpiles, SIPRI, 1983). The history of nuclear development is an excellent example of a few men exercising power over many. Starting with the commitment of the American government in 1941 to undertake a secret research and development program (the Manhattan Project) in order to create an atomic bomb, and continuing until the present full-scale deployment of weapons and plants, the nuclear industry and its promoters in the government have exhibited a blatant disregard for human life and the environment. The accumulation of a nuclear arsenal that is sufficient to wipe out the entire world many times over is in itself an indication of an insatiable hunger for power.

Susan Koen and Nina Swaim (1980) see this hunger as an expression of the nuclear mentality, which they describe as a belief system, an ideology, that will foster the use of destructive technology in order to sustain the expansion and domination that characterize capitalist patriarchy. They see patriarchy as a society characterized by violence, exploitation, a reverence for the scientific as absolute, and systematic "rape" of nature for man's enjoyment. This result comes about when the intellect and the dominating, controlling, aggressive tendencies within each individual are defined as the most valuable parts of their being, and those same attributes are emphasized in the political and economic arena. When the patriarchal paradigm becomes operational on the economic and political level, and the exploitation of nature for the sake of technological advancement, profit, and domination becomes the "modus operandi" of society, "we find ourselves in the interlocking horror story of the nuclear mentality" (Koen and Swaim, 1980, p. 6).

Women have been in the forefront of the antinuclear movement since the first demonstration of nuclear destruction—the dropping of bombs on Hiroshima and Nagasaki. At the end of the fifties a group of women from every political stance, from the east as well as the west of Europe, formed the European Movement of Women against Nuclear Armament and held a conference in Brunate, Italy in 1959. The subject of the conference was the responsibility of women in the atomic age. Well-informed women gave lectures about the dangers of nuclear tests and explained their technical details. The women who were at Brunate drew up a petition requesting the following:

1. putting a stop to nuclear tests
2. instituting proceedings to establish nuclear-free zones
3. prohibiting the making and use of nuclear weapons
4. destroying all existing stocks
5. setting up international control of all these measures

In 1964 a new peace movement was started in the United States. It was a women's movement that called itself WISP—Women's International Strike for Peace. European women adopted the same tactics, and women from many countries arrived in Scheveningen in the Netherlands in 1964 on the occasion of a NATO conference held to plan the setting up of a multilateral nuclear force. A list of the names of thousands of women from around the world who protested against the nuclear proliferation was handed to U Thant, the Secretary-General of the UN. Later a meeting was held. It was opened by Gonnie Scholten-van Iterson (1982) from the Netherlands with the following words: "We have heard in all our media that it is an honour to receive NATO in our country, so I reckon it be an honour to greet the women who have come from all over the world to proclaim the rejection of the plans of NATO and of the whole train of thought which underlies these plans" (p. 114). The women conducted a march in front of the conference place, a silent march with flowers.

In *Handbook for Women on the Nuclear Mentality* by Susan Koen and Nina Swaim (1980) we learn about the strong opposition of some outstanding women against nuclear arms and plants. We learn about bio-statistician Rosalie Bertell and physicist Helen Caldicott, both using their academic backgrounds to inform others about the dangers of radiation exposure. We learn about nuclear lab technician Karen Silkwood and the extensive search she did to show that the company she was working for, Kerr-McGee—the largest uranium producer in the United States—violated safety and health regulations. She detected a conscious effort on the part of the corporation to conceal faulty welds in the fuel rods. She did her work on behalf of the Oil, Chemical and Atomic Workers Union and collected evidence against the corporation. While working on this talk her apartment was contaminated and her food poisoned. She had her notes and collected evidence in a brown manila folder and in a reddish-brown spiral notebook. These she was going to hand over to the *New York Times* at an evening meeting on November 13, 1974. One her way to that meeting she was killed on the highway, her documents had been taken from her car when it was found. On the first anniversary of her death, Karen Silkwood memorials were held all over the United States. Her parents filed suit in an Oklahoma federal court against the Kerr-McGee Corporation and won. The corporation had to pay the Silkwood family $5,000 for the contamination of Karen Silkwood's apartment, $500,000 for damage to her health, and $10 million in punitive damages.

We further hear about songwriter, singer, and political activist Holly Near, writer and peace activist Grace Paley, and Dolly Weinhold—also called Earthquake Dolly. The description of these women's fights against nuclear power is fascinating. The handbook is recommended for further study. Here I shall simply describe in some detail one other woman who is also an antinuclear activist and is also described in the handbook, Winona La Duke. She is a Chippewa Indian and a founder of Women of All Red Nations (WARN). WARN was founded in September 1978 by 200 native women "to bring back the traditional role of women in the Indian nations and in the leadership and guidance of the American Indian Movement." La Duke says: "Women are considered to be the backbones of Indian nations because the responsibility for future generations belongs to the women" (p. 35). She further clarifies the way in which Native American women view the battle over uranium mining and other examples in the following passage:". . . we view ourselves as an integral part, almost a representation of the earth. The earth is our mother—a woman. As women are exploited, so is our mother. And we must fight both battles simultaneously" (Koen and Swaim, 1980, p. 36).

As a Native American woman, La Duke is concerned with the historical exploitation of Native people, the colonization of Indian lands, and the current dangers facing Native people as a result of uranium mining and milling. She states: "In 1974, 100% of all federally controlled uranium production came from Indian reservations. . . . We predict that about 80% of federal uranium production comes from Indian lands now" (p. 34). It is her belief that the major focus of antinuclear efforts should be on the issue of uranium mining and milling as the real source of the problem. The push in the United States to create more nuclear power plants and weapons results in the direct "rape" of Indian lands by uranium mining. The high unemployment rate on Indian reservations has further forced Native people to take the hazardous jobs of uranium mining offered by industry, resulting in increasing incidences of lung cancer, death from radiation and respiratory diseases. In addition the practice of the mining industry of leaving mill tailings scattered on the land ensures the continued exposure of all Native peoples to the dangers of radiation. Winona La Duke organizes her people and especially the women against this crime against the Indian and Mother Earth.

Australian women are also protesting against uranium mining and the employment of nuclear weapons. One Friday, November 11, 1983, and for some days after, Australian Women for Survival organized a peace camp at the U.S. satellite communication base at Pine Gap, close to Alice Springs. The protest was organized to highlight to the public Australia's role in the nuclear arms race. The camp and the march were also focusing on aboriginal land rights issues.

WOMEN IN THE MILITARY

Since women in the industrialized world have had more of a choice to decide on the number of children they want to give birth to, the population has been declining. Women are not fulfilling the task assigned them by Nietzsche: to be there for the recreation of warriors. Or rather, they are not producing enough sons, not enough manpower for the military. The fact that women produce less cannon fodder now than they did some years ago seems to be one of the main reasons behind the growing tendency in several countries to actively encourage women into military careers.

The military, the prototype of patriarchal institutions in male society, uses arguments from the equality debate to further its aims. This fact alone should make feminists suspicious. An institution that cultivates the masculine virtues of detachment, coldness, lack of caring for other human beings, strength, and hardship and actively degrades the feminine, invites women to join in the name of equality. We must ask ourselves the questions: Whom are we required to be equal to? Equal to do what? Equal to kill? Before we accept the invitation to join, we should also ask what we are invited to defend? Our lives, yes. But what type of society? Are we merely invited to defend the continued existence of patriarchy? Do we have any guarantee that we or our sisters and daughters will be less oppressed if we help men to fight some enemy?

Since the argument of equality is persistently used in the current propaganda to recruit women into the military, I shall spend some time here looking at the actual conditions of some of those women who have chosen a military career. Then I shall return to the question of whether women should join the armed forces.

But before looking at the unequal treatment of women in the military, it is useful to remember that the arguments for recruiting women into the armed forces have varied according to the position of women in the society. It is also important to know that women have not decided whether they as a group will participate in the military apparatus. Historically it has been male state elites and their subordinate male strategists who have decided whether women should participate in the military apparatus and in what form. In a paper on women in the Army, Cynthia Enloe (1979) concludes: "For women to assess meaningfully what they believe should be their proper relationship to security structures, they must explore how they are utilised by male-run states and why. Otherwise, they risk labeling as progress what in reality is an adjustment to the state elite's own latest manpower imperatives" (Enloe, 1979, p.37).

In 1972, the Vietnam War had made military service so politically unpopular that the United States ended compulsory service for men (the draft). Almost simultaneously, the Department of Defense began a policy of deliberately increasing the recruitment of women volunteers. Women were to make it possible for the government to end the unpopular draft and yet maintain a large Cold War military establishment. Wendy Chapkis and Mary Wings (1981) point to the fact that this change in government policy coincided with —and they claim was facilitated by—the rise of feminism. A large part of the U.S. women's movement defined liberation as equal opportunity, and hence saw the increased involvement of women in the armed forces as an avenue to achieving liberation. The U.S. National Organization for Women (NOW—a large, moderate, well-funded and high-profile women's organization with more than 125,000 members, which claims to be the world's largest feminist organization) identifies itself as an "essentially anti-military group" according to Judy Knee of its national office (Tiffany, 1981). Yet in its brief to the U.S. Supreme Court encouraging draft registration (the first step to compulsory military conscription) for women, NOW writers relied heavily on traditional, promilitary rhetoric. "A male-only draft," they write, "tells all women that solely because of their gender, they will not be called upon to serve and defend their country, that they will not be relied upon in time of greatest national need" (Tiffany, 1981, p. 38). The male-only draft, they write, "also harms women by excluding them from the compulsory involvement in the community's survival that is perceived as entitling people to lead it and derive from it the full rights and privileges of citizenship." They further hold that "compulsory universal military service is central to the concept of citizenship in a democracy."

Attitudes like these have made it rather easy for the U.S. government to make use of feminist rhetoric. Military recruiting materials often take up the chorus: "Today's Army is Leading the Way in Opportunities for Women." Critical feminists should ask, opportunities to do what? Women are further enticed to join the military by promises of expanded horizons: economic security, job training, travel, and adventure. Critical feminists should ask why they will be traveling to such exotic places. What is the U.S. military doing in these places—making new friends in order to kill them? The U.S. Army stresses the unique occupational opportunities for women in the military: "No longer is a women restricted to a traditional role. . . . You can be a missile repairer, carpenter-mason, a construction equipment operator. . . . You can improve physically and mentally and still be feminine." And it goes on: "You won't be asked to do things you can't. You will get the chance to learn what you want. . . . You can make it in the U.S. Army and still be a women. And you will get equal pay all the way" (Tiffany, 1981, p. 38). The U.S. Army proudly proclaims that only 28 out of 348 occupational specialities are closed to women. (What the recruitment material fails to mention is that these 28 specialities comprise 42 percent of all army jobs and are often prerequisites for promotion.)

When analyzing recruitment material used to recruit men and women to the U.S. military, Ine Megens and Mary Wings (1981) found a great difference in the type of pictures used. The women in the pictures are almost always smiling, and in some situations seem to play a purely ornamental role. The men seldom smile. Women are more often shown with men than with other women or alone. Women often get instructions or information from men, but rarely conversely. Several pictures show women soldiers putting on lipstick. The text on a poster picturing a smiling woman soldier states: "Some of the best soldiers wear lipstick." While women's recruitment material in this way tries to bury the real function of the Army under smiles and feminine imagery, recruitment material for men glorifies the machismo of the armed forces. You see men in combat, men with machine-guns, and you read: "Men who respect the tat-tat-tat of the machine-guns" or "Our M60 monsters are things of beauty only to the guys who ride them . . . " Of course, neither men's nor women's recruitment material ever addresses the important questions of who controls the military and for what purposes it is used.

The proportion of women in uniform in the U.S. military in 1981 was 8.4 percent. In spite of all the promises these women have been given by the military, they end up doing traditional "women's work" without civilian women's rights. Enlistees rarely possess much power in the armed forces, and women enlistees possess even less. The appeal of "equal opportunity" is used to draw women into the service, but they end up in the lowest jobs and are completely powerless within a rigid patriarchal hierarchy. The advantages and disadvantages of having women in the military are constantly evaluated by the Pentagon, and reports are made to other NATO countries. A couple of years ago the experiences had been so good that the United States encouraged other NATO countries to recruit more women into their military ranks. Even though 8 percent of the women in the U.S. armed forces were absent from work, mostly because of pregnancy, childbirth and menstruation, this was just half of the proportion of men absent, mostly because of drug or alcohol abuse. Women were drinking much less than men and seldom used narcotics. They were also more obedient and more pleasant to command. They took orders well and caused fewer disciplinary problems than men (Elster, 1982). Women also were more highly educated than men: On the average 92 percent of the women had a college degree against only 66 percent of the men. At the same time women were cheaper labor. Nevertheless, in 1981 the U.S. Defense Department began to alert Congress and the public that it found the once hoped-for 12 percent level of female participation in the military to be unrealistic and harmful to American military preparedness (Enloe, 1981). Was the presence of women demoralizing men? Or was it making them less macho, less apt to excel in military values? Little do we know. But we know that women are used and dismissed by the military institutions according to the policies of those institutions and not because of women's wishes or feminist policies.

There have been women in a number of NATO military forces since their inception in 1949, but they were not worthy of explicit alliance attention until the manpower shortages of the mid-1970s. The first meeting of senior women officers from NATO forces was held in 1961. The women officers hoped to share information among themselves; they sought also to act as a pressure group to gain better treatment of women in uniform throughout NATO. Cynthia Enloe (1981) notes that the group was given little serious attention by the male defense elite. It only met sporadically for the next 13 years.

But when the heads of the Women's Services in NATO met in 1974, their work was suddenly taken seriously. The male defense planners by this time were worried by the problems they were experiencing in filling manpower quotas. Recruiting more women into the armed forces could compensate for the declining birth rates and also for the need for more highly educated enlistees and military personnel. A 1980 NATO publication, *Women in the Allied Forces*, notes that "women in the military tended to be older, better educated and present fewer disciplinary problems." The same publication noted that a "successful recruiting programme for women volunteers in France was started in 1974 and has since been extended" (Chapkis and Wings, 1981, p. 19).

NATO's Committee on Women in the NATO Forces reports annually on the status of women in the alliance. Cynthia Enloe (1983) in her recent and thorough book on the militarization of women's lives tells that these reports are a response to pressures from NATO's Conference of Senior Service Women Officers. The 1982 report on women in uniform reveals considerable differences within the alliance. Enloe (1983, p. 127) quotes figures from Belgium, Canada, Denmark, France, Federal Republic of Germany, Greece, Italy, Luxembourg, the Netherlands, Norway, Portugal, Turkey, United Kingdom, and the United States. According to her, the variation found in the degrees and ways the 15 national forces of NATO use women can be explained in various ways. The variations reflect, firstly, the degree of ideological conservatism of the current regime; secondly, the ambitiousness of the given military's regional or global mission; thirdly, the country's birth rate; fourthly, the level and quality of civilian unemployment; fifthly, the social status of soldiering, and lastly, the country's ethnic or racial groups' "trustworthiness" and "competence" in the eyes of military officials.

Bosses within NATO as within liberation armies (e.g., Che Guevara) and in civilian life seem to like to be surrounded by helping and serving women. The Norwegian newspaper *Arbeiderbladet* (January 17, 1984) reported that 3,500 soldiers from the British Royal Marines on maneuver in Norway had to do without tons of equipment that should have reached them from Britain. The ships carrying the equipment had to return to England due to heavy storms in the North Sea. "But we have got the most important thing," an officer told the newspaper as he smiled. He was talking about the 22 women soldiers from Women's Royal Naval Service who had arrived. The newspaper tells that the female soldiers are there to take care of trivial matters like cooking, serving, typing, managing the switchboard "to free the men to go out in the snow to do their job." The head of the female soldiers was Teresa Kitchen (an appropriate name). She was an exception, however, for all of the other women were private soldiers. But they were to *serve* the officers only. Since they have a lower military rank than the officers they serve, they are not allowed to mix with their bosses in their spare time. The female soldiers have their own bar in the basement of the hotel where they are staying, the newspaper reports. The officers have their bar on the first floor of the same hotel.

In West Germany, the state has been circulating proposals to increase the recruitment of women in the armed forces in the late 1980s, arguing that there will not be enough young men to fill the ranks. As in the United States, such proposals have gained support from parts of the women's movement. In 1978 Alice Schwarzer wrote an article in the feminist magazine *Emma* arguing for military service for women as a right and a responsibility. In Belgium, the government decided to recruit women into the armed forces as part of its International Women's Year Program. And in the Netherlands in 1978, the State Secretary for Emancipation proclaimed a step forward for women as all formal barriers to women's full participation in the Dutch military were abolished. And in the spring of 1981, the military went further, taking the dramatic step of being the first industrialized country to open combat duty to women recruits. In April 1980, the British government issued a White Paper on Defense that gave particular attention to the "increased contribution of women in the Armed Forces." In Norway a committee appointed by the Norwegian Ministry of Defense delivered a paper on "the equality of men and women in the armed forces." The paper, delivered in 1982, concluded that women ought to be encouraged to seek a career in the military and that they should be allowed to occupy any job. In December 1982 the Council for Equality invited women's organizations and some individual feminists together with women in military careers and representatives from the Defense Ministry to discuss "defense and equality." We were invited to discuss the best way to implement the following conclusion from the paper: "Campaigns to spread information and change attitudes must be conducted as well within the military as in civilian life in order to ensure full equality between men and women in the armed forces" (p. 3). Some feminists were amazed by the fact that the Conservative government, which has not otherwise been known to fight for women's rights, was now using feminist language, talking about equal rights between men and women and putting an end to the discrimination of women: Women must be allowed leadership; they were as clever, strong, and reliable as men. But there was no reason to be amazed. The effort to integrate women into the military was a joint NATO effort that had little to do with the actual Norwegian government leading the country. It was simply a coincidence that the government in charge happened to be a Conservative one. I was invited to the meeting but was unable to attend it. For this reason I wrote down my arguments against it in an article entitled "Equal to kill" (Brock-Utne, 1982d). I did not see it as the business of the Council for Equality to initiate a hearing on the background of the paper from the Ministry of Defense. Were we aiming at a mechanistic equality, at becoming like men? Should we try to implement everything that was advertised under the label equality?

Women have been recruited to serve in the Israeli army ever since the establishment of the state in 1948. They are recruited on the basis of a national recruitment law. Nira Yuval-Davis (1981) sees this as one of the reasons for the existence of the myth concerning the egalitarian status of women in Israel. Out of the 850 military professions in the Israeli army in 1980, women were engaged in only 270. The percentage of female soldiers who were performing clerical work was estimated to at least 65 percent. The other most popular areas of female military labor are in the fields of welfare, education, and communications (Yuval-Davis, 1981). The female roles in the Israeli army are roles that belong to the "rear," as women are legally banned from the "front" war zones. In an article on women in the Israeli army, Yuval-Davis concludes: "The overwhelming majority of military tasks in which women are engaged is no more than a mirror image of the roles women mostly occupy in the civilian labour market" (Yuval-Davis, 1981, p. 75). She tells that in February 1980 the judge advocate general came out with a judgement that "coffee-making and floor washing cannot be seen as being outside the legitimate duties of military secretaries" (Yuval-Davis, 1981, p. 75). Debates about coffee-making and cleaning of the office between the male boss and his female secretaries are well-known from the civilian sector. Here, however, in addition to the common imbalance of power between a boss and a secretary, the boss has the added power of his military authority. And unlike the civilian sector, resignations are not accepted.

Another aspect of the work of women soldiers is reflected in the name of the women's corps, "Chen," meaning charm. A central demand for the women in the army is "to raise the morale" of the male soldiers and to make the army a "home away from home." During the basic training of women, they are coached to emphasize their feminine characteristics and their neat appearance; the benefits of cosmetic guidance are to help them in this respect.

Though women only serve auxiliary functions in the life of the Israeli army, they have another national military function that is perceived as *primary* to them. That primary function is motherhood, as national producers of the future military force. Women with small children are exempt from doing military service. Women who enter the military may not assume roles that could expose them to any danger of not being able to fulfill their reproductive role in the future. Yuval-Davis tells that it has been a common reaction in Israel, when greeting a pregnant woman to say: "Congratulations! I see you are soon to bring a small soldier into the world."

These facts from the Israeli experience should show that the manpower strategy that has been adopted is bipartite. On the one hand the state needs women in the army to do the menial jobs (since it will not enlist male Arab Israelis) and likes to give an image of "progressive" Israel to the outside world, playing up to the thoughts about equality stemming from the feminist movements. This also fits well into the Zionist stereotype of women as rugged frontier pioneers. But on the other hand, the state is careful not to alienate the male-led conservative religious parties who want women to be home-centered wives and reproducers of the nation's Jewish population. By stressing the feminine qualities of women in "Chen," by exempting young mothers from doing military service, and by not allowing women to have jobs at the front or leading jobs, the state is trying also to satisfy the male-led conservative groups.

In a country burdened by an oppressive government or by occupying forces, the people as a whole may rise up and revolt. Caroline Heikens (1981) claims that under these circumstances women are always among the first to take the initiative, perhaps because they know what it means to endure isolation and oppression. Seeing how little women have to lose may make a woman even more radical. In a liberation struggle men often have to hide, since they are more sought after than women. Women can take more risks and often do so. Women may take great risks in civil disobedience and in demonstrating against an oppressive government. I shall later describe the brave nonviolent fight of the Argentinian Mothers of Plaza de Mayo. A nonviolent civilian disobedience struggle calls for inventiveness, creativity, and endurance. Here women have been leading figures, though they are often forgotten when the battle is won and history is written. Good examples both of courageous nonviolent fighting and of having been "forgotten" when praise is delivered and busts made can be found in the Norwegian women's struggle against the German occupation of Norway (Stene, 1982; Wormdahl, 1978). But what about women in military operations—women carrying arms in the guerilla wars, for instance?

What we usually find is that when the situation shifts to a "normal" military operation, the structure of resistance—once loose and anarchically organized —becomes hierarchical. Women are the ones who are again gradually forced into marginal positions. Enloe (1979), after having analyzed the situation of women in various liberation armies around the world, concludes: "While the ideological rationales behind women's recruitment in liberation armies are indeed different from statist rationales, actual practices of liberation militaries and state militaries frequently look strikingly similar" (p. 28). Women enlist in armed units and are prepared to fight alongside the men, but often encounter male ambivalence. Enloe (1979) quotes a Lebanese woman: "On the surface, men were proud to have women fighting in their ranks. This conformed to the scheme of 'people's war.' In actual fact, the presence of women was felt to be an intolerable blow to their virility." Military commanders would give women fighters the least prestigious weaponry "on the excuse that they had not had enough training" (Enloe, 1979, p. 33, taken from Sharara, 1978, p. 14). The Lebanese war has been an urban war where neighborhoods have been the "front." Lebanese women commentators have noted that women on all sides participated largely by providing food to armed combatants, sewing sheets for hospitals, administering first aid, and donating blood. A Lebanese journalist writes: "Very few militants took part in this work. . . . This was considered women's work, and regarded with contempt, men who participated in it felt themselves diminished, and were mocked by their comrades" (Sharara, 1978, p. 19). This attitude corresponds well with the attitude toward women guerillas expressed by the revolutionary leader Che Guevara. In his book on guerilla warfare, he writes that among the worst things during the Cuban war was the fact that the guerillas were forced to eat the tasteless and sticky food they were making themselves. A female cook usually makes better food, he maintained, and besides, it was much easier to get a woman to perform such household chores. It constituted a great problem in all guerilla warfare, according to Che Guevara, that the more civilian jobs were looked at with contempt.

In a special issue of the *Women's Studies International Forum* on Women and Men's Wars (no. 3/4, 1982), Nhiwatiwa from the national liberation struggle in Zimbabwe and Delia Aguilar-San Juan, who writes about the national liberation struggle in the Philippines, both pay homage to women who directly participate in armed struggle in the cause of liberation. Delia Aguilar-San Juan (1982) holds that Filipino women are convinced that "freedom from oppression as women can become possible only when the nation is liberated from U.S. domination and when the majority of the people can be released from poverty, illness, malnutrition, and other forms of deprivation rampant in a neocolony" (p. 254). The Philippines have experienced 350 years of Spanish rule followed by the takeover by U.S. imperialism in 1898. This long colonial history did not go unresisted by the Filipino people, and while foreign domination resulted in the loss of rights women formerly possessed, they did not suffer for lack of heroic examples. There was Gabriela Silang, a general who led an uprising against Spain in the eighteenth century. Using assorted weapons to ward off a heavily supplied enemy, she valiantly led an army of 2,000 men. Filipino women of today also have joined the armed fight. Lorena Barros, the leader of the organization Makibaka (Free Movement of New Women), declared in 1971: "If an armed conflict does arise, we will fight alongside with the men, we should take arms if necessary" (from Aguilar-San Juan, 1982, p. 256). Makibaka was driven underground in 1972. And in 1976 Lorena Barros was shot to death by the Philippine Constabulary as she stood by the doorway of her hut. She stumbled and stood up and fell and stood up again, many times, until a bullet hit her in the head. Every time she stood up she also fired a shot. She had fired six shots from her .45 caliber pistol before they managed to kill her.

Aguilar-San Juan (1982) tells about a mother and her two children who packed up to follow their worker-father who had joined the New People's army four months earlier. Asked whether she would cry if her father should die in combat, eight-year-old Lisa answered: "I'll be angry and I'll kill our enemies." Aguilar-San Juan comments: "The mother's role as prime shaper of her children's world view cannot be underestimated" (p. 260). I would add that in many ways this mother seemed to have imbued her daughter with the same values, virtues, and thinking that the Viking mother strove to imbue in her son. But one can understand Filipino women fighting U.S. oppression by all means. With the sale of Filipino women going on now, with the prostitution in connection with the U.S. Air Force and Subic Naval Bases, conditions for women could hardly become worse. My question will always be: Will resorting to violence, using men's ways to solve conflicts, better the situation?

By looking at women in the militaries of several countries it is clear that women are not treated equally in the armed forces. They are oppressed even more than in civilian life; rape and sexual harassment are common, and macho attitudes prevail. This should not be surprising, but to some women these facts do not represent good enough reasons for women not to join the army. They maintain that if women in uniform become an increased presence (making excuses for the Israeli example) and are better organized, they can fight their way to leading positions in the military ranks. I shall here briefly summarize some of the arguments advanced by those who find that women ought to join the armed forces:

* To defend one's country is the duty and right of a citizen. To be full-fledged citizens and have real equality with men, women should also defend their country in the same way that men are defending it.
* The military institution with its monopoly on using organized physical force is such an important institution that women have to participate in it if they want to have power. Women cannot ask for rights and privileges without taking on the burdens and duties of this society.
* An integration of women in the army will also further the civilian rights of women. It will give women more self-confidence and teach men that women are capable fighters too.
* Integrating women in the army might be an advantage to the army, since women are loyal and dependable and easy to command and give the army a more human touch.

These are among the arguments most frequently heard in the ongoing debate. Not all of them are advanced by feminists. The last argument is heard from military establishments. The most frequent counterarguments also stem from various groups who usually adhere to one or two of the arguments cited:

* Women should defend their country, but not by copying men's ways, not by using physical violence. We are asking for equality, but not on men's premises. We do not want to become equal to men.
* We do not believe that we are able to change the military institution by joining it. If we join it, we shall have to join it on its premises, which are antithetical to those of the feminist movement. If you are in disagreement with the main ideology of an institution, you do not join it, if you don't have to.
* Women have too many burdens and duties in society as it is, being the ones doing all of the housework and the caring for small children, the old, and the sick; mostly this work is unpaid. Until men take over some of these burdens and share the unpaid work and our long workdays with us, women should not take on any extra duties.
* Women who give life and represent life should not take life.
* Women have a tradition of nonviolent fighting and represent a peace force that will be destroyed if they are integrated in the army.
* Integrating women in the army means a higher militarization of society and will make work in the peace movements more difficult.

To me the most important of these arguments is the first one. In the new feminist movement we make a clear distinction between equality and liberation. We want equality, but on our own premises. We do not want equality on men's premises. We do not want to become like men or copy men's ways. We are trying to build up other patterns of communication, other ways of relating, of organizing work. We are trying to build egalitarian structures where everybody has a say. We are fighting hierarchies. We are trying to cooperate and to break down competition. We use assertiveness training so that women become self-assertive, independent, critical, but at the same time we want to keep the caring aspects of our education and to teach men to also care about living beings, children and grown-ups, plants and animals, Mother Earth.

When the army promises to make a man out of a young boy, what do they mean by that? I agree with Celina García (1981) when she says that this facetiousness means that the army will strip a young male of his individuality, his spontaneity, his fears and compassion for his kind, and make him a walking being that obeys orders without questioning. He must be taught to be tough and strong, to not show compassion, to not care for other human beings—some of them he must learn to define as "enemies" who deserve to be killed. He must not show tenderness or weakness because such traits are womanly. And so he is taught to kill the woman in him. Are we too to kill the woman in us? Are we too to let the army make men out of us, make men of women?

My answer to this is: No. If we too become men, then there is no hope for humankind. Rather than joining the army we should help men refuse to do military service, refuse to kill. It is too easy to copy men's ways and label it "equality." There has always been a tendency for the oppressed to imitate the oppressor. Women have to counteract such a tendency. We have to discard as utterly dangerous to the human race all those values developed by men that are based on violence and oppression.

2 Peace Activities Started and Led by Women

ARE WOMEN MORE PEACE-LOVING THAN MEN?

It seems likely that the old matriarchies were peaceful, and as a sex, women have never institutionalized violence. But women who "succeed" in the patriarchal societies of today are usually not very different from men: they would not be allowed top positions if they were. The fact that Vigdís Finnbogadóttir with her declared pacifism won the presidential election in Iceland is encouraging, however. Also, going through the training in patriarchal thinking in formal school systems and political life generally guarantees that women will think like men, will compete the way they do, and hold the same value systems. This is the dilemma described by Virginia Woolf in her book *Three Guineas* (1938). If women are to save the world, we must involve ourselves in a different education, especially in the institutes of higher learning. And we must have power. But can we see any signs that women as a group in our patriarchal societies hold different attitudes from men—about important questions concerning peace and the arms race?

I believe there are some such signs. Opinion polls in many western countries show that women are far more negative in their attitudes toward the raise in military expenditures and the deployment of new weapons than men are (Brock-Utne, 1981a). A higher percentage of Norwegian women than Norwegian men, for instance, were against plans for stationing weaponry for the U.S. Marines in the middle of Norway, thus making Norway even more of a base for U.S. warfare against the USSR. While 54 percent of Norwegian men sampled said they accepted these plans, only 29 percent of Norwegian women did.

While men are designing new technology and building new industries based on the philosophy that any specific advance is progress and that economic growth is the yardstick to measure by, women are thinking of the effects on their children. Women protest and march against pollution and nuclear power plants. When a referendum on the continuation or abolition of nuclear power plants was held in Sweden in 1976, 88 percent of the women within the Social

33

Democratic party in Sweden said no to these installations as compared to only 25 percent of the men within the same party. When the board of the Norwegian Social Democratic (Labor) party took its stand on the question of installations for the U.S. Marines in the middle of Norway, only six board members voted against these plans. Of these six, five were women (the sixth was a young man; the leader of the youth organization of the same party). But the prime minister voted yes. Had *she* not done so, she would most likely not have been the prime minister.

Another Norwegian poll from November 1982 asked for the opinion on whether Norway ought to grant 49 million Norwegian Kroner (approx. $6 million) as Norway's contribution to NATO's infrastructural preparations for the stationing of the cruise missiles in Europe, and showed that 76 percent of the women answered no to this question compared to only 46 percent of the men.

Opinion polls from the United States show a gender gap when it comes to questions concerning economic distribution, the development of weapons and peace initiatives. Bella Abzug (1984) refers to a large opinion poll conducted by *New York Times*/CBS in June 1983. That poll showed for instance that only 39 percent of the women against 60 percent of the men were satisfied with the economic policies of the Reagan administration. It further showed that 74 percent of the women held that the development of the nuclear bomb was a bad thing against only 56 percent of the men interviewed.

A majority of the Dutch population is against the deployment of the new missiles. Research shows that within this majority, 10 percent more women are against nuclear weapons compared with males of the Dutch population (van der Gaast, 1981).

In earlier opinion polls concerning military questions there are more abstentions among women than men (Brock-Utne, 1982). Now the previous abstainers among women are voting no to the continued arms race. Organizations such as Women for Peace in which women undertake study-group activities and organize teach-ins, have probably been instrumental in giving women enough self-confidence to be able to rely on their own judgement about questions concerning peace and war.

We may quote great feminist peace heroes like Bertha von Suttner, Fredrika Bremer, Ellen Key, and Clara Zetkin, who all believed that women had a special role to play in the creation of peace. In her peace appeal in 1915 to women in all countries Clara Zetkin said: "When the men kill, it is up to us, the women, to fight for the right to live. When the men are silent, it is our duty as we are filled with suffering, to raise our voices in protest" (Zetkin, 1957–1960, Vol. I).

But even male peace activists like Johan Galtung today and Mahatma Gandhi, who led the Indian nonviolent fight against British colonial rule, have been among those who have announced publicly that women have a special role to play in the creation of peace. Gandhi went so far as to maintain that *only* women were able to save the world. He looked at women as the incarnation of *ahimsa*. Women have a different upbringing than men, are a more peaceful sex, and more capable than men of solving conflicts in a nonviolent manner. He warned women against imitating men, becoming like men. He said: "She can run the race but she will not rise to the heights she is capable of by mimicking man" (Gandhi, 1940). This sentence resembles a feminist adage of recent origin: "The woman who strives to be equal to man lacks ambition." Gandhi said that he had learned the techniques of nonviolence and civil disobedience from women, mainly from the British suffragettes. Gandhi was convinced that women should take the lead in the civil disobedience or *satyagraha* movement in India. He said: "I would love to find that my future army contained a vast preponderance of women over men. If the fight came, I should then face it with greater confidence than if men predominated. I would dread the latter's violence. Women would be my guarantee against such an outbreak" (Gandhi, 1939). It is a fact that more than 60 percent of the participants in the Salt March, which took place in March 1930, were women. And out of the 30,000 people arrested in connection with the march, 17,000 were women (Thomas, 1964).

Gandhi saw that if women were going to play the leading role he wanted them to play, they had to have more power and also fight their own oppression. He was of the opinion that even in the context of marriage, women should guard against serving as mere tools of enjoyment for their men (Ryland, 1977, p. 135). He urged women to refuse to play along by dressing to please men, which could only confirm their subordinate status in the world. In an address to women in Ceylon, Gandhi (1927) said: "What is it that makes woman deck herself more than man? I am told by feminine friends that she does so for pleasing man. Well, I tell you, if you want to play your part in the world's affairs, you must refuse to deck yourself for pleasing man. If I was born a woman I would rise in rebellion against the pretension on the part of man that woman is born to be his plaything." Gandhi's vision of the role of women in Indian society and his stand on specific social reform issues were remarkably similar to those of leading feminists in India in the 1920s and 1930s, women leaders like Saraladevi Choudurani and Kamaladevi Chattopadhyay. In theory and public speech he was a co-feminist, but it would be unjust not to mention that in his private life, in his relationship to his wife, he was a male chauvinist (Sharma, 1981). To most feminists a male who deserves the term co-feminist also shows a high degree of congruence between his private and public life. A co-feminist does not only take feminist stands publicly, but he also seeks to promote his wife's independent career and shares household chores with her. If you are working for an egalitarian society, you also have to arrange your household in an egalitarian manner. The means must be in harmony with the ends you want to promote.

While male peace activists like Johan Galtung and Gandhi talk about women being more peace-loving than men and also see that fighting the oppression of women is a necessary element in the fight for peace, other male peace activists do not agree. Some peace-loving men have trouble understanding that the more women are oppressed in a society, the easier their own viewpoints will be disregarded if they are labeled feminine. Riane Eisler (1982), the co-director of the Institute for Futures Forecasting, points to the following ironic fact: Those on the liberal left and center who speak of freedom, equality, and disarmament continue to see sexual equality and other "women's issues" as peripheral concerns, requiring action *after* more important things are done. But those on the right, who relentlessly work for hierarchical orderings, authoritarian controls, and increased armaments, correctly perceive that sexual inequality is the cornerstone of the system they seek to impose on us all and work relentlessly against sexual equality. President Reagan has found his ideologue (much as Hitler did in Nietzsche) in George Gilder, whose book, *Wealth and Poverty*, the President gave all his cabinet appointees. Gilder claims that discrimination, both racial and sexual, is a myth, and that women get paid less than men because they produce less. This thesis, which is actively promoted by the Reagan administration, is that women destroy their husbands' productivity by working: Men work hard only if they have women and children at home who would starve without them. To get women out of the labor force will restore the American family's viability. By the recriminalization of abortion—another goal of the Reagan administration—they evidently hope to create another baby boom. We might cite Nietzsche (1885) (Hitler's ideologue) here: "Men should be trained for war and women for the recreation of the warrior" (p. 81). Gilder also claims that feminism is incompatible with the objectives of black males. It is a consoling fact that where polls according to sex have been taken, it appears that for the first time since women have had the vote they are voting quite differently from men. They are turning away from Reagan and from the Republican party in very large numbers.

Those on the right see the women's liberation movement and feminist ideas as dangerous threats to the society they want to create. And they are right. Evidence strongly suggests that the more militaristic a society, the more sexist it tends to be. Gloria Steinem (1980) shows in a series of articles how Hitler crushed the German feminist movement as he militarized Germany. The Nazi movement was an essentially male organization. German women's virtue, according to Hitler, was to bear children, preferably sons, who were to become soldiers and propagate with the sword the ideology of Nazism around the world.

HOW WOMEN WORK FOR PEACE

Looking at peace movements started and led by women, I have asked the question: What characterizes women's fight for peace? Analyzing this question I have found three main characteristics (Brock-Utne, 1981d):

* It is connected to the concern for human life, especially for children, but also for themselves and other women.
* It makes use of a varied set of nonviolent techniques, acts, strategies.
* It is transpolitical, often transnational, aimed at reaching other women in the opposite camp.

One of the earliest organized incidences of women's fight against men's wars that we know about has been recorded by Aristophanes, in his play "Lysistrata." The ancient Greek city states were at war with one another—or rather the men in the cities were, to the great despair of the women. Aristophanes tells how the women from the various city states met and discussed what to do to have their men stop the constant wars and fighting. Lacking any powerful means at their disposal, they decided on one that, according to Aristophanes, led to the end of the war: they decided to go on a sexual strike against their men until the men had stopped fighting. Women were here fighting across the city states in a collective, nonviolent action to put an end to the war.

Bertha von Suttner—A Forgotten Peacemaker

The focus in this section will be mainly on peace movements started and led by women. As has already been mentioned, there have been some outstanding women of our time who are fighting bravely against the threat of a nuclear holocaust, women like the physician Helen Caldicott. It is also important that earlier women who have dedicated their lives to the work for peace be remembered. They are too easily forgotten. Not many years ago I did not know about Bertha von Suttner myself. She has been "forgotten" in our history books. I have discovered that my mother and her generation knew quite a bit about the peace campaign of Bertha von Suttner. My daughter and her generation have never heard of her. I have asked large audiences of Norwegian youngsters if they had ever heard the name Bertha von Suttner. Nobody had! But they all knew about Alfred Nobel, they all knew about the invention of dynamite. They also knew about Fridtjof Nansen, not only as a polar explorer, but also as someone talking about peace and working for peace. And of course they knew about the writer Bjørnstjerne Bjørnson as a political activist, and some of them about the Russian writer Leo Tolstoy and his work for peace. But the work of Bertha von Suttner was made invisible to them. Since that time I have been talking about her whenever I deal with the fight for peace. So consequently several pages about her life are included here.

Austrian author Bertha von Suttner (1843–1914) devoted her life to the fight for peace. She was well-known in Europe at the turn of the century, yet she has received little attention in history books. No wonder. Those books are about men and war, not women and peace. They are about the way men solve conflicts violently. They are not about nonviolent conflict resolution or fights for peace. And women—both as a group and the outstanding women of various times—are made invisible.

Bertha von Suttner was born in Prague as Bertha Sophia Felicita, Gräfin Kinsky von Chinik und Tettau. Her father, who had been a field marshal, died before she was born. Her mother then moved to Vienna. Those she mixed with were officers, mostly belonging to the nobility. Bertha moved with her mother from Vienna to Paris, Baden-Baden, and Italy. Her mother was a passionate gambler and moved between cities that had casinos where she could gamble. After some years she had gambled all her money away. Up to that time Bertha had some of the benefits of an upper-class background. She had a private tutor who had taught her basic skills like reading and writing, arithmetic, music, and some knowledge of other languages. She had a great talent for music. She also loved to read and read far more than anyone had inspired her to do. She was rather critical of her mother's group of acquaintances. She grew up in an atmosphere where to win glory on the battlefield was the hope for most men. Men were to be tough and brave.

When her mother's fortune came to an end, Bertha with her aristocratic upbringing had to look for a paid job. There was no money left for a dowry should she marry. Bertha was at this time in her late twenties. The only job that would be commensurate with her social background was the job of governess, private tutor to some upper-class children. She was employed by Freiherr von Suttner to teach his four girls, who were between 15 and 20 years old. The four sisters also had a brother, Arthur von Suttner, who was studying law. Bertha and Arthur soon fell in love with each other. His parents were very much against their relationship. Bertha was ten years older than Arthur, was poor, and had no dowry. Arthur's parents decided that they had to get a replacement for Bertha even though she was a good teacher for their daughters, because they heartily disliked the influence she had on their only son. One day Arthur's mother showed Bertha an advertisement in a newspaper: A very rich and distinguished elderly gentleman living in Paris was looking for a respectable woman of good breeding in command of several foreign languages who could work as his private secretary and also see to the proper management of his home. She applied for the job and got it. The distinguished elderly gentleman turned out to be the inventor Alfred Nobel, a man who at that time was totally unknown to Bertha. Nobel was kind to Bertha, showed her around Paris, and did what he could to make her feel welcome and happy. But she was desperately unhappy, longing for Arthur. Arthur was filled with the same despair and longing. After several weeks Bertha left the job as

Nobel's secretary to meet Arthur and marry him, in secrecy. The couple eloped and supported themselves in Caucasia by giving private lessons, she in music, he in German. At this time the Russian-Turkish war broke out. They both helped by collecting money for the victims of the war. But when it became increasingly difficult to earn a living solely by giving private lessons, Arthur started writing about the war in Austrian newspapers. His articles were well received and also helped them financially. Then Bertha also started writing. She insisted that she became an author not as a result of any inner drive, but because she wanted to prove that she could do anything her husband could. If he could write and get articles accepted, she surely could too. She was ten years older than he was and did not want to be intimidated by him. Their marriage was, by the way, an extremely happy one, based on an equal partnership.

When Bertha von Suttner first started writing she used the pseudonym B. Oulot. She began with a series of short stories called *Fans and Aprons*, which was immediately printed in *Neue Freie Presse* and for which she was well paid. From this time, in the beginning of the 1880s, until her death, Bertha never stopped writing. In these years in Caucasia she also started writing novels. Still using the name B. Oulot she wrote the novel *Es Löwos* (1883), which is about the happiness of living and working together with the person one loves. The novel is a tribute to Arthur. Around this time, 1885, she also wrote *Ein schlechter Mensch* (A Bad Person), which dealt with the way new and more radical thoughts were making their way into conservative social settings. Her first popularized scientific novel, *Inventarium einer Seele* (Inventory of a Soul, 1883), also stemmed from these years in Caucasia. This is the first novel in which her pacifist viewpoints, which she had developed through wide reading and discussions with her beloved Arthur, are evident. This book became a success and was widely read. The great author and literary critic of the time, Georg Brandes, wrote a chapter in praise of the book in his collective works.

After the couple had lived and worked nine years in Caucasia, Arthur's parents finally accepted the marriage and asked the couple to return home to Austria. Here Bertha wrote *Das Maschinenzeitalter* (The Age of Machines), which is considered one of her best books. Apart from *Die Waffen nieder* (No More Arms), which she wrote a couple of years later in 1889, it was the most widely read novel around the turn of the century. Because of the wide discrimination against women and the lack of belief in women as creative beings, Bertha still felt obliged to have her writings published under various pseudonyms. *Das Maschinenzeitalter* (1888) was published under the name *Jemand* (Someone). The critics were enthusiastic about the book, which they claimed must have been written by: "an intelligent man of the highest knowledge and ability." In her book about Bertha von Suttner, Ursula Jorfald (1962) mentions that Bertha and Arthur happened to be enjoying a meal in a restaurant on the very day when *Das Maschinenzeitalter* had been discussed in the

Austrian Parliament and was, consequently, the talk of the people in the restaurant. Bertha listened eagerly to what people had to say. When she heard a group of men at a neighboring table recommend it so highly, she smiled to them and said: "I think I shall have to buy myself that book and read it." The answer she received was: "If you want to take some good advice, nice lady, don't do that. That book is not for ladies" (Jorfald, 1962, p. 25).

After the publication of this book, Bertha and Arthur went to Paris to stay with Alfred Nobel for some days. Bertha had kept up the contact with Nobel through all the years since she had been his secretary those few weeks in Paris before she eloped with Arthur. She sent him her writings and they constantly wrote letters to each other. Their correspondence ought to have been dramatized, since it illustrates so well the fundamental issue of the relationship between means and ends.

Alfred Nobel was a kind and hospitable host to Bertha and Arthur von Suttner when they visited him in Paris. But Bertha was shocked to hear the many rumors of a new war and the plans for revenge that were being harbored by many men of influence. This anticipation of a new war seemed quite immoral to her. In Paris they also learned that a peace organization had just been created in London, The International Peace and Arbitration Association. Bertha's main thought was how she could best help this new peace movement. She decided that since her aim was to mobilize as many people as possible for the peace movement, an engaging and provocative novel would accomplish this more easily than a fact-oriented thesis. She wrote *Die Waffen nieder* in 1889, a novel that must be read. It is the most fervent, intense, and heartfelt argumentation against war and against the "rationale" behind wars. Though she is dealing with "old-fashioned wars" where men went to the battlefield to kill other men, she is nevertheless dealing with what we have called the nuclear mentality, the quest to conquer and win, to be the strongest, the bravest, the best. Von Suttner writes about Prussia and Austria singing a never-ending chorus:

> My weapons are defensive,
> Your weapons are offensive,
> I have to arm, because you arm.
> Because I arm, you arm.
> Consequently we both arm—
> and continue to rearm.
> (Kempf, 1964, p. 34)

Besides being an ardent attack on the mentality leading to war and permitting war, the book is also a beautiful love story. In the pacifist male hero of the book, Bertha painted a beautiful portrait of her own husband. The book was extremely popular and was immediately sold out when it appeared in 1889. In Germany alone it was reprinted in 31 new editions, and it was translated into numerous languages. But Bertha originally had great difficulties in finding a publisher who would take the book. Her manuscript was returned from one publishing house after another. One publisher wrote her an honest letter telling her why he could not have the manuscript printed, saying that the military establishment would be offended. Another publisher said that should he print it, he would have to have an experienced statesman go through the manuscript and delete anything that could give offense to political and military circles. Bertha replied that she would rather have the manuscript burned than subjected to a diplomatic and opportunistic censorship.

The manuscript was finally published in its original version. Ursula Jorfald (1962) tells both about Bertha von Suttner's own reactions to the success of her book and about reactions from great men of the time like Rosegger and Tolstoy. Bertha von Suttner gave the following reason why it immediately became such a bestseller: "In order for a tone to reach the most beautiful sound the acoustic surroundings must be the best. The militarism of the day has reached such heights and put so much pressure on people that the solution—to abandon arms—met the most responsive audience." The novel went to the hearts not only of the masses, but also of the great men of that time: Leo Tolstoy, Alfred Nobel, Bjørnstjerne Bjørnson, Peter Rosegger, and Friedrich von Bodenstedt. Rosegger wrote in his book review: "the reading of "Die Waffen nieder" was a strong experience. When I had read it, I had but one wish: that this book be translated into all languages, that all libraries in the world will have copies of it and it be read in all schools. Societies have been created for the spreading of the Bible. I wish I could form a society which would deal with the spreading of this book, a book I find has fundamental consequences and is of fundamental value" (Jorfald, 1962, p. 29). Leo Tolstoy wrote to Bertha von Suttner: "I look at the publication of your book as a good token. The book Uncle Tom's Cabin by Harriet Beecher Stowe contributed towards the abolition of slavery. God give that your book will serve the same purpose when it comes to the abolition of war" (from Jorfald, 1962, p. 30).

But the book was also met with harsh words and ridicule. Bertha was a woman who had ventured into an area she was not supposed to be able to understand. One critic wrote: "The conclusions she draws can only be met with a smile from any serious politician." Professor Felix Dahn criticized her through a poem addressed to weapons-resisting women and men. In his poem he answered: "Yes to arms," to her "No to arms." The main message of the poem was that men were free and wanted to fight. Fighting was a job and duty of real men, a duty that women had no understanding of, and consequently should not talk about. Women ought to keep quiet. It was not their business to deal with questions concerning war and peace. Such questions should be left to those men who had the capacity for dealing properly with them. He used sexist language to describe those men who did not want to fight, calling them "men in petticoats."

Bertha von Suttner answered Felix Dahn: "But women are not going to be silent, Mr. Professor. We are writing, making speeches, working, acting. Women are going to change society and ourselves" (Jorfald, 1962, p. 34). At that time Bertha had not yet undertaken any major speeches to larger audiences. She wanted her husband to open an important peace conference, which she had the main responsibility for organizing. When he became ill, she had another man open the conference. But she realized after having written the successful *Die Waffen nieder* that she wanted to do away with her fear of addressing big audiences. She wanted to dedicate her life to the work for peace. The success of her pacifist novel had given her an important platform for the continuing fight for peaceful solutions to conflict. From then on, peace conferences, congresses, and peace meetings formed the most important ingredients in her life, together with hospitable moments with peace-friends from all over the world.

The first time Bertha von Suttner spoke to a large audience was at the Peace Conference in 1891. This conference was held at the Capitol in Rome; it was the first time in history that a woman spoke at this ancient and historical site. The newspapers in Rome did not like the fact that a woman was allowed to speak there. But von Suttner was calm and self-assured; she knew that she was fighting for a just cause and had important things to say. She was received warmly by the audience.

Besides writing, speaking, and arranging peace congresses, she also traveled from one country to another to win the hearts of well-known, influential people for the sake of peace and disarmament. She was in continuous correspondence with Alfred Nobel, who looked upon himself as a pacifist even though he was the inventor of dynamite. Ursula Jorfald quotes letters he wrote to Bertha von Suttner. On one occasion he wrote to Bertha: "I am doing more for peace with my cannons than you are doing with your speeches on peace and disarmament" (Bertha von Suttner, 1909, pp. 370–371). On another occasion he wrote: "When the day arrives that two armed nations can destroy each other within minutes, then all nations will shrink back and will dismiss their troops. We shall have a disarmed world" (Bertha von Suttner, 1909, pp. 370–371). Of course, we are now in that very situation described by Nobel, yet the world is still armed and rearming more steadily than ever before in history.

Since Nobel constantly insisted that they were fighting for the same cause but by different means, Bertha von Suttner tried to talk him into donating some of the money he had earned on dynamite to the creation of a peace prize. At last, in January 1893, Alfred Nobel wrote to von Suttner that he had decided to donate a part of his fortune to the creation of a peace prize that would be given each fifth year to "that person or those persons who have worked in the best way to further the brotherhood of man, for disarmament and for the organization of peace conferences." He believed that the prize would be awarded six times in all, "Because if we have not succeeded in thirty years in improving the current situation, we are witnessing barbarism" (from Jorfald, 1962, p. 96).

Bertha von Suttner never stopped working for peace, using every opportunity she could find. For instance, she contacted the Norwegian polar explorer Fridtjof Nansen when she learned that he was going to talk about his polar expedition to an audience in Vienna in 1889. She asked him if he could use this opportunity to say something about the important work for peace and disarmament. He agreed and devoted the last part of his speech to that topic.

Bertha saw that a question of vital importance to the peace movement was the creation of a newsletter. She found enthusiastic support for such an idea in the young German publisher Alfred Fried in Berlin. Together they created a monthly peace magazine which she edited and he published for seven years (1892–1899). The magazine contained 48 pages and was called *Die Waffen nieder* after the successful novel. The magazine published news about the peace movement and detailed accounts of the 1892 Peace Congress in Berne. Among the delegates to this congress, Bertha von Suttner was the only woman. Yet she played a leading role as one of the three members of the important drafting group. The three important issues dealt with were: the solution of conflicts through arbitration, the creation of an international High Court of Justice, and disarmament. Bertha was eagerly advocating the use of arbitration to settle international conflicts and corresponded with statesmen from many nations about this. Present at the Peace Congress of 1892 were not only peace activists from many countries, but also leading statesmen, politicians and writers. She corresponded with the Norwegian author and political activist Bjørnstjerne Bjørnson, who told her that the Norwegian Parliament had unanimously adopted a resolution favoring international arbitration. The creation of an international Court of Justice was further discussed at the Peace Congress in 1894, and steps were taken to have this plan realized within five years, in time for the next peace congress, which was to be held in The Hague. This was also the place where the court was to be located.

Peace promoters from all over the world met in The Hague in 1899, among them many statesmen. Just before this congress, in August 1898, the tsar of Russia had published a manifesto in which he urged all peace-loving nations to meet at the Peace Conference in The Hague and form an alliance of nations to fight for world peace and abandon all wars. Pope Leo XIII wrote to the same effect. Bertha was excited; the manifesto of the tsar made the fight for peace into a campaign involving governments, just as she had hoped. Together with other peace activists she traveled from country to country to promote the message of the tsar's manifesto. It must have been gratifying for her to know that he was moved to write it after having read *Die Waffen nieder*. But she was disappointed at the way they were received in most countries; England was the only one that distributed news about the congress and encouraged people to attend.

Throughout these years, Bertha von Suttner wrote a diary and kept careful notes of all the proceedings going on at the congresses. The Peace Conference in The Hague in 1899 marked the first occasion that statesmen from many nations discussed how a guarantee for a lasting world peace could be attained. In her diary Bertha described the hostility with which the conference was met.

At the 1899 Peace Conference Bertha von Suttner was again the only woman to participate in the negotiations. While they were still in session there was a meeting of the International Federation of Women in London. For this meeting Bertha had written a speech about the important role of women in the peace movement. The speech was read in her absence.

In 1902 Arthur von Suttner died, and Bertha never recovered from the blow, grieving until she died herself 12 years later. At first her grief and despair were so deep she did not feel she could go on, working alone at what they had always shared. He had been her moral supporter, her intellectual partner, her lover. She said that had it not been for a letter he had left for her to be read after his death, she would not have been able to continue her work. Among other things he wrote: "The good memory of your life's companion must give you strength to continue our work for promotion of peace until you too reach the end of your life's journey. Have courage. Do not give up. You must go on doing your best" (Bertha von Suttner, 1909, p. 539).

And she went on. In December 1905 she was awarded the Nobel Peace Prize. Public opinion in many countries had been in favor of awarding her the prize many years before; she ought to have been the first one to receive it. But the Nobel Peace Prize Committee was reluctant. Ursula Jorfald (1962) says: "When one reads all the angry protests against the Nobel Committee from all parts of the world because it delayed over and over again giving the Peace Prize to Bertha von Suttner there is only one conclusion to be drawn: It looks as if the Nobel Committee did not want to stoop to the position of giving the Prize—especially not the first one—to a woman. This fact tells something about the worth of women at the beginning of the century." At the Nobel Institute in Oslo there are three busts, all portraying men. There is no bust of Bertha von Suttner, who was the spiritual godmother of the prize (Jorfald, 1962, p. 112).

The work at the next Peace Conference in The Hague in 1907 was even more difficult. The Conference had become more official and there were many official representatives present. Bertha wrote about the Conference in her diary:

The agenda set up for this Conference and the composition of it resemble a Congress of free-thinkers to which each nation has sent ten archbishops and just one free-thinking scientist and in which just one item was set aside for "the right to worship" while ten items concerned liturgical matters and where there was no item covering the right to be without a religion at all. In The Hague we are going to discuss the use of contrabands, mines, the cannonading of cities and other such "practical matters," but not a word about the abolition of the instruments for murder.

Bertha died just before the outbreak of the First World War, the war she had long dreaded and warned against.

Women's International League for Peace and Freedom

In 1915, at the beginning of World War I, women from 13 countries came together in The Hague to protest the war and think of ways to have it stopped. There were women from countries that were at war with each other and from neutral countries as well. This meeting was the starting point of the Women's International League for Peace and Freedom (WILPF). These women worked out a manifesto that included a proposal for a permanent institution of arbitration. The first task of this new institution would be to arbitrate between the two sides then at war with each other. This, we should note, was in 1915, before the League of Nations had come into being.

The meeting appointed two delegations of women who were to travel to all the states at war and also to the neutral states and present the manifesto to governments and top leaders of the states. The women were received by 35 governments. Ursula Jorfald (1962) tells that one Prime Minister in one of the largest states said: "Your proposal is the most sensible which has come to this office." The Prime Minister of another state said: "I agree with you that it would be better to follow your proposal which could lead to an early end to this war than just to go on and waste more lives and damage more property and land." But, as we all know, the states did not follow the advice these women gave. After the war, WILPF sent a proposal to the Peace Conference in Paris in 1919 suggesting measures aimed at avoiding a new war.

When Emily Greene Balch, the first Secretary General of WILPF, received the Nobel Peace Prize in 1946, the Director of the Nobel Institute, Gunnar Jahn, said:

> I want to say so much that it would have been extremely wise if the proposal WILPF made to the Conference in 1919 had been accepted by the conference. But few of the men listened to what the women had to say. The atmosphere was too bitter and revengeful. And on top of this there was the fact that the proposal was made by women. In our patriarchal world suggestions which come from women are seldom taken seriously. Sometimes it would be wise of the men to spare their condescending smiles.

Women's International League for Peace and Freedom is still active on all continents today, with chapters in 24 countries. It is the only truly international women's organization solely devoted to the work for peace. The first aim of the organization as stated in the Statement of Aims of WILPF as revised at the Stockholm Congress in 1959 is this: "The WILPF aims at bringing together women of different political and philosophical tendencies united in their determination to study, make known and help abolish the political, social, economic and psychological causes of war, and to work for a constructive peace; (Bussey and Time, 1980, p. 232).

The WILPF has consultative status with the UN Social and Economic Council and with the specialized agencies, UNESCO, ILO, and FAO, where it regularly makes known its views on all sorts of current issues that come before these bodies. The WILPF maintains a secretariat in Geneva (address: 1. rue de Varambe 1211, Geneva 20, Switzerland). The member bodies are national sections, each with its own officers and programs, suited to the needs of the area. Individuals may also be members. Every three years a Triennial Congress is held where plans and policies for the organization include issuing publications, sending out appeals and petitions, organizing delegations, sponsoring conferences and seminars, and publicizing findings. In recent years the annual summer schools have also attracted quite a number of younger women to the organization. The league takes a keen interest in promoting education for peace and has published a number of brochures and study guides for teachers. These are available from the United States section (address: 1213 Race Street, Philadelphia, PA 19107, USA). The former president of WILPF, Kay Camp, published a booklet in 1977 describing the work of 50 world feminists, all leaders in the effort to obtain peace, social justice, and freedom in the world. The booklet is entitled *Listen to the Women for a Change* and is available from the WILPF offices.

One of the largest meetings that the WILPF has sponsored during recent years was Women of Europe in Action for Peace, which was held in Amsterdam in the Netherlands from November 27 to 29, 1981. More than 500 women from 25 countries and 4 continents belonging to 112 national and international organizations and movements came to the meeting. The meeting was initiated by WILPF with the support of Dutch Women for Peace and Dutch Women against Nuclear Weapons. A conference report is available from WILPF.

Irish Peace Women

The incident that gave rise to the work of the Irish Peace Women was the killing of three small children in their pram and the mutilation of their mother. When the aunt of these children, Mairead Corrigan, was told what happened, she expressed such a passionate anger and despair on television that she reached the hearts of most mothers, who all felt that they'd had enough. In another part of Belfast, Betty Williams expressed her spontaneous disgust for the act that had led to this tragedy. She got the night editor of the local newspaper to print her name, address, and telephone number along with an invitation to all women who wanted an end to the war to notify her. Women responded in great numbers; they called each other; they organized themselves.

In less than 48 hours Betty Williams and the women who called her had gathered more than 6,000 signatures to a petition demanding an end to the acts of war. Betty Williams presented these results on local television. She and Mairead Corrigan came together and planned a peace march the day after the funeral of the three small children. The news of this march spread like wildfire. More than 10,000 people came to this march, many of them in buses from other parts of Northern Ireland. Participants were mostly women; middle-aged women, mothers with small children, and also grandmothers. A number of them joined the march as it proceeded. It took place in total silence. This march in August 1976 marked the starting point of the Peace People movement in Northern Ireland. From that time on, peace marches were arranged throughout Northern Ireland, as were sympathy marches in England and other countries. Three months after the first march, more than 150,000 people had participated in marches to demonstrate their strong desire for lasting peace in Northern Ireland.

Two weeks after the first march, the Peace Women marched through Shankhill, a working class district in Belfast. The two leading Peace Women, Betty Williams and Mairead Corrigan, are Roman Catholics; but the Protestant women ran out of their houses, embraced the demonstrators, and cried. The Peace Women had managed to get women from both opposing camps to march together; Protestants and Catholics were in the same march for the same cause.

Great courage was required of the marchers. Those who marched were often attacked by extremist groups from both of the opposing parties; often young boys threw stones at the peaceful demonstrators. On several occasions they destroyed the banner that the women carried and used poles to beat the peaceful participants in the march, who never returned this violence. The Peace Women gradually widened their range of activities to include other nonviolent actions, like tea-party actions. Here women from one "camp" would invite women from the opposing "camp" to a tea party. These tea visits were returned and extended to arrangements where children from the two parties met. Holiday camps for children were arranged.

In Norway, more than 10,000 people took part in a march in Oslo in November 1976 to demonstrate their support for the Irish Peace Women. The Peace Women were given the Norwegian People's Peace Prize, a sum of $400,000 collected by Norwegians in the course of a few days in protest against the Nobel Committee, which had not granted the Nobel Peace Prize to the two Irish women. (They did receive that prize the year after, however.)

Nordic Women for Peace

The peace action among Nordic women, named Women for Peace, was started directly after NATO had made the decision, on December 12, 1979, to install a new generation of land-based intermediate-range nuclear missiles (cruise and Pershing missiles) in west and central Europe. Norway is a member of NATO, but the Norwegian Parliament frequently has too little say in decision-making on important aspects of NATO membership. In the case of theater nuclear weapons, people felt that they had been deceived and betrayed by their own government. People refused to believe in protection by nuclear arms, which destroy what they were meant to protect. The argument for the new turn of the arms screw was, as always, that we had to become stronger, we had to rearm in order to start a real disarmament. Nordic Women for Peace was started by Danish and Finnish women at a kitchen table in Copenhagen around Christmas 1979 and spread to other Nordic countries. A common text for the action was adopted in Oslo on January 22, 1980. It states:

> We have more and more come to realize that women all over the world nourish the same thoughts and the same fears: Do my children have any future? Together with women all over the world we want to turn our power-lessness into strength. We cannot any longer silently accept the power game between the superpowers. All acts of aggression must be stopped and the disarmament negotiations must be continued and must lead to action and real disarmament. We demand:
>
> • Disarmament to secure a lasting peace!
> • Food instead of arms!
> • No to War!

This manifesto was translated and spread, with petitions to sign, to all women in all the Nordic countries: Denmark, Finland, Greenland, Iceland, Norway, and Sweden. By June 1980, more than half a million signatures had been collected. The signatures were delivered, together with the manifesto, to UN Secretary General Kurt Waldheim immediately before the official opening of the UN Conference on Women, held in Copenhagen in the summer of 1980. The campaign also addressed itself to President Carter and President Brezhnev. At the Copenhagen Conference, the leaders of the Nordic Women for Peace were urged by women from all over the world to carry on their work. And so they have done. After the conference they started building up study circles in their countries for women to learn more about the arms race. In several instances, former knitting clubs have become study groups on arms and disarmament. From these study groups, the idea of the Peace March of summer 1981 arose.

Two young Norwegian women who belonged to one of the study groups of Women for Peace but who had never before been politically active decided that they wanted to do something more for peace. Would organizing a peace march to go through several countries be a good idea? The two young women, Wenche Sørangr and Rachel Pedersen, were advised to contact Eva Nordland, who had been engaged in peace work for many years and had many contacts. Together they made plans for the 1981 Peace March from Copenhagen to

Paris. Ten women from each of the Nordic countries had to promise to walk all the way from Denmark to France, while others would join the march, some for hours, some for days. Since this was in the summer when the newspapers do not have much to write about and since people had not been marching for peace for quite some time, this Peace March was rather well covered by the media. By the time the march reached Paris on the 8th of August, the day before the anniversary of the bombing of Nagasaki, many thousands of people had joined. Marchers sang and danced in the streets.

There was considerable discussion about the march in the newspapers. Opponents maintained that the women had chosen the wrong countries to walk through. For their mission to have any effect, they would have to walk to the Soviet Union; the Soviet leaders were the ones to be held accountable for the arms race. And when the women were fighting nuclear weapons both in the East and the West, why did women from the Soviet Union not march with them? We have an explanation for this in a statement made by Margarita Maksimova from the Soviet Union at the 1981 Amsterdam conference initiated by WILPF. Margarita Maksimova (1982) said: "In the summer this year we decided to participate in the Peace March 1981. Unfortunately only the government of the Federal Republic of Germany gave us visas. The other governments denied visas to the Soviet women who wanted to participate in the Peace March" (Maksimova, 1982, p. 67).

These experiences led to the planning of a new Peace March for the summer of 1982, this time to the Soviet Union. Militaristic men who had been opposing the Peace March of the summer of 1981 on the grounds that it would weaken the West and that the Soviet Union would not allow such a demonstration on its soil, had some difficulty responding when the Soviets not only accepted the idea of the march, but also the slogans which criticized armaments in the East as much as armaments in the West. This Peace March must also be described as a success, although it was quite different from the one in the previous year. Because the distances were too great to walk, much of the march had to be undertaken by train. The Nordic women felt warmly received in the Soviet Union. Many of them had never met a Soviet before and did not realize how terribly afraid they were of war, how scared they were of the U.S. military strategy and NATO. Their experiences were valuable, and they made warm personal friendships.

But those who were against the 1981 Peace March because it did not go to the Soviet Union still kept complaining and writing letters to the editors of the biggest newspapers in Scandinavia. They claimed that the women had been too naive, that they had been fooled by clever propaganda from the Soviets, that they were traitors to their country, destroying the spirit of defense in their countrymen.

But Women for Peace continue working, arranging teach-ins and seminars, writing songs, and giving concerts. As they make a point of having women speakers, I have often been called upon to talk about disarmament, the arms race, the Special Session for Disarmament at the UN, peace education, or women and peace. I frequently talk about the same issues to male-dominated audiences. It strikes me over and over again how different these audiences are. Everything is different: the questions I get, the tone of the discussion, the atmosphere, and the personal care given to a busy and often exhausted speaker. I often find the level of debate much higher in these all-women groups. Questions are asked out of genuine concern, not as a point of discussion. I am also impressed by the knowledge these women possess of military doctrine, numbers and types of weapons, and military research and development.

Mothers of Plaza de Mayo

There is another group of courageous women who are working for peace and human rights in their own country, the Argentinian Mothers of Plaza de Mayo. Since the military coup in Argentina in 1976 and until 1983, thousands of Argentinians have "disappeared." They have been murdered, tortured to death, or held in one of the many prisons that the generals erected. Almost every family in Argentina has a close relative who has "disappeared" during this period. Since the beginning of 1977, mothers, wives, and other women relatives of the murdered, imprisoned, or "disappeared" persons carried on a silent demonstration in front of the Palace of the President at Plaza de Mayo every Thursday. To be easily recognized they wore white handkerchiefs on their heads. The number of women was steadily growing. They wanted their sons and husbands back, and they wanted to know what had happened to them. They protested against the torturing, killing, and lack of respect for life in their country, and they protest against war. They were among the very few Argentinians who were involved in direct action against the Argentinian occupation of the Malvinas (the Falkland Islands). They did not want this war (Brekke, 1982).

Several of the Mothers were imprisoned, and some also have "disappeared." From January 1979 it was impossible for the Mothers to demonstrate at their usual place. But they still met at the same time each Thursday, in the surrounding churches. After the occupation of the Falkland Islands, they again demonstrated in the Plaza de Mayo, and were removed by the police.

The Mothers of Plaza de Mayo viewed their fight as a fight for peace. "If you want peace, you must defend life," they claimed. They worked for peace, human rights, and democracy and against violence and all sorts of terrorism in Argentina as well as in other countries in the world. They claimed that their courage, strength, and perseverance came from a universal feeling of motherhood and caring.

Women of Greenham Common

Inspired by the Nordic Women for Peace who marched from Copenhagen to Paris in the summer of 1981, 40 Welsh women (several of whom had young children in strollers) and a few men set out from Cardiff on August 27, 1981 to march 125 miles to Greenham Common Air Force Base in protest against the 96 cruise missiles that the government planned to base there in 1983. According to British military plans, cruise missiles will be installed in all of the 102 NATO bases in Britain during the 1980s.

Women came from all over Wales and represented a diversity of ages and backgrounds, though most had never before been involved in any sort of political action. On September 5 they arrived at Greenham Common (located near Newbury in Berkshire) and delivered a letter to the base commandant stating their reasons for undertaking the march. Despite having attained this goal, the general feeling was not one of satisfaction. For all of their efforts the women had obtained almost no media coverage, which led them to conclude that some direct action would be appropriate. Following the example of the suffragettes, four women chained themselves to the fence at the main gates. This *did* interest the press, but the coverage tended to focus on "women in bondage" rather than women opposing nuclear weapons, so that this tactic was soon dropped (*Brighton Voice*, [Great Britain], no. 87). However, by this time most of the women were so frustrated because an issue they felt to be of vital importance was virtually ignored by the press that they determined to stay at Greenham Common until they got their way. They decided to camp outside the base and form a peace camp. At first, they simply slept under the open sky in sleeping bags. Then they got tepees, round tents that the Indians used, where you can sit in circles to talk. After some months they also got several caravans, one of which is used as an office.

In December 1983 when the first of the 96 cruise missiles were sited at the base at Greenham Common (the first place in Europe where this new generation of nuclear weapons has been installed), the women had camped outside the base for more than two years. There are constantly about 15 to 20 women in the camp, on weekends many more. Though men are admitted to the camp, they have never been permitted to play a leading role. The march was organized by women, the camp was set up by women. The women feel that it is important to show that they do not need men to lean on when they make decisions. On the contrary, they develop their own democratic forms better without the interference of men. This means that the men who stay in the camp or visit it have to play a supportive role and keep somewhat in the background. This is an unusual role for a man to play, but men coming to Greenham Common know about this and behave according to the rules. Only women from the camp are allowed to talk about the camp to the press, Helen John (1982) told the Danish newspaper *Information*. She says that the reason why the peace camps have not been cleared away by the police is that the government does not know how to deal with them. They first thought that the women would give up camping when the winter came, but that did not happen. Then they thought that the public would lose interest, but that did not happen either. On the contrary, the women in the peace camp at Greenham Common have become the symbol of the growing peace movement in Britain. Demonstrating by the seven gates, the women have been moved several times. But they return, asking the workers at the base to think about the type of work they are doing and about the future of their children.

For centuries women have watched men go off to war. Now women have left home for peace. The women at Greenham Common say that they can no longer stand by while others are organizing the destruction of life on our earth. In an invitation distributed by the women at Greenham Common to an international action at the base on December 12 and 13, 1982 they said: "As women we have been actively encouraged to stay at home and look to men as protectors. Now it is time to reject this role."

The women who set up the peace camp have made personal sacrifices because they feel so strongly about this issue. They have left families and friends and given up jobs to live in tents and borrowed caravans without electricity or heating throughout the cold of three winters. They have already faced two evictions, and some of them have spent time in prison, but they have returned to Greenham Common and are still there. The women who have left their families feel that they are taking the greatest responsibility in caring for their children by stopping cruise missiles from coming to Britain.

The women at Greenham Common have met with heavy criticism from all sides. They have been criticized not only by state officials and the police who have arrested them continuously, but also by radical feminists. In *Breaching the Peace* (1983), a collection of radical feminist papers, several British feminists attack the ideology behind Greenham Common. They find that this ideology is not feminist. The papers were written for a radical feminist halfday workshop called "The Women's Liberation Movement versus the Women's Peace Movement" or "How Dare You Presume I Went to Greenham?" held at A Woman's Place in London in April 1983. The introduction to the collection of papers from the workshop states: "We see the women's peace movement as a symptom of the loss of feminist principles and processes—radical analysis, criticism and consciousness raising." From reading the papers presented, I understand the main criticism to be that peace is defined too narrowly by many peace women. When they fight for peace they fight against a nuclear war or a war of mass destruction. They fail to see that "women are always having a war waged upon us" (Green, 1983, p. 9). To continue citing Green in her paper, "Not Weaving but Frowning":

> Because the violence of this war (against women) is so widespread, it is not
> seen as such by many of its victims and certainly not defined as such by those

who do the naming—the war makers. It's the very fragmented and personalised nature of the war against women that allows it to be so normal as to render it invisible. . . . As far as I am concerned the ultimate act of male violence happens everyday. And when I am walking around thinking of this and I hear phrases like "women for life on earth" and "women for peace" I feel completely bemused. What on earth do they mean? What peace? (Green, 1983, p. 9).

Since in this book and throughout my work as a peace researcher and educator I am using a wide peace concept, I can certainly understand the criticism voiced by Frankie Green. According to my definition of peace and according to UN and UNESCO definitions (see the first chapter) we would still not have peace if all nations were disarmed but there were no other changes. If structural violence was still built into the system as it is today, and women were still oppressed and exploited, there would be no peace.

I think we are naive if we believe that our work in movements to prevent a nuclear war will give any guarantee of more equal rights or less oppression of women once the antinuclear battle is won. We have seen over and over again how women have fought against the abolition of slavery, in the civil rights movement, and in revolutions and liberation struggles only to be sent back to their previous inferior position when things "went back to normal." The way we work in the peace movement, even in an all-women peace movement, ought to be a constant issue for debate. Questions to be asked should include: Do we also further women's liberation by our work or are we perhaps working against the aims of our liberation? Are we working to raise our consciousness not only on military matters, but also on the ideology of militarism and how it relates to sexism and the oppression of women? I agree with Lynn Alderson (1983) when she declares in the same collection of papers: "Women's oppression is fundamental to maintaining the system which is the backbone of our oppressive destructive society. It is not a secondary issue to be attended to 'after the revolution' or after you've saved the world. You can't do either without it" (Alderson, 1983, p. 13).

Feminist writers remind us that the suffragettes were co-opted both into the peace movement and the pro-war movement. It has taken us decades to regain the position they thereby lost. Must we lose it again? they ask. Trisha Longdon (1983) feels sure that when male peace activists, who may be as male chauvinist as any men, look at the Greenham women as the symbol of the peace movement in Britain and admire and support their work, it is because Greenham women are not naming their own oppression but have been co-opted into male struggles, accepting their terms and receiving in return their approbation and status. And she asks: "Can't we see what they're doing?" Absorbing our justifiable anger, using our fear and directing them away from their original source—where men would lose and women would win—towards their own ends. It has happened before—and proved a very successful tactic" (Longdon, 1983, p. 16).

I do not think that male peace activists are consciously trying to take women away from women's liberation movements, but they are happy that women are doing important and necessary work in the antinuclear movement. They do not care about issues they see as "women's issues": rapes, wife-battering, dowry deaths, infanticide of baby girls, exploitation of women all over the world through the longer working hours women have than men, all the unpaid housework and child care done by women. Men, even radical peace activists, do not see the connection between the oppression of women and the nuclear threat. Even many peace women who have come to the peace movement with a previous personal history in the women's liberation movement do not see this connection, or at least, prefer not to talk about it.

It is the responsibility of feminists in the peace movement to point to this connection, to speak out about it, even though it might disturb the calm of the peace movement. We cannot expect anyone else to do that consciousness-raising task for us. It took a woman to point out how the military institution depends on women playing traditional roles for its continuation. Cynthia Enloe (1983) in her recent book analyzes the way the military uses women and depends on the exploitation of women, previously as camp followers, now as subservient military personnel, hospital nurses, loyal military wives, prostitutes, and arms-manufacture workers. Feminist analysis of the military institution, of militarism, and especially how it relates to sexism, is of urgent importance. Feminist analysis of the work in the peace movement is also highly needed. What sort of peace are we fighting for? What do we understand by peace? These questions must be asked over and over again. Most Greenham women say that they are raising the issue of male responsibility for the nuclear threat and see the nuclear threat as just one form of male violence. This is the basis of some feminists' involvement in Greenham, but it has not emerged in the public forum. Linda Bellow and associates, London Revolutionary Feminists, (1983) ask: "How do the feminists involved feel about the public image and why are no feminist politics coming across either in the media or in the movement?"

The criticism voiced in this collection of feminist papers ought to be taken seriously by all women in the peace movement. Many of the rather general points made may even be more relevant in other parts of the peace movement than to the women at Greenham Common. The criticism pertaining to Greenham Common is weakened by the fact that it seems as though none of the writers have been to the peace camp themselves and are relying on the public image that has been created about the campers. They seem to know little or nothing of the internal debates going on in the camp. It has further surprised me that the policy adopted by the Greenham Common women—of only allowing men in support roles and of doing the speaking and appearing in newspapers and on television themselves—has not been commented on.

In an article on the Women's Peace Camp at Greenham Common, Lynne Jones (1983) tells about the intense discussions in the camp on the question of having men at the site and what roles they were to play. The march and the camp had always been women's initiatives, with women talking to the press, representing the camp, and doing the decision-making. But at some periods, especially at the start, men had been allowed to live in the camp. Under the threat of eviction, a majority of those living at the camp at that time decided that only women would be allowed to live in the camp for the next two weeks. After that time the decision would be reviewed. The two weeks passed, and the decision was reviewed and confirmed. Jones (1983) quotes one of the women, Shushu, in the camp: "It was the best decision we ever made," she said at a much later date. "The men were a problem. They put us in the role of mothers, 'Mummy show me how to do this' and always rushing to see how far they could go" (p. 88). In the same article Jones cites the press release issued by the Women's Peace Camp on this occasion. The press release starts by announcing that while the camp is under threat of eviction, only women will be living on the site. It further announced: "We intend to deal with women representatives of the authorities and wish to communicate our actions through women in the media. We would appreciate it if the press would respect this request."

Certainly the women at Greenham know that allowing men to play a role at Greenham would mean that they would be relegated to subservient and traditional roles. Most of the initiators and many of the other women who have joined Greenham Common have not called themselves feminists. This fact seems to annoy the writers of the feminist collection of papers criticizing the ideology of the women at Greenham Common. To me it seems more valuable that these women work against the siting of nuclear missiles rather than stay in their protected homes and go to tea parties. I also believe that if a woman starts becoming politically conscious on any issue, she usually will end up as a feminist. The feminists in the peace movement should be able to help her in that process.

Shibokusa Women

At the north foot of Mount Fuji in Japan some Shibokusa women have built a cottage where they maintain a permanent peace and protest camp. The land beneath the mountain has previously been used by the local people since the Edo period, around the seventeenth century. This was called the Iriaiken, the right of common people to cultivate and earn a living from a certain place, in this case the Shibokusa area. In fact, it was rather poor land, but years of work had enabled them to grow beans and radishes there and even create a silkworm industry. Then in 1936, the militarization of Japan disrupted the fragile prosperity of the community: The army began to execute drills on the Shibokusa land. After the war, the U.S. Army stationed troops on the site, which led to a startling increase in prostitution in the area. A Shibokusa woman told Leonie Caldecott (1983) who visited the Shibokusa women in their camp: "We women were treated like the dust on the ground" (p. 99). Even after the 1952 San Francisco peace treaty was signed between Japan and the United States, the land was not released by the military. Finally on June 20, 1955, 70 farmers staged a protest on the Shibokusa land. They were arrested as rioters, but as they were taken by jeep to Fuji Yoshida, the jeep crashed and the chief of police was killed. It was an accident, but it drew attention to what they had been doing. Officials from Tokyo came and promised another 50 hectares of land to compensate those people who had lost their livelihood, and these people planted pine trees on it. Now that the trees are fully grown, the government claims it as state land again.

The Shibokusa people feel that they are being treated little better than slaves. Because of the poverty of the land, men in the area have tended to go away to find work, leaving the subsistence-level cultivation to the women; this is even more common since the loss of the Shibokusa area to the military. And so the women took over the struggle, building a series of cottages on or around the military base and occupying them, small bastions of ordinary life among the soldiers' incessant preparation for death. In December 1982 they had built 15 cottages.

The Shibokusa women make it their business to disrupt military exercises. In groups of up to ten they make their way into the exercise area, crawling around in the undergrowth and popping up in the middle of firing. They plant scarecrows to decoy the troops. Sometimes they'll build a fire and sit around it singing and clapping their hands, totally ignoring officials who try to move them on. They are frequently arrested and taken to the police station. Leonie Caldecott (1983) quotes one of the Shibokusa women telling about the frequent arrests: "They are quite gentle, because they are afraid of provoking us—they hate it when we start screaming, and they have realised that though we are physically easier to arrest than men we're more trouble afterwards. Men put up a fight, but once it's over they just give everything away. We never give our name, age or anything. We just say we're so old, we can't remember when we were born or who we are . . ." (p. 104).

What do the Shibokusa women hope to achieve in the long run? They say that they work for much more than simply getting their land back. According to a Shibokusa woman:

> As we carried on with our campaign we realised that the whole phenomenon of militarism wherever it takes place is violence against the land. So we are really a part of the wider anti-war movement. You see, Mount Fuji is the symbol of Japan. If they are preparing war on her flanks, how can they say Japan desires peace?

This kind of longterm resistance is the first of its kind in Japan. We will continue it to the end. I have seen time and time again how Japanese men will not endure the worst: they have no patience, they give up or become violent, rather than sitting it out. . . . We are not clever. Many of us have not been educated at all. But we are strong because we are close to the earth and we know what matters. Our conviction that the military is wrong is unshakeable. We are the strongest women in Japan and we want other women to be like us (Caldecott, 1983, p. 105).

Australian Women for Survival

Women from all over Australia have recently organized Women for Survival groups in all the main centers in Australia and in some rural areas as well. Their aim is to reach out to as wide a group of women as possible. In a letter I received from the Women for Survival (address: PO Box 3603, Alice Springs, N.T. 5750) to announce their peace camp outside Pine Gap, the organizers claim that they see it as a great challenge "to involve women who up until now have not been active either in the women's movement or in the peace movement, but who are becoming increasingly concerned at the dangers of the arms race."

When Women for Survival organized their peace camp outside Pine Gap, the U.S. satellite communication base, on November 11, 1983 they collaborated with the aboriginal women of Alice Springs, believing that they also involve the support of aboriginal people in their struggle for autmy and land rights. The aboriginal women also oppose the presence of Pine Gap and support the women's camp. Women for Survival were given permission to camp on one side of the road outside the gates of Pine Gap by the traditional aboriginal owners of the land. The presence of Pine Gap military base represents an act of imperialism—this time by the United States against the aboriginal people.

Pine Gap is one of the key satellite communications bases outside the United States. It is a CIA controlled base, which has been described as the eyes and the ears of U.S. defense. The base is so top secret that not even the Australian government is informed as to what exactly goes on there. Some of its known functions are:

- to monitor Soviet missile launches, military communications, and radar transmission, etc.
- to provide an early warning system
- to map out targets for U.S. missiles
- to work on the "star wars" scenario through research into laser beam technology

It is clear that with one of its prime functions to pick out Soviet targets, Pine Gap itself becomes a number one target. Even if there were only a limited nuclear exchange, Pine Gap would be one of the first places in the world to be hit.

Women for Survival in Australia have chosen November 11 as the first day of their protest action because it was on that day in 1975 that the democratically elected Labor government was sacked. Many Australians remember this date as marking the coup in which the CIA in collusion with the Governor General and the Liberal Party engineered the displacement of Whitlam and his government. There was reason to believe that the Labor government was considering a refusal to the United States on the renewal of the lease for Pine Gap, which was due the following year. November 11 is also Armistice Day, when the world remembers the signing of what turned out to be an all too tentative peace agreement at the end of World War I.

In a circular letter sent out by the Women for Survival before the peace camps took place, they mention that another reason for choosing November (when it was already getting rather hot in Alice Springs) was that they wanted to express their solidarity with

> the peace movement in the US and Europe as the pressure to struggle against the imminent deployment of the Pershing II missiles in West Germany and the Cruise missiles in Britain and in Sicily comes to its height. Especially we want to link hands with the women in Comiso in Sicily and with the women at Greenham Common in Britain. These women have given us inspiration and we hope to generate some energy back to them at this crucial time.
>
> We have sent letters off to contacts we have all over the world. We are particularly anxious to reach women's groups and peace groups or individuals in Russia and in eastern Europe. We also want to make contact with women who are struggling in the so-called Third World. Many of us feel that one of the best hopes for the kind of transformation that is needed if we are to reverse the arms race can come from the women's movement which is growing and strengthening throughout the world.

On November 11 and 12, 1983 the Australian Women for Survival organized actions not only at Pine Gap, but also throughout the country, since women who could not reach Pine Gap wanted to join in the expression of their profound opposition to the base and to all it represents in the terrifying build-up of the arms race. Women for Survival were asking for a cancellation of the lease for Pine Gap and in the meantime that more information be sent to the Australian government and people as to what actually goes on there. They further demanded that Australia should become independent through a foreign policy of nonalignment. The women planning the peace camp and demonstration at Pine Gap on November 11, 1983 appealed to women elsewhere in the world to mark that day, so that "we can all draw strength from the knowledge that though enriched by our diversity, we are united and strong in our opposition to a situation—largely controlled by men—which threatens to perpetrate the ultimate violence on this planet."

The march on Pine Gap on November 11 to mark the opening of the peace camp was "a peaceful affair . . . quite unlike other demonstrations Australia has experienced," the Australian newspaper *The Sydney Morning Herald*, reports (November 12, 1983). Instead of loud chants, there was quiet singing. Instead of angry slogans there were long banners with people painted and embroidered on them. The speeches were analytical and rather sad. "The boys discovered the philosopher's stone of nuclear fission. They called their bombs 'the baby' and the 'little boy.' The patriarchy has reproduced by parthenogenesis and created enough funds to kill everyone, all the world over," one of the chief organizers, Biff Ward, told the crowd. (*The Sydney Morning Herald*, November 12, 1983).

The women marched in a column, led by a contingent of local aboriginal women. Several aboriginal women made speeches. All the women joined in an antiuranium song entitled "Come on Bob":

Come on Bob, you've got the job
Now what are you gonna do?
What'll you gain with your power and fame?
If they blow us all in two
Don't sell uranium for dollars and for pounds
Keep the spirit of Australia—leave it in the ground.

After the march, women set up their peace camps outside the base. On Sunday, November 13, the women tried to enter the base. One hundred and eleven women were arrested after they had climbed into the U.S. communication base. On the following day they were all subjected to all-day hearings in the Magistrates Court. They were charged with trespass, and Mr. Dennis Berrit, SM, fined each $300. One the following day another 18 women were arrested by the police at Pine Gap when they demonstrated to mark the deployment of Cruise and Pershing missiles in Europe. Following the arrests the demonstrators pulled down the gates and performed a mock funeral with a woman lying on one of the gates carried by "pall bearers." They removed a section of the front gate from its hinges to use it for the mock funeral. The women arrested were again charged with trespass and fined $250 each.

An article in the *Sydney Morning Herald* (November 16, 1983) claims that the peace women at Pine Gap met with little sympathy from the townsfolk of Alice Springs. "They should drop a bomb on the lot of those filthy lesbians," a taxidriver said. The local newspaper in an editorial headed "Ignore the Peacenicks" said the local women did not see either Pine Gap or the Americans as a problem. "On the contrary, the Americans are an important part of our community. They and the base itself have become involved to a considerable degree with community service and activities. Individual Americans and Australians have become friends." Senator Bernie Kilgariff (NT) said: "Such protests as we see now do not take place in Russia and we do not see protests to Russian embassies entreating them to join a disarmament program. Soviet funding has been traced to so-called peace movements."

The first part of this argument is often put forward by right-wing politicians. If we were to stop criticizing because political criticism is forbidden in the Soviet Union, it would be tantamount to abolishing our own democracy because the Soviet people are denied democracy. I thought that the right to criticize one's own government was one of the rights we were fighting for, one of the reasons for our so-called defense or military build-up. And if the Australians look on the Americans as their friends, there should be even greater reason to know more about the military installations on Australian territory. Certainly one expects openness from one's friends and that they would want to listen to well-founded criticism and make behavioral changes accordingly.

The accusation that the peace movement is receiving money from Soviet Russia has been voiced several times and has been mostly proved wrong. Certainly groups of people, especially from peace committees, may sometimes be invited on trips to Soviet Russia or to eastern European countries. However, these trips are few in comparison to the many trips funded by NATO and other official channels to sponsor groups to visit western countries.

American Pentagon Action

On November 16, 1981 thousands of American women rallied in front of the Pentagon. One of the participants, Ynestra King (1983), writes: "The Pentagon emerged as the symbol of all the male violence we opposed. It is the real workplace of the American generals who plan the annihilation of the world as their daily work, far removed from the lives they imperil and the murders they commit. We wanted it to be clear to women around the world that there is a feminist awareness of, and opposition to, the imperialist role of the United States military around the world" (pp. 40–64).

The action at the Pentagon consisted of four stages, each signaled by a different "larger than life" puppet. First, the white mourning puppet, accompanied by a slow, constant drum beat, was moved around the parade grounds while women placed hundreds of tombstones in the ground to commemorate their sisters who had been victims of individual or state violence. The next puppet was red to symbolize rage. The women expressed their anger by yelling and shouting: "No more war" and "We will stop you." The following puppet was the yellow puppet, which signaled the beginning of the empowerment stage. The puppets led the women out of the parade grounds to encircle the Pentagon. As they walked, they wove a continuous braid which encircled the entire Pentagon. Susan Pines (1984), one of the organizers of the Pentagon action, tells how affinity groups blocked entrances to the Pentagon during the fourth and final stage. This stage was the defiance stage, signaled by a black puppet. Many women were now weaving a web of brightly colored yarn across doorways. At the end of the day 65 women were in custody. Sixty-two women were charged with obstruction of entrances, and three were charged with defacement of federal property for marking the entrance of the building with blood. That night 43 women were sent to the Arlington County Jail, either sentenced to ten days in prison or held for trial. In later trials women were sentenced to ten, fifteen, or thirty days of imprisonment. In a statement written from jail and endorsed by many of the women who participated in the civil disobedience, Nesta King explained: "We went to the Pentagon in an action which embodied our resistance to coercive authority. . . . The every day oppression of living in an increasingly authoritarian, militarized society is . . . a feminist concern . . . We believe it is essential to resist directly. . . . Civil disobedience might help save our planet and usher in a free feminist future. That's why they put us here" (Pines, 1984, p. 247–248).

PEACE ACTIVITIES INITIATED BY WOMEN

I have mentioned several examples here of peace activities initiated by women. I have characterized women's fight against war between states. I have also dealt with the way women are trying to prevent further rearmament.

In Latin America as a whole, women have been very active in movements oriented toward social justice (land rights, civil strikes, student movements, etc.) and sometimes have become the main protagonists, as in the case of the Mothers of the Plaza de Mayo. The Colombian feminist researcher Magdalena León (1983) finds that such participation represents women's involvement in the struggles against class oppression and to a lesser degree, against patriarchy. In this sense, she claims, women's participation has been consistent with the definition of politics as the locus where topics pertinent to the public sphere find expression: capital, social classes, state, basic needs, and so on. She also thinks it important to mention that the active role assumed by women in the general social struggle has not been translated into a question of their subordinate condition in society. According to León (1983), the feminist debate in Latin America today supersedes and questions this restricted form of participation. This, she finds, is precisely the reason why the human rights movement has not "met," either in its philosophy or in its struggle, with the feminist movement. She finds that human rights have been confined to the public sphere, while the feminist movement has centered an important part of its social practice on the task of unveiling the public character of the private sphere. She mentions sexual aggression against women, exploitation of women through domestic work, and domination of men over women in the family as examples of inequality between the sexes in the private sphere that are not taken into account by the human rights movement. She could also have mentioned the degrading custom of dowry in India, which Indian feminists try to drag out of the private sphere and make public along with the dowry tortures and deaths camouflauged as "kitchen accidents."

Many of the atrocities against women that have been mentioned in the first part of this book have not officially been treated as a violation of human rights. León maintains that if the feminist and human rights movements in Latin America are to meet, the human rights content would have to be widened to integrate the issue of equality between women and men economically, socially, and in the domestic sphere. The denunciation of violence made by the human rights movement should also include domestic violence.

Women often find when they work in mixed-sex peace movements against the arms race or against the oppression of other groups that they are oppressed themselves, relegated to less important jobs, or "forgotten" when the fight is over. This is happening again in some of the more recent western disarmament movements (Romstad, 1982). This fact forms the basis for the strict position taken by the Greenham Common women that no man is allowed to play a leading role in their undertaking. They are fighting against the oppression and invisibility of women at the same time as they are fighting against the stationing of more nuclear missiles.

South African women have played an important role in the struggle for national liberation and against apartheid. They played a very important role in 1913 when they demonstrated against the enforcement of the pass law, in 1943 against the rise in bus fares, and in the defiance campaign of 1952. And on August 9, 1956 the Federation of South African Women organized a demonstration of 20,000 women outside the Union Buildings in Pretoria to protest to the then racist Prime Minister Strijdom against the extension to black women of the hated regulation enforced against black men by the white majority: one requiring blacks to always carry identification papers, without which they could be put in jail. Since that year August 9 has been a day used by South African women for conferences and demonstrations. The first conference of the African National Congress Women's Section in the external mission took place in Luanda, People's Republic of Angola from September 10 to 14, 1981. The conference was held to celebrate the 25th anniversary of the historic march of the Federation of South African Women. (*Voice of Women*, special conference issue, 1981). This was the first conference held since the banning of the ANC Women's League in 1960.

Though the women of South Africa have primarily fought against colonial oppression and domination through nonviolent means, it looks as though *Voice of Women*, VOW, which is the official organ of the African National Congress Women's Section, also supports women using arms and violence in the fight against oppression. The Federation of South African Women at its first conference in Johannesburg on April 17, 1955 declared that: "We women of South Africa hereby declare our aims of striving for the removal of all laws and regulations, conventions and customs that discriminate against us as women, and that deprive us in any way of our inherent right to the advantages, responsibilities and opportunities that the society offers to all sections of the population" (*VOW*, 4th Quarter, 1980). The federation at that time issued a list of its demands, which included demands for four months maternity leave on full pay for working mothers, birth control clinics, the right of all women to vote, equal rights with men in property, marriage, and the guardianship of children. In the later issues of *VOW*, it seems that topics that may divide the sexes and point to the oppression of women are avoided. Unity in the struggle against apartheid is sought. But this may be a unity on men's terms.

HOW HAS WOMEN'S FIGHT FOR PEACE AND HUMAN RIGHTS BEEN RECEIVED?

The first mechanism that patriarchal society uses to combat women's fight for peace is to make this work *invisible*. This is a mechanism used not only by those who are opposed to the causes women are fighting for (they try to use the same mechanism against fighting for peace); it is also used by men fighting together with women for the same cause.

In the United States, it was the women's fight within the antislavery campaign that gave rise to the early struggles for women's rights. And it was women's work within the civil rights movement that gave rise to the new feminist movement. In both cases women realized that even when they were fighting together with men for the liberation of other groups, they were being relegated to the lower positions. They were kept away from leading positions; they were not asked to appear on television or make speeches; they were asked to embroider banners, to collect signatures and money, to hand out leaflets. In the American delegation to the big antislavery congress in London in 1840 there were seven women. All had fought courageously for the abolition of slavery in their own country. Several of them wanted to take the floor at the congress, but the men did not allow it. Because of the importance of the cause they had come to fight for, the women did not make any fuss then and there. Sitting quietly in the gallery and watching the men speak, they realized that they would have to fight for their own rights to be able to help others.

The Norwegian historian Yngvar Ustvedt, who has recently written a book on World War II, said in a newspaper interview that he had found out that of all the brave Norwegian women who fought alongside the men during World War II to resist the German occupation and had been killed during that fight, not one had her name inscribed on the memorial slabs erected in honor of those who were killed during the war. He also mentioned that the men had not wanted the women they had been fighting alongside in the underground movement to celebrate the victory with them at the end of the war.

Celina García (1981) asks whether male workers for peace are reluctant to incorporate the work of women because they themselves have not understood clearly the relationship between violence and oppressive sex roles. "In other words," she says, "will peace issues be another male-dominated project to be accepted 'for the sake of peace'?" (García, 1981, p. 163). Patriarchal society tries various ways to make women's work for peace invisible. Articles and letters to newspapers are not printed. Women's actions for peace receive scant attention from the mass media: For instance, the massive signature campaign of the Nordic Women for Peace in the spring of 1980 was hardly noted on the Norwegian television. It only was mentioned briefly twice in the news (all together three minutes coverage).

A patriarchal society does not want to give women credit for creative work or for their brave fight for peace and justice and against oppression. According to patriarchal thinking, women are not creative, brave, or strong. Creative women seem to have greater difficulty than men in getting their articles and books printed, their paintings and compositions accepted, and in receiving scholarships to continue creative work. Women for Peace in Norway has a much harder time getting financial support than No to Nuclear Arms, and they are less likely to receive media coverage of their arrangements (Romstad, 1982).

There are basically three ways in which women's creative work or work for peace and justice is made invisible:

1. It is not brought to the attention of the media at all. Women are allowed to do the menial work, all the organizing, but not allowed to have their works printed or to appear in the newspapers or on television
2. A distorted picture of women's activities is given and feminist work in the peace camps is distorted or made invisible. It suits the patriarchal society to have women pictured as mothers and wives fighting for their children rather than as feminists also fighting against their own oppression and analyzing the relationship between sexism and militarism. I have already mentioned that rapes committed by "our" side are often not reported and are made invisible while rapes committed by the "other" side are reported.
3. Even though the creative work of women or the work of women fighting for peace and justice is brought to the attention of the public when it is actually happening, it is often made invisible when history is written or when memorial slabs are erected.

A recent analysis of a history book currently in use in the secondary schools of Norway revealed that of the 610 persons mentioned in the book there were only 5—five!—women (*Videregående opplæring* [Secondary education] no. 4, 1980). The book deals with the period from 1850 to 1914 and is claimed to be a world history book. Whose world?

Because our foremothers tend to be "forgotten," made invisible in male history, feminists have to drag them out of oblivion. This is the intention of the German book *Frauen gegen den Krieg* (Women against War), edited by Gisela Brinker-Gabler (1980). Here we find speeches and extracts from original works by earlier women peace fighters, women like Bertha von Suttner, Clara Zetkin, Selma Lagerlöf, Olive Schreiner, Helene Stöcker, Rosa Luxemburg, Hedwig Dohm, Claire Goll, and Lida Gustava Heymann. We find a similar intention of uncovering the words of women in Dale Spender's book: *Women of Ideas and What Men Have Done to Them* (Spender, 1982). In this book Spender traces 300 years of women's ideas. She uncovers not only the ways and words of women, but also the methods of men. While men control knowledge, she argues, they are in a position to take women's ideas. If they like them, they use them and get credit for them. If they don't, they "lose" them or make them invisible. Spender provides convincing evidence that women's absence from the record as creative intellectual beings is not women's fault, but men's. In the introduction to the book she claims that when she learned that in 1911 there had been 21 regular feminist periodicals in Britain, a feminist book shop, a women's press, and a women's bank run by and for women, she could no longer accept that the reason she and other feminists knew almost nothing about women of the past was because there were so few of them, and they had done so little. And she asks: "Why didn't we know about these women? Was it possible that we were not meant to? And if women who raised their voices against male power became but a transitory entry in the historical records, what was to be the fate of the present women's movement?" (Spender, 1982, p. 4).

The invisibility of women, especially women opposing male norms and values, is fundamental to patriarchy. Spender finds that the simple answer to the question she posed—why did she not know about all the women of the past who have protested about male power—is that patriarchy does not like it. These women and their ideas constitute a political threat and they are therefore censored.

When the first mechanism does not work, then ridicule is tried. Women are laughed at, accused of being naive and having no knowledge about vital defense issues. The Swedish author Fredrika Bremer, a major pioneer in the fight for women's rights, was made a laughing-stock when she tried to mobilize women to end the Crimean War. On August 28, 1854, her invitation to all the women of the world to draw up a peace treaty to end the war was published in *The Times* and later in other newspapers. She asked all women to feel like sisters. "Each of us is weak," she said, "but together and united we are strong. If we stretch out our hands to each other, we shall be able to carry the world in our arms like a baby." This was met by a sarcastic editorial in *The Times* and scorn and ridicule in Sweden.

It is not difficult to find recent examples of the use of the same mechanism. The women who had started the signature campaign for peace in the spring of 1980 were constantly ridiculed in Nordic newspapers and called naive. How could they possibly think that Brezhnev and Carter would take notice of signatures from some Nordic women, let alone have such a campaign influence their important decision-making on questions concerning military expenditures? Such an assumption was ridiculous. Women fighting for peace and disarmament are constantly being ridiculed in the Norwegian press. One of the leaders of the Peace March to Paris in 1981 and to the Soviet Union in the summer of 1982, Eva Nordland, is frequently accused by the military establishment and its supporters of being naive, unrealistic, and having no competence in matters dealing with defense.

Since women are oppressed everywhere in patriarchal society, we should not be surprised that we are oppressed in a mixed-sex peace movement. One of the leading personalities of the Norwegian Women for Peace, the now retired physician Bett Romstad, gave some clear examples of the discrimination against women within the No to Nuclear Arms movement. At a seminar on women and militarism sponsored by the women at the Peace Research Institute of Oslo (Romstad, 1982), she told about the difference between working in Women for Peace and in No to Nuclear Arms. Because she was mainly working in Women for Peace she did not have anyone to do her typing or other routine work. These serving spirits (women, of course!) worked in No to Nuclear Arms, where they worked in the office without pay. The men who had jobs there got paid for their work. The women in Women for Peace shared all the work, both the routine and the more prestigious chores. Women also always have other routine work to do—household chores, looking after kids, husbands, relatives who get sick. And since women are poor, it was infinitely more difficult for Women for Peace to get financial support than for No to Nuclear Arms. They had a harder time getting money both from the state, from trade unions, and getting voluntary contributions, even from women.

Women for Peace was started before No to Nuclear Arms as a protest against the December 1979 NATO decision to station cruise missiles in Europe, a decision in which only men—100 percent men—had participated. The women worked in study groups, developing all sorts of new songs, poems, brochures. The groups all had different approaches. Their motto was, "Let a hundred peace study groups blossom." They made fun of military secrets and handed out leaflets stamped "Secret." They arranged teach-ins in various towns where they stayed overnight in each other's apartments and houses, cooked together, and talked about the world situation. Most of them were glad when No to Nuclear Arms was started; they thought it was important to get men to work for disarmament too.

Bett Romstad gave a heartfelt account of how she experienced the opening meeting of No to Nuclear Arms. Women constituted the great majority of those present in the audience, but the speakers, with only one exception, were men! Two women were "entertainers." Men were doing all the talking—serious and learned talking with technical details and references to 'balance of power' and 'deterrent-weapons counting.' And the one slogan was: No to Nuclear Arms. There was nothing about using money spent on weapons to satisfy the needs of hungry and starving people. There was nothing against war itself. Is war all right as long as it is not a nuclear war? The war in Vietnam was not a nuclear war, yet 90 percent of those killed belonged to the civilian population, including innocent children.

Later meetings organized by No to Nuclear Arms have often revealed the same tendency: Men speaking while women make up the majority of the audience. When the council of No to Nuclear Arms set up an expert group to give a recommendation about the construction of a nuclear weapon-free zone in the Nordic countries, it "happened" to be an all-male group. I was on the council myself and reacted immediately when I heard the proposal but hesitated in drawing attention to the fact that the proposed group was an all-male group. The reason for my hesitation was that I was a rather likely candidate myself. There were several other women present who would also have been likely candidates, but I had not talked to them beforehand and was afraid they did not have the time. Some of them later told me that they did not want this to be a "woman's issue." They disliked the talk about sexism in the peace movement. The fight against nuclear weapons was too important, as one of them later told me. So we kept quiet for the sake of peace, as women usually do. When I afterwards read about this expert group in the No to Nuclear Arms newsletter, I regretted my silence. Here the expert group was mentioned by name and accorded the following comment: "The composition of the group should guarantee a good result." When the women in Women for Peace read this sentence they decided not to follow up a letter they had just received from No to Nuclear Arms asking them to collect more signatures for another campaign organized by No to Nuclear Arms.

Romstad pointed to the differences between the academic-looking leaflets handed out by No to Nuclear Arms, written in academic language, displaying the titles of all the important people on the council, and the flower-decorated letters handed out by Women for Peace, with drawings, poems, and facts about the arms race, but written in ordinary language aimed at ordinary people. She told how women were the ones who were handing out leaflets and selling buttons for No to Nuclear Arms. Very often these women were also members of Women for Peace, but they were not permitted by the leaders of No to Nuclear Arms to hand out their own leaflets or sell their silver peace dove with the feminist symbol in its beak. She told how the women in Women for Peace in Trondheim (a city in the middle of Norway, the third largest city) came to Oslo to help No to Nuclear Arms to get signatures in their campaign against the use of nuclear arms in Norway in case of war and for making the Nordic countries into a nuclear weapon-free zone. These women found that the collection of signatures was not going as well in Oslo, as in other parts of the country. The weather that particular weekend was especially bad. No to Nuclear Arms had promised to bring material and equipment to put up a stand, and a woman from the movement brought it and then disappeared. Five or six of the Women for Peace from Oslo helped the women from Trondheim to collect signatures. They had also brought with them doves and other material from Women for Peace, but were told that they would not be allowed to hand that material out or to sell it. Nobody from No to Nuclear Arms helped the women who collected signatures. On that Saturday night the Oslo group of Women for Peace gave a party in honor of the Trondheim group. No to Nuclear Arms did nothing, simply collected the money for buttons sold and the lists of signatures. A woman from No to Nuclear Arms fetched the material that was left over and the equipment. There is little doubt that it was mainly women who collected signatures in the signature campaign run by No to Nuclear Arms. Two women from the organization were also allowed to hand the signatures over to the government and have their photos taken by the press on this occasion. But in the evening only men were interviewed about the signature campaign on television, only men were allowed to explain its importance.

Romstad could also provide evidence of many other instances, where Women for Peace had done all the work, and No to Nuclear Arms claimed the honor, the prestige, and the money. She told about a big peace meeting that a group of people had organized in one of our largest cinemas. They had arranged for good artists, well-known politicians, and peace activists as speakers. No to Nuclear Arms did not want to have anything to do with the arrangements beforehand. Women for Peace stepped in, and the cinema was hired in their name; they were the sponsors for the event. The peace meeting turned out to be very successful, even netting a profit. When that happened, it was "forgotten" that Women for Peace had sponsored the meeting, and the men wanted to give the money to No to Nuclear Arms. A woman protested, and as a compromise the money was donated to the People's Peace Prize for Alva Myrdal.

Romstad also told how the Women for Peace in the town of Sarpsborg arranged a peace march to a lake near the town on Hiroshima Day, with music, peace appeals, and the lighting of candles to float on the lake. They did all the work, though the local branch of No to Nuclear Arms supported the event and were mentioned as co-arrangers. But afterwards, No to Nuclear Arms grabbed all the profits from the event—Women for Peace, who had done the organizing, got no share in the money earned by this event.

But the peace marches from Copenhagen to Paris in 1981 and to the Soviet Union (Moscow and Minsk) next summer were organized entirely by Women for Peace. No to Nuclear Arms did not want to have anything to do with these peace marches. Yet when one of the bigger local branches of No to Nuclear Arms in the Oslo area picked out two participants to talk about the Peace March to the Soviet Union in the summer of 1982, they picked out two of the very few men who participated. The march was an all-women initiative, and the great majority of the participants were women. Of course, Women for Peace protested when only men were asked to speak about the march. Because of this protest, the organizers asked one woman and one man to speak. Before the march took place the leaders of No to Nuclear Arms had been rather reluctant about the march. They were not merely refusing to support it morally but were commenting on it rather negatively. In a local branch of No to Nuclear Arms in the city of Haugesund, where I was asked to speak in the spring of 1982, the local leaders were rather upset by a letter they had received from the central office of their organization after they had told them that they wished to support the Peace March to the Soviet Union and wanted to encourage their members to participate in it. They were requested to do nothing of the sort and were told that the Board had made a decision that No to Nuclear Arms should not have anything to do with the Peace March and not encourage their members to take part in it or give money for it. And with the hierarchical structure typical of male organizations, everyone had to follow decisions made by a very few.

The concrete examples of sexism within the mixed-sex peace movement have been taken from my own country, Norway. I happen to know these examples best. They could easily have been taken from any other country. When feminist peace activists are rather hesitant about making an issue of the sexism of the mixed-sex peace movement, as I have also seen here, we do so because we often feel that we must not make a nuisance of ourselves, that we must be quiet for the sake of peace. But perhaps it is exactly for the sake of peace that we ought not to be quiet. We are not merely saying no to nuclear arms, but to the whole nuclear mentality, to the use of violence and oppression and also to the oppression of women. There is no doubt that we shall also have to fight our oppression within the mixed-sex peace movements if we join them.

3 Peace Education

In 1981 I was working as a guest researcher at the International Peace Research Institute of Oslo and had been asked to join the staff primarily in order to deal with peace education. That particular field had interested me for several years. I viewed the principles that govern peace education as very similar to those that are basic to the study of the rather recent subject, Social Education, at the University of Oslo. This area of study seems to be one of the few tangible and still surviving results of the student revolution of 1968. It is built on principles of shared decision-making, nonhierarchical or flat structures, rotation of jobs, group work and group exams, and helping and caring for each other. We try to play down competition, and grades are pass or nonpass only. Students help each other to pass and are guided in this process by the teachers, who meet them more frequently than teachers normally meet students. I have been teaching this subject since its earliest days and have held a tenured position at the University of Oslo since 1977. A book that has inspired much of our thinking is Paulo Freire's *Pedagogy of the Oppressed* (Freire, 1972). We are concerned with dialogue, cooperation and action, with building symmetrical relationships between people.

It was only after I had joined the study of Social Education as a full-time teacher that I became concerned about sexism in education and started to work professionally to investigate how girls were oppressed through education. Yet when I undertook to write the expert paper for UNESCO, I had not really started to combine my insight into the study of sexism in education and women's studies with my previous work on peace education and the principles governing such education. But my awareness of the fact that a combination of such fields of insight would be vital to the field of peace education was steadily growing. It was further stimulated through the meeting with other feminist peace educators within the Peace Education Commission of the International Peace Research Association in Canada in the summer of 1981. In spite of the fact that several of us defined ourselves as feminists and were well trained within women's studies, we had nevertheless accepted sexism as a nonissue in the formal debates in our commission in the daytime. But when we got together informally in the evenings we decided that this silence had to be broken. Not only because we could no longer accept the oppression of girls as a nonissue within peace education and peace research, but because we realized that insight resulting from feminist research had to be brought into peace education to develop the field and make it more complete.

I brought this new awareness with me when I sat down to work on the assignment given me by UNESCO. I very soon realized that I could not write about the "education of *young people* for peace." Young people are young girls and young boys, and the education we give the two sexes is so different. And I did not want to write about the role of mothers without also mentioning the fathers or without mentioning the fact that mothers usually have little power. When giving talks about peace education, often some man in the audience will start the debate after my talking by saying: "But if it comes to creating a different mentality in the education of people for peace, you women are the ones who have the power to do that. You are the ones who take care of the children before they have preconceived ideas and when they are easy to mold. Certainly if mothers would unite and give a proper peace education, the whole world would change. How can mothers be made more aware of the possibilities they have to change the world through the education they give their children?"

Perhaps the thoughts inspiring this question were also thoughts inspiring the assignment given me by UNESCO. In both cases my answer was to give some facts about mothers around the world and also to stress the role of the father and the general oppression of women in society. It is also necessary to look at education given in the preschool and school, in the peer group, and through the media and leisure activities. This education is very different for girls compared with boys, a fact that has to be taken into account by all peace educators.

In the rather extensive literature on peace and disarmament education one seldom finds any mention of the fact that boys and girls are educated differently. In a very thorough German book on peace education, Hermann Röhrs (1983) gives advice on how to teach peace to children in kindergarten, to their parents, and to teachers and pupils in various school subjects. He uses the term *parents* (or rather *Eltern*) when he describes a project in a kindergarten when only mothers were interviewed. He stresses the importance of knowing how the parents educate their children before starting to work with peace education in the kindergarten. But he only asks the mothers, and he asks them about the education they give their *children* without making any distinction between the education they give their sons and the education they give their daughters. We know so much by now about the difference between the upbringing of girls and boys that to write about them as if they received a unisex education becomes rather unscientific.

I intend here to stress the difference in girls' and boys' upbringing and how this pertains to peace education, and I shall concentrate on the out-of-school influences. In Röhrs' (1983) book on peace education, Johan Galtung is cited as not believing much in peace education within the normal, competitive school system. I tend to agree with Galtung that it is difficult to teach peace in a setting where children are taught to compete against each other. In many countries, including my own, children are given grades according to a relative scale. That means that a certain percentage of the children will always receive bad grades. They are not able to get a better grade unless one of their class-mates gets a worse grade. This grading system is a good illustration of struc-tural violence. The whole schooling situation is normally one of dominance. The teacher dominates the pupils, and the boys in the class dominate the girls. They interrupt them and call for the teacher's attention. It is difficult to teach about equality between states large and small, when there is so little equality between teachers and pupils; to teach about the equality of the sexes when the boys in the class are allowed to dominate the girls. Is it at all possible to teach democracy in a highly authoritarian school or university?

In another article on peace education, Johan Galtung (1975) discusses this dilemma and asks: "Will it not merely sound hypocritical?—or even worse, remain empty words that are nullified through the much stronger message of verticality and dominance being normal and acceptable, conveyed through the structure itself?" (p. 80). One of the reasons why I do not go into peace education in schools in any depth is that most of the peace education litera-ture in existence deals with peace education in schools (see for example, Haavelsrud, 1975, 1981; Röhrs, 1983).

Peace educators usually distinguish between education *for* peace and education *about* peace. While education for peace starts before the child is born and continues through life, education *about* peace is usually undertaken by the school at some stage. Teaching about peace seems to be of little value and to have no effect if it is performed within a competitive and hierarchical structure. I see it as my task to deal with education for peace in the broad sense, starting when the child is born and even before that. An education for peace is an education for cooperation, for caring and sharing, for the use of nonviolence in conflict-solving. An education that fosters competition, con-quest, aggression, and violence is an education for war. But in many ways, as I shall show here, these values are the ones that dominate our society today, the values boys are taught.

If then, we are going to work seriously for peace, we are going to have to rethink some of the values and beliefs that are at the core of our society, which help to glorify conquest and mastery. Such rethinking is very difficult and will encounter much resistance, particularly by those who are viewed as leaders within the present framework and would feel a distinct loss of status if the framework were changed and their characteristics no longer glorified. But how do we begin to rethink? And how do we teach the whole society to reeducate itself? This is the task that peace education has set itself: By *peace education* I mean the social process through which peace as I have defined it is achieved. This includes the practicing of equality of rights and equal power-sharing for every member of a given community. It further includes the learning of skills of non-violent conflict resolution. It also includes respect for human rights (Author's definition).

Peace education, then, integrates numerous strands of thinking which have been evolving for some time. In a paper I presented at the Ninth Conference of the International Peace Research Association I tried to bring together disarmament education, development education, and human rights education, and to show how they are all an integral part of peace education (Brock-Utne, 1981b). Common to all these educational programs is the belief in the rights of individuals and the concept that all human beings have *equal* rights. This is an important part of peace education—the equality of all human beings, regardless of color, class, or creed. Only through respect for the equal rights of others and through work for the cessation of all forms of oppression on a major and minor scale will the concept of peace become a reality. I certainly agree with black women who hold that the issue of peace has to be widened (Brown, 1983). And while we might start with the major focus of ending oppression of one country by another, on this same continuum we come to the microcosmic implications and find that we must be equally determined to end the oppression of any one individual by another. So, logically, a commitment to peace education leads to a commitment to end sexism and racism and to the quest for ending the inequalities that are manifested in every aspect of society—in the home, at school, in the workplace.

But acknowledging what peace education aims to achieve does not necessarily provide an answer to the question of how it can be achieved: One fundamental issue is *how* peace education can be taught. As a peace educator it seems clear to me that peace education can be taught, but it demands a different value system. And this is why I make much use of the quote that "peace starts in the minds of women."

This statement needs clarification and I am going to begin with the "minds of women" to illustrate what is meant. I am going to begin with a consideration of women as mothers.

THE ROLE OF MOTHERS IN PEACE EDUCATION

The German philosopher Nietzsche, who was widely read and used by the German Nazis, saw the role of women as producers of sons who would become warriors. In her book *Gyn/Ecology* (1979) on the metaethics of radical feminism, the American philosopher and professor of theology Mary Daly claims that Nietzsche was right not only in the obvious sense that the war state requires mothers to produce sons to become soldiers, but also on the deeper psychic level: The psychic sapping of women in patriarchy functions continually to recreate its warriors. The state of patriarchy is the state of war, in which periods of recuperation from and preparation for battle are euphemistically called "peace." As long as the state of patriarchy continues to exist, women will go on recreating warriors. In a patriarchal society, men have placed themselves at the top of a hierarchy with women and children at the bottom. Women are exploited, victimized, and oppressed. In the above-quoted work (*Thus Spake Zarathustra*), Nietzsche (1885) gives men the following advice: If you are meeting a woman, do not forget the whip. In a patriarchal society women are mutilated and physically abused, with the same claim that Nietzsche used: Women are to learn who their masters are; they are to learn "their proper place." Their proper place is not in the Senate, not in the government, nor in the leading positions of big newspapers or transnational companies. They find their proper place in doing unpaid household chores or taking care of children. And children are to be brought up to reproduce the patriarchal society. What else can mothers do, when they themselves are part of this society? Women are often so totally oppressed as to have internalized the value system and beliefs of the oppressor, even concerning their own worth. It is not an uncommon experience of women working in crisis centers for battered women in the western industrialized world that battered wives blame themselves, claiming that they deserved the whipping, beating, or torture of their husbands.

How is it possible for a mother to teach her daughter that she has as much value as her brother when the mother herself does not believe so and has much less value than her husband? How is it possible for her to teach her daughter to stand up for her rights, to be self-assertive, to change the world, when she is so oppressed herself that she is unable to envisage any other world? And how is it possible for a mother to let her son grow up in a noncompetitive way when she believes men must be trained to become winners? How is it possible for her to let her little son be weak and allow him to cry and show emotions when she believes men have to be strong and tough?

These questions resemble the question asked Virginia Woolf by an educated man who wanted her opinion on how war could be prevented. Her answers to him in *Three Guineas* (Woolf, 1938) also resemble the answers I am trying to give here, though in a different form. In short, the answer is that if women are to help men prevent war they have to fight for their own liberation—not for equality on men's premises, but for liberation from capitalist (both private and state) and patriarchal structures. They have to fight to better their own conditions as women and mothers.

In the western world, the classic picture that comes to mind when one speaks of "the family" consists of a male wage-earner, a female homemaker-mother, and one or more (usually two) dependent children. Yet even in the United States, this pattern actually accounted for only 16 percent of all families in 1977 (*Ms*, 1978). In Norway in 1984 it accounted for only 10 percent of all families. Kathleen Newland (1979) claims that the twin myths of the nuclear family, with its male breadwinner and female housekeeper/child-raiser, and the extended family, which cares for its disadvantaged or dispossessed members through all adversity, have nearly blinded planners to the problems of the woman looking after herself and, most likely, raising children on her own. In the realm of middle-class attitudes and government policies, the woman-headed household hardly exists; and when it does command attention it is viewed as an aberration, the product of a disaster.

But woman-headed households can no longer be considered exceptional in countries rich or poor. In most countries such households comprise a substantial minority, and their number is constantly growing. According to Buvinic and Youssef (1978), one quarter of all Venezuelan families are headed by women, in the United States, the figure was 14 percent in 1978 and growing very rapidly; in Indonesia the figure given is 16 percent; and in parts of Kenya the proportion of households with female heads reached 40 percent. In most of the Commonwealth countries of the Caribbean, at least one family in three is headed by a woman.

The picture that emerges of mothers all over the world is a complex and varied one. But all over the world mothers have one thing in common: They are exploited by male-dominated society. Most societies in the world are sexist societies, though the degree and form of sexism vary. We talk of sexism when the sex roles assigned to men and women function in such a way as to assure the power of one sex over the other. All over the world, sex roles function to the benefit of men, to secure their power and control over women. Sexism, like racism, is a belief system rooted in a world view that assigns varying levels of worth to different groups of human beings. The worth assigned is based upon innate characteristics like skin color or sexual characteristics. As with racism, the assigned social worth under sexism also serves as a rationale for assigning less valued functions to those accorded the lower social worth. Betty Reardon (1981) maintains that in a form of circular reasoning typical of such belief systems, the assertion is made that men do more socially valuable work; therefore, such work is assigned to them because they are more socially valuable. Women are held to be inferior to men and have no legitimate claim to authority. Fulfillment of their social roles fixed by this "natural inferiority" requires submission to the exercise of authority. The socialization of women is distinctly different from that of men, and the more sexist the society, the more distinct is that difference. If women are raising children on their own, their households belong to the poorest in the world. They must make do with shockingly low incomes. They are exploited by employers and frequently receive little child support from the fathers of their children. They have to work long hours. If they are living together with a man, they are usually exploited by him in addition to being exploited by the employer if they are gainfully employed. It is not easy in such a situation to try to change the world through peace education, and yet there is no other hope for womankind.

Elena Gianini Belotti (1973) tells that when a son is born in Lucania, Italy, a mug of water is poured down from a window. The running water is seen to symbolize the boy running down the street and into the world. When a daughter is born drops of water are splashed on the fireplace, symbolizing that a new citizen is born who is going to find her place within the house, near the fireplace. Mothers know well enough the disadvantages that daughters inherit; low status, low earning power, lack of autonomy, long working hours, exploitation. If they are married, they know that their husbands usually prefer sons; especially the first born has to be a son. To be the father of a son adds to the husband's self-image of being masculine. These combined factors produce in mothers the cruelest misogyny of all: son preference.

To be received into the world with a sigh of disappointment is not a happy beginning for any child, but it is the fate of many girls. The natural ratio is about 105 boys to 100 girls born. In parts of North Africa and India, according to Newland (1979), parents' choice would be to have anywhere from three to six sons for every daughter. The desire for sons is usually explained in practical terms: economic contribution, support in old age and continuity of the family line.

Newland (1979) claims that son preference serves as a kind of barometer of woman's overall status in society, except that it registers changes in the social climate *after* they occur rather than before. The very mild degree of son preference found in Thailand can be seen as one manifestation of the relatively egalitarian nature of Thai society. Newland (1979) reports that in Korea, by contrast, customs and economics combine to generate a preference for sons that is among the strongest and most persistent found anywhere. A woman's status is closely tied to her ability to produce sons.

The German philosopher Karl Marx never concealed his strong preference for the male sex and for sons. He usually wrote letters to Friedrich Engels when his wife had given birth to another child. In 1851 he wrote to Engels: "My wife has unfortunately given birth to a daughter, and not a son." And in 1955 he writes again: "Unfortunately another being of the female sex. Had the child been a boy, I should have rejoiced." And when a son is born, he exclaims: "Vivat, le garçon. Il faut peupler le monde des garçons" (Long live the boy! The world must be populated with boys; cited in Janssen-Jurreit, 1976). Living with husbands who hold attitudes like those of Karl Marx, it is not surprising that women desperately want boys.

When I gave birth to my eldest son, Karsten, at Tynset—a farming district in Norway—23 years ago, I was shocked to experience the great difference in status between mothers who had born a son and those who had "only" born a daughter. A mother of a girl in the bed next to mine confessed to me that her husband had told her he would only come to visit her if she gave birth to a son. She also told me that at the farm where she lived they would hoist a flag if a boy was born, but not if a girl was born. At that time only the sons could inherit the farm. It was the eldest son who would inherit the farm, even though he had several older sisters. This property law was changed some years ago so now daughters may inherit.

Nancy Williamson (1978) describes the disturbing development of techniques for intervening in conception or gestation so that parents can choose the sex of a child. Some of the preliminary results are chilling. A clinic in Singapore treated over 1,000 women in a sex preselection experiment carried out in the mid-seventies; over 90 percent of the women wanted boys. The Chinese have experimented with an early sex-determination technique that permits selective abortion early in pregnancy; in the first trial, of 30 women who chose to have abortions, 29 aborted females. In India private clinics that perform a sex-determination test by amniocentesis followed by an abortion if it is a female fetus are thriving (Hoskins and Holmes, 1984; Roggencamp, 1984). The rapid development of new reproductive technologies including easy and cheap sex determination techniques (both prior to and post conception) makes it highly likely that the specific abortion of female fetuses will be practiced even more widely. (For a discussion of the imminent threat to women through the development of new reproductive technologies, see Arditti, Rita, Renate Duelli Klein and Shelley Minden [eds.], 1984). Such developments are often explained by saying that they will help 'control' the population explosion. Yet the grave problem of rapid population growth cannot be dealt with by selectively preventing the birth of girls. Doing so would be a capitulation to sexism at its most brutal.

It does not seem surprising that a wife who has given her husband the son he wants, would also like the son to grow up in a way the husband would approve of. We have historic examples of mothers who wanted their sons to grow up tough and strong men. On the Swedish island of Gotland is located a large stone carving of a proud Viking mother saluting her son with a drinking-horn on his homecoming from a Viking raid. Norwegian professor of education Eva Nordland (1968) thinks it likely that this Viking mother, Gerd of Gotland, was proud of the education she had given her son. She had contributed toward the continuation of the Viking culture by raising such a self-assertive, daring, and aggressive son who fought for himself and his kind. She had trained him to endure hardship and strain, to compete, and be a winner. And any signs of weakness she had frowned upon, because the best that could happen to a real Viking was to die in battle. The worst type of death was a death in bed, a death caused by illness or old age.

The mother of Saint Olav (the Holy Olav, Norwegian King, who reigned from 1015 to 1028, and lived 995–1030) is known to have said to her son: "I feel all the prouder the more successful you are, my son. Should I have to choose I would prefer that you became King of all Norway though that might involve a short life for you, rather than witness that you would not surpass your stepfather and die of old age as he probably will" (taken from Nordland, 1968, p. 3). The mother of another of the ancient Norwegian kings is said to have been very proud when her seven-year-old son, fighting with a boy who was older, bigger, and stronger than he was, got hold of an axe and almost killed the older boy, who was not using any weapons. The mother said that her son deserved a Viking ship as soon as he was old enough.

We may retrace this educational philosophy at various times and in various settings around the world. In the *Forsyte Saga*, (Galsworthy, 1933) the violence the sons are educated to pursue is more of an indirect than a direct kind. They are taught how to exploit others, to excel, to build vast empires by oppressing other people. In the world of today there is no more room for Vikings, empire-builders, exploiters. But is not the spirit of the Viking mother still very much present in the education mothers give their sons? If mothers were to educate their sons to adhere to other ideals than those of their fathers, they would either have to be strong and independent themselves or at least be willing to tolerate constant quarrels with their husbands over the education of their sons.

A mother who endured such quarrels is one of the main characters in the beautiful novel *The Woman and the Black Bird* by Nini Roll Anker (1945). This pacifist novel is written in Norwegian and has not been as widely read as it deserves. The peace researcher Johan Galtung (1967, p. 209) admits that it was his reading of this novel that turned him into a pacifist. It also made a great impact on my eldest son, Karsten, who grew up to become a pacifist. The mother in the novel reads fairytales to her sons and she often plays with them when they are small. She lies down on the carpet with her two sons, and they play with the patterns in the carpet and imagine all sorts of things. Her husband, who is a military man and wants his sons to become tough, strong soldiers, does not approve of his wife's fantasy plays with his sons. She creates in them empathetic and tender beings. When the war comes, one of her sons becomes an invalid. But she helps the other son to desert from the army. He leaves the army because he does not want to kill. His mother hides him in their holiday cabin. Together they play on the carpet again. But they are discovered. The son is shot, and she is taken to jail. It was the father who helped the police find his wife and son.

When I give talks in small Women for Peace groups it often happens that the women introduce themselves and say something about their private lives. It has often struck me how many of these women's grown-up sons are conscientious objectors like my own son, Karsten. Often these women start talking about the upbringing they have given their sons and how difficult it has been to counteract all the influences toward masculine, violent, and competitive behavior that their sons have been subjected to elsewhere. I know what they are talking about and think of all the time I have spent with Gunnar to educate my boys for peace and to counteract an education toward violent and aggressive behavior.

Feminists who become mothers of sons are faced with a difficult problem and also a challenge: Is it at all possible to bring up boys in a non-sexist way? Judith Arcana (1983) tries to answer this question in her recent book on the socialization of males. The first part of her book—the book of Daniel—is about the upbringing of her son. The last part of the book is built on interviews with other mothers of sons—both feminist and non-feminist.

BOYS, THE PREFERRED SEX; GIRLS, THE CARETAKERS

In Chapter 1 I mentioned that considerable evidence shows that women and girls feel the pinch of food scarcity earlier, more frequently and more severely than men and boys do. This leads to a higher incidence of severe malnutrition among women and girls and to their dying at an earlier age. Alice Stewart Carloni (1981) has made a study of sex disparities in the distribution of food within rural households in Bangladesh. She concludes that in order to eradicate malnutrition, it is not enough to increase the supply of food available to households among the rural poor, unless at the same time steps are taken to ensure a more equitable distribution of food within the household by enhancing the perceived economic value of females in rural society. The preferential treatment of boys starts before birth and continues in all sorts of ways after the children are born.

Belotti (1976) refers to several studies that show that mothers breastfeed their sons much longer than they do their daughters. In one study 99 percent of the mothers who had just given birth to sons breastfed their children, against only 66 percent of the mothers who had given birth to girls. Other studies (referred to by Belotti) show that infant boys are also allowed to stay longer at their mother's breast than the infant girls who are breastfed. The mother's body is placed at the small son's disposal to a much greater extent than in the case of his sister. Belotti claims that even the smallest specimen of a male symbolizes an authority the mother knows she has to be subjected to and obey. She lets her baby boy be greedy at her breast and rather enjoys his greediness, while a baby girl is punished by being taken away from the breast if she shows the same behavior as her brother. A girl is not supposed to be greedy and should not become accustomed to having her own immediate desire satisfied. She is taught to let herself be commanded and to wait for satisfaction. Where resources are scarce, the little there is will go primarily to the men and boys. Where resources are more abundant, girls will also get enough to eat and will also have an education. But the preferential treatment of boys will still be there. The early education of the boy will make him "opt" for curricular choices that will lead to well-paid jobs, while his sister "opts" for curricular choices preparing her for jobs with low salaries or no pay at all

(Brock-Utne, 1981a). The fact of preferential treatment of boys in most coeducational classrooms in the western world has now been firmly established by research (Brock-Utne, 1981b; Spender, 1981a, 1981b; Spender and Sarah, 1980; Wernersson, 1977). Boys in an elementary school class with the same number of boys and girls usually receive two-thirds of the teacher's time and attention (no matter what the sex of the teacher is; but usually teachers at this stage are female).

The relationship between mothers and daughters is from the start more complicated than the mother-son relationship. Of course, it is easier to let a child have its way, to show it a lot of attention, than to restrict the child the way mothers often do with girls. Mothers report that from a young age they have many more conflicts with daughters than with sons (Belotti, 1976; Brunet and Lezine, 1966). They usually attribute this to the more difficult character of their daughters. At the same time the mothers admit that they bring up their girls more strictly than their boys. Belotti (1976) reports that those girls who are in for the most trouble with their mothers are those who are born with a high activity rate and have mothers who are rigid and place great value on tidiness, stability, and neatness.

A Korean proverb states: A daughter lets you down twice: once when she is born and then again the day she gets married. In many parts of the world the father's ownership of his wife and children is symbolized by the fact that the whole family uses the father's family name/surname. The name is given to the son forever for him to pass on to a future wife and children. But the daughter keeps her father's name only until the day she gets married and is given her husband's name (the name of *his* father) as a token of her new identity as a member of her husband's family. Feminists increasingly refuse to change their name on marriage. Some British feminists have replaced their surname (*sir*name) with the first name of a girlfriend, e.g., Elizabeth Sarah (Spender, 1980).

Daughters are taught to be less demanding than sons. They are taught to help their mothers with unpaid housework and child care from the time they are very young. They are taught not to show signs of outward aggression, which often means that the aggression is turned inward—against themselves. In short, daughters are taught to be feminine, which means behaving and acting in a way that suits men. A feminine girl never tries to surpass a boy. She is happy to be "The second sex": Simone de Beauvoir's world-famous term.

So the girl is taught to be submissive, to allow her brothers the best part, as the fathers have theirs. And she is taught to look neat, to care for her appearance. Mothers start to toilet train their daughters earlier than they do their sons, and they restrict their daughters' thumbsucking more severely. A pretty appearance is important to someone who is going to be looked at as an object.

In the glossy magazines young girls read in the western world this indoctrination is continued. The important thing for a girl is to get married. To trap the right man, she must be good looking and gentle. In countries where divorce is common, women have to go on taking care of their appearance the rest of their lives: They must try to stay young so that their husbands will not desert them for younger and prettier women. In the winter of 1983 a factory in my immediate surroundings arranged a ski contest for girls and boys aged 8 to 12. Winners of the girls' contest each received a cosmetics kit. Winners of the boys contests received a shotgun.

Jeanne Martin Cisse (1975), Ambassador to the United Nations from Guinea, writes that a characteristic feature of traditional African education was the initiation system, which served primarily to develop in boys a sense of honor and duty to serve their country, while cultivating their lofty feeling of superiority over girls, who were taught what was necessary to fulfill their functions as women in charge of family life. In her own words:

> Women were educated in this way for family life in order, first and foremost, to serve men to whom they owed complete obedience. They had to show submissiveness to their husbands, fathers and brothers, so that education was a form of alienation and a means of ensuring the subordination of woman to man. This education was given by the older women who decided that all the girls in the clan would be required, on reaching a certain age, to undergo a period of special training to harden them and teach them to bear the lot which was and had to be theirs. Such conditioning was intended to improve what were held to be qualities of wife and mother in the African woman and, at the same time, to strengthen her inculcated feeling of inferiority, thus justifying the Maninka proverb which says that a woman's devotion and unconditional submission to men will make her worthy of giving birth to a hero. (Cisse, 1975, p. 348)

All over the world females tend to be more nurturant than males (Hutt, 1972). Little girls are more attentive to their younger brothers and sisters. Pope and Whiting (1973) found in a large cross-cultural study of children that between the ages seven to eleven, girls emerged strongly as the more helpful sex.

In a country like Norway, time studies show that at the age of 15 girls spend an average of 1 hour 26 minutes per day doing unpaid housework at home, while boys in the same age group spend on the average 16 minutes. At the age of 15 both girls and boys in Norway are attending the nine-year compulsory school and living at home (*Time studies*, Norwegian Central Bureau of Statistics, 1972). This means that already at this age boys have more time at their own disposal, time they can use to watch television, or can spend on competitive sports, experimenting with their science kits, or earning extra money by doing occasional paid work.

Belotti (1976) tells from her studies in Italian kindergartens how small girls are trained and expected to wait on boys, lay the table for them, put the boys' toys away when they have played with them. The teacher may ask all the children to tidy up; the boys won't do it, and she lets them get away with it.

("Boys will be boys.") Then she asks the girls (who are usually already putting away their own toys) to put away the toys the boys have been playing with as well. The girls seldom protest; they have seen their mother clear up their father's things, clean and tidy up his clothes, cook his dinner and have it ready on time.

The kindergarten teacher, instead of intervening and making the boys tidy up, loads all the work on the girls. She will not do the work herself; that would lower her prestige, but she has the girls do it. And she gets away with such sexist behavior. If she asked black boys to serve white boys and to clear up their mess and tidy up their toys, she would be accused of racism. Her rationale is similar to a racist one: She is asking individuals who are considered to be of less worth to serve those considered to be of higher worth. There is a striking parallel between racism and sexism, both of which comprise such a a large part of our culture that most people do not even recognize them. Girls—and later mothers—are considered to be of less worth than boys—and later fathers. Girls are helpful, they wait on their brothers, yet they are oppressed by them. But there is one situation in which young boys also are expected to wait on others, to sacrifice themselves, to be oppressed. That is if and when they are soldiers.

"THE IDEAL MOTHER" AND "THE IDEAL SOLDIER"

There certainly are some interesting similarities between the ideal mother and the ideal soldier, though mothers do not normally see this. And it is precisely because they are so exploited and oppressed themselves that they do not see how the patriarchal state also exploits their sons as soldiers and creates the patriarchal mind within them.

Both mothers and soldiers are asked to take orders from men who have more power and a higher status than they and to sacrifice their lives for others who are judged more important. "Not to reason why," but to accept the system is a considered virtue. The American peace researcher Betty Reardon (1981) maintains that what the soldier has done for the nation or the warrior for the tribe through the centuries, woman has done for the family. Woman has been trained to sublimate her own needs to the service of others. Soldiers and mothers have days dedicated in their honor, when society offers thanks for their sacrifices by, in Reardon's words: "reminding them that for such they were born and by such they will continue to be identified and find meaning; for war and domesticity are in the natural order of things, as are the fixed roles of soldiers and mothers within that order" (Reardon, 1981, p. 8).

The military chain of command is conceptually close to the patriarchal family, both being essentially hierarchical organizations. In both institutions, obedience is a virtue and disobedience severely punished. Obedience to authority is the cornerstone of an effective military machine and the fundamental principle of the patriarchal family.

Namelessness is also a common trait of mothers and soldiers. Although mothers sacrifice their lives for their children, the children will usually be known by their father's name. Their mother is forgotten in the history books, as most women are. Most soldiers who sacrifice their lives are also nameless. The grave of the Unknown Soldier under l'Arc de Triomphe in Paris has become a symbol of the nameless soldiers killed on the battlefield. In history books we read about Alexander the Great and the battles *he* won. Bertolt Brecht has asked: Did he win them all by himself? Was he quite alone? Did he not even have a cook with him?

Though the similarities between the "ideal" mother and the "ideal" soldier are striking, there are also distinct differences in their training. Both are asked to sacrifice themselves, both trained to be obedient and submissive; but mothers give life and seek to protect the life they have given, while soldiers are trained to be prepared to take life.

George Gilder (1973) writes of training in a Marine Corps boot camp:

> From the moment one arrives, the drill instructors begin a torrent of misogynistic and anti-individualist abuse. The good things are manly and collective; the despicable are feminine and individual. Virtually every sentence, every description, every lesson embodies this sexual duality, and the female anatomy provides a rich metaphor for every degradation. When you want to create a solidarity group of male killers, that is what you do, you kill the woman in them. That is the lesson of the Marines. And it works.

Thus, the behavior that many fathers and some mothers think sex-appropriate for the little boy is carried to extremes in the training of the soldier. He must be tough, strong, never weak or troubled by soft feelings for the "enemy." And a mother who has trained her son to play with dolls rather than with guns may see much of her education destroyed by the military training her son is forced to go through.

Militarism and Sexism

There is a clear relationship between militarism and sexism. Both militaristic and sexist societies are built on power and oppression. Militarism is a belief system emerging from a world view founded on the basic assumption that human beings are by nature violent, aggressive, and competitive, and from the corollary assumption that social order must be maintained by force (Reardon, 1981). The Australian peace researcher Robin Burns (1981) sees sexism as the practice of violence and oppression in a fundamental way, which gives rise to attitudes intimately associated with militarism and authoritarianism, which socialize the young into accepting conflict and its repressive "resolution."

Celina García (1981) from Costa Rica finds that androgynous* societies are less violent. Oppression seems to increase in cultures where there is more clarity between sex roles, where men are ridiculed and humiliated when they exhibit "feminine" behavior and do not assert their masculinity in acts that involve the subjugation of others.

It is claimed that more matriarchal societies have not represented oppression of the male sex or a military organization (Daly, 1979; Davis, 1971; Garcia, 1981; Janssen-Jurreit, 1976). The Great Goddess seemed interested not in the battlefields but rather in spiritual and intuitive development. In her book *The First Sex*, Ellizabeth Gould Davis (1971) tries to repudiate the last 2,000 years of propaganda concerning the inferiority of women. She claims that this myth of feminine inferiority has prevailed so long that women themselves find it hard to believe that their own sex was once, and for a long time, in great power. In order to restore women to their ancient dignity and pride they must be taught their own history, as the American blacks are being taught theirs. She shows how the deterioration in the status of women went hand in García, 1981; Janssen-Jurreit, 1976). The Great Goddess seemed interested not in the battlefields but rather in spiritual and intuitive development. In her book *The First Sex*, Elizabeth Gould Davis (1971) tries to repudiate the last great world civilization, the Celts, maintained the tradition of female supremacy until the fall of Rome, when the Celts were crushed by the Germanic barbarians and the oriental Christians, two promoters of masculinism. Celtic feminism was condemned as sinful by the patriarchal conquerors.

Evidence suggests that the more militarist a society is, the more sexist it tends to be. Gloria Steinem (1980) shows in a series of articles how Hitler crushed the German feminist movement as he militarized Germany. Lionel Tiger (1969) points to the significant fact that the Nazi movement was an essentially male organization.

Mary Daly (1979) brilliantly shows how extreme militarism degrades all attempts at creating equality between the sexes, degrades women and anything associated with softness and emotions. The male who is not willing to go forward blindly on the march of massive destruction is a "female" or a "transsexual." Thus, in recent years, U.S. President Lyndon B. Johnson was known to respect the opinions only of tough, "real" men. Only those who were confident and hawkish about Vietnam were listened to. Daly quotes David Halberstam (1972), who writes that on hearing that one member of his administration was becoming a dove on Vietnam, Johnson said, "Hell, he has to squat to piss." . . . Doubt itself, Johnson thought, was almost a feminine

---

* androgyny—a union between the masculine and feminine principles, choosing the best qualities of both sexes. García uses the word to identify and expose the myths that justify direct violence in the male sex and indirect violence in the social context.

quality, doubts were for women. . . . Another example of this prevailing attitude was Spiro Agnew. Marc Fasteau (1975) points out that Agnew "compared then-Senator Charles Goodell to Christine Jørgensen, a man surgically changed into a women, in describing Goodell's shift from hawk to dove."

How are these tough, "real" men created? The men who go "forward blindly on the march of massive destruction?" How are they taught to prefer violence to nonviolence, aggression to nonaggression, to degrade anything associated with softness and emotions?

NONVIOLENCE INSTEAD OF VIOLENCE

Masculinity and Violence

In our type of society being masculine is practically synonymous with being aggressive. A survey conducted for the United States National Commission on the Causes and Prevention of Violence revealed that 70 percent of over a thousand respondents agreed with the statement: "When a boy is growing up it is very important for him to have a few fistfights" (Stark and McEvoy, 1970, p. 52).

When my youngest son, who like my eldest son, Karsten, had never been given war toys and was taught not to fight, was five years old he had a hard time in a kindergarten. He exhibited behavior at home that I had never seen in him before: He started hitting us although he had never been beaten by us, and he cried more often. I had the feeling he was not happy in the new kindergarten. When I called one of the teachers, she said: "We were just about to call you about Gunnar. You must teach him how to fight. Because he does not know how to fight and does not want to fight, all the others want to fight with him. And then he cries, and they call him a sissy and fight him more. You must teach him how to fight or the situation will get worse when he starts school." I replied that it was not my responsibility to teach my son how to fight. On the contrary, it was her responsibility to teach the other children *not* to fight. It was her responsibility to intervene in fights, stop them, and help children to solve their conflicts through nonviolent means. It was difficult to teach her from my position as a mother. I asked her if she would have given us the same advice had Gunnar been a girl. She admitted that she wanted to change his behavior precisely because he was a boy and not a girl.

From toddler age on, boys engage in angry outbursts roughly twice as often as girls and are much more likely to attempt physical injury of their target. They grab toys, attack other children, and ignore requests from parents and peers. They quarrel with children more often, and are more aggressive generally in all areas of behavior than girls. Corinne Hutt (1972) has made extensive studies of the social behavior of preschool children. She concludes that boys are twice as aggressive as girls (aggression here including verbal aggression). Even more interesting, she sees the fact that it is predominantly boys toward whom this aggression is directed. The boys manage to irritate each other enough for aggression to be the outcome twice as often as it is with girls. The sex difference in aggression is in evidence in all age groups that have been studied. Thomas Detre (1974) has found that there are approximately twice as many aggressive boys throughout the school grades as girls and three times as many aggressive boys in kindergarten as girls.

Some researchers maintain that the greater aggressiveness of boys and men may be partly biologically determined, which I shall discuss later. But as educators, we can mainly do something about the environment surrounding the child. When we compare these findings showing the greater aggressiveness of boys to the lesson Gunnar's kindergarten teacher tried to teach him and us, we see that aggressiveness is encouraged in boys. She admitted that she would not have encouraged him to fight had he been a girl. In the case of a girl physically attacking another girl, she would probably have stopped the attacking girl verbally, the way she ought to have done with the boy attacking Gunnar.

If boys are encouraged to be violent and aggressive from infancy onward, it is not strange that researchers on aggression seem to agree with Arnold Buss (1971) in his conclusion:

> Human aggression is a problem for men, not women. It is men who wage wars, engage in bitter competition, fight each other individually, and maintain vendettas lasting for years or even decades. . . . Status as a male is to be achieved by being aggressive, and masculinity is perhaps the most basic aspect of a man's identity.

A study conducted by Maccoby and Jacklin (1974) of play patterns of American preschool children playing with children of the same sex and with children of the opposite sex showed that boy-boy pairs were more likely to engage in a tug of war over a toy than girl-girl or boy-girl pairs. While both boys and girls were somewhat more likely to cry or retreat toward their mothers (who were quietly seated in the room) when playing with a boy partner, girls were particularly affected by a male partner and tended to retreat or stand quietly watching the boy play with the toys. Girls with female partners rarely exhibited such behavior. Apparently even very young boys do something that makes their partners wary. Maccoby and Jacklin state that they do not know what this "something" is.

Another American study referred to by Maccoby (1980) and conducted in 1977 by DiPietro of same-sex preschool children who were allowed to play freely in a room with a trampoline, a beach ball, and a big Bobo doll (a child-size inflated toy with weighted feet) showed that some of the girls' groups developed a distinctive pattern of interaction that was almost never shown by boys. They organized their play by making rules. If one girl insisted on going first or taking a longer turn than the others, her partners would react by invoking the rules and arguing, rather than by using force. The children may very well have learned this behavior from their parents. Sandra Kronsberg (1981) has shown experimentally that parents intervene physically when the child is a boy and verbally when the child is a girl.

DiPietro found little sex difference in level of physical activity. The girls jumped on the trampoline and moved quickly with the beach ball like the boys did, but they seldom engaged in roughhousing. The girls seldom tried to hit each other with the beach ball or push or play tug of war—things the boys did quite frequently (usually accompanying the activity with shouts of glee or excited laughter). The friendly rough-and-tumble of boys' play is sometimes hard to distinguish from more serious encounters with mutual intent to hurt, and roughhousing can turn into aggression quite quickly. Both types of interaction are typical in boys' groups in the western world, but not in girls' groups.

These results have recently been confirmed in a Norwegian study of kindergarten children, five to seven years old. Tone Reithaug (1983) collected data from periods of free play where the children were allowed to choose their own activities. She found that the girls would gather in the doll corner and the boys in the building and construction corner. She then looked at the interaction between the groups and found that the interaction between the boys in the construction corner was highly competitive. They competed in building the nicest ploughs, the nicest trains. In the dolls' corner, where mostly girls gathered, there was a role play without competition. She also found that the boys shouted and called for attention much more than the girls and that more than 80 percent of the threats uttered during the free play period were threats from boys.

Eric Erickson (1951) worked with 150 boys and 150 girls who were ten, eleven, and twelve over a two-year period. Among other things Erickson gave them the task "of constructing a scene on a table which they would find exciting as a set for an imaginary motion picture." After they had constructed the setting, they were asked to tell the plot of the movie they were imagining. Erickson found that the girls' scenes were expressly peaceful while the boys' scenes showed that they were already confirmed in their interest in violence.

The greater aggressiveness of boys seems such a universal feature that some parents take this aggressiveness as a biological fact. Aggressive behavior on the part of their son simply indicates that their son is "normal," a "real boy." They are unaware of the fact that their own expectations have been working like self-fulfilling prophecies, or that the attitudes and expectations their little son is met with from his immediate surroundings, especially his father, may determine whether his aggressive disposition will cause him to commit acts of violence, become a delinquent, or whether they will be used in a nonviolent struggle to better the conditions of others.

A large number of studies have been conducted on the question of sex differences, specifically on the question of different levels of aggression between women and men. Many of them are tainted by conventional assumptions about male and female roles (thus revealing an unquestioned amount of sexism). In others the researchers do not question the methods they use and believe that counting, measuring, and collecting data will reveal *the* link, rather than providing an answer to the specific question they have asked. Despite the problems inherent in scientific work (endocrinological as well as behavorial; see also Chapter 4), I shall discuss some of the research conducted on aggression.

Psychobiology and Violence

Maccoby and Jacklin (1974) have compiled a most extensive survey on research data on sex differences. They consulted more than 1,400 scientific works. The sex differences found were divided into three parts: (a) myths, (b) poorly substantiated findings, and (c) well-established findings. Within the third group we find the greater aggressiveness of boys. This greater aggressiveness on the part of boys seems to show up at the age of two years, but not before. Maccoby and Jacklin suggest that boys may be biologically more prepared than girls to learn to become aggressive. But even if this is so, it is all the more reason for parents to work to channel their sons' aggressive drives into a worthwhile challenging activity.

Researchers do not agree on the question of whether differences in the brain or in the glandular secretion of men and women make men more predisposed toward aggression. Lars Jalmert (1979) maintains that most researchers working in this field have had a hard time defining aggression, or have not defined it at all. This also seems to be the case in the extensive psychobiological work of Laurel Holliday (1978) on the violent sex. Sometimes she equates aggression with physical violence, sometimes with verbal assertion. When she started studying the psychobiological differences between males and females she also started asking why males are so different from females.

> I wanted to know why, for example, sex is the most reliable predictor of how violent a person will be in all cultures, races and classes in recorded history. And why are 90 percent of all violent crimes committed by men? Why are males the violent sex? Because daddy encouraged them to be tough and play with guns, because teacher said they were stronger and faster than girls and didn't cry, because Mommy took away their dolls? (Holliday, 1978, p. 11).

After extensive reviewing of studies showing how fathers treat their sons, how the rod spoils the boy, how media violence affects the male child, Holliday still reaches the conclusion that there is an inborn disposition toward greater aggressiveness in the male of the species. She claims that the relation between the male sex organs and aggression has been obvious to animal breeders for centuries; castration has been used to tame aggressive bulls for at least 5,000 years. Only in the last two or three decades, however, have scientists technologically corroborated folk knowledge and shown that phylogeny, androgens, the male sex hormones, are prime facilitators of aggression. From her studies she concludes that male aggressiveness (whether in mice, monkeys, or humans) is connected with the level of androgen circulating in the bloodstream. She does not doubt that environment and conditioning influence an individual's propensity for aggression, but "the fact remains that the male of the species does not begin life with a propensity for peacefulness anywhere near that of a female, and equalization, in most cases, requires social inhibition of the male's inborn biological proclivities" (Holliday, 1978, p. 28).

Holliday argues convincingly that androgen levels are correlated with aggressiveness. Alcoholics have androgen levels five to ten times higher than normal men. The reasons for this are not clear, but alcoholism causes severe liver damage, which in turn causes an increase in androgen levels. Normally the liver inactivates much of the androgen in the bloodstream, but a severely damaged liver is unable to perform this function; thus androgen levels rise precipitously. Alcoholism and violent crimes are strongly correlated. A four-year study in Philadelphia, for example, found that alcohol was involved in 70 percent of all physical assault murders and 50 percent of all murders (Wolfgang and Strohm, 1956). It is easy to agree with Holliday when she advises men who want to decrease their aggressiveness to cut down on alcohol. It is not so easy to follow her when she makes a case *for* the smoking of marijuana. But she is able to show that marijuana has been found to decrease men's potential for aggressive behavior as well as plasma testosterone levels. It has been suggested that the active ingredient in marijuana, THC, has a chemical structure very similar to estrogen and that it works as an antiandrogen in men who are heavy marijuana smokers. Holliday claims that there are clear indications that marijuana may be a valuable "herbal remedy" for aggressiveness.

Holliday not only points to the androgen levels in males, but also to the structure and function of the brain and the work of the Y chromosome to explain the greater aggressiveness in males. If we assume that males really are born with greater dispositions for violence, if we think their biological make-up predisposes them for aggressiveness (which, of course, cannot be "proven"), what should be the consequences of such insight? I can see three obvious categories.

Limit the number of male children. Holliday claims that the most important step we as individuals can take to reduce the harmful effects of masculine psychobiological programming is to have fewer male children. In Appendix One of her book she gives what she calls complete directions on how to have a girl. Her directions are based on a woman knowing the exact time of ovulation, and Holliday gives instructions on how to determine this.

I would be afraid of recommending such a practice. If a mother is able to choose to have a girl, she is also able to choose to have a boy. I have already mentioned how mothers normally prefer sons, perhaps primarily to satisfy the wishes of their husbands. Given the position of women in society today, I am afraid that, the practice of choosing the sex of an infant would work to the detriment of the female sex. I have greater belief in another of Holliday's recommendations: trying to look for a father for your children who belongs to the least aggressive of males. There seems to much truth in the saying: "like father, like son."

Have women rule the world. The greater aggressiveness of males is sometimes used to explain why men hold leading positions. There is reason to ask if this trait should not make them unqualified to occupy such positions. I have already mentioned that the great peace activist Gandhi believed that women were the only ones who could save the world. The peace researcher Johan Galtung has voiced a similar faith in women.

Buckminister Fuller, Lionel Tiger, Lyall Watson, and many other men who have given thought to the problem of male aggression have concluded that the only hope might be to turn the world over to women. U.S. Admiral Gene R. La Rocque, Director of the Center for Defense Information in Washington, D.C., asked the women members of CDI's Board and the wives of men on the Board to join together and develop a women's project to prevent nuclear war. The first National Women's Conference to Prevent Nuclear War was the outcome (September 12, 1984 in the Capitol, Washington, D.C.). Admiral Gene La Rocque stated that his generation had failed to stop the arms race and now it was up to the women.

Lionel Tiger and Robin Fox (1971) make this prediction in their book *The Imperial Animal*: "So long as the use of nuclear weapons could be banned for one year, if all the menial and mighty military posts of the world were taken over by women, there would be no war." Elizabeth Gould Davis (1971) related how Buckminister Fuller, on a television broadcast in 1968, shocked his studio audience when he suggested that society might be saved by restoring women to their age-old leadership in government while men confine themselves to gadgetry and games.

Holliday (1978, p. 171) tells how the Iroquois Indians have long recognized that there is a basic difference in the propensity of men and women for aggression, and for that reason gave to women the sole right to declare war of their nation against another.

Make men change. The third consequence of the insight that men's biological make-up predisposes them for violence and aggression would be to counteract these predispositions either through clinical surgery and/or medication or through changes in the social and educational environment of boys. Though I feel rather hesitant about the first of these two roads, I shall briefly mention some of the insights here. For instance, it has been known for some time that castration decreases criminal practice (Hawke, 1950; LeMaire, 1956). It has also been known that boys whose mothers were given estrogen during the critical period of gestation (eight weeks of life) are programmed to be less aggressive and less dominant than males who have no hormonal interference in utero. Dr. Richard Green (1974) studied the behavioral effects on male offspring of giving pregnant diabetic women estrogen in an attempt to reduce fetal mortality. They assessed the male offspring of these women at age six and sixteen and found that at both ages they show less assertiveness, aggressiveness, and rough-and-tumble play when compared to normal controls and to sons of diabetic mothers who were not exposed to high levels of estrogen. In this case, the evidence is strong that the estrogen interfered with the process of fetal androgenization and had a dramatic effect on the boys' subsequent behavior. I have already mentioned that marijuana decreases a male's androgen production, while alcohol increases it. But I am not going to recommend here either castration of men, hormonal interference in utero, or the smoking of marijuana.

It is important to emphasize at this point that the correlation between aggression and androgens is only a correlation and not necessarily a causal link. Most of the evidence would seem to indicate that high androgen causes high aggression, but sometimes social influences can cause a change in androgen levels. Maccoby and Jacklin (1974) summarize this, saying that hormone levels constitute an open system and that at the present state of our knowledge, it would appear that a high testosterone level can be both a cause and result of aggressive behavior. This of course means that it is important to look at the social and educational environment we give our boys whether it encourages aggression and violence or cooperation and caring. What sort of toys are our young boys given? What kind of entertainment do they receive on television? What are they encouraged to participate in? Is the education and upbringing we give them likely to counteract their aggressive dispositions or, on the contrary, are we encouraging them and thereby increasing their androgen levels? It is my conviction that the biological components of sex-role behavior, while definitely of some consequence, are relatively small by comparison with cultural influences.

Early Socialization and Violence

Most parents provide different socialization experiences for their daughters and their sons at the same time that sex-typical toddler behaviors are emerging. Parents tend to buy their sons more transportation toys, sports equipment, and military toys, while they buy their daughters dolls, stuffed animals, and domestic toys (Rheingold and Cook, 1975). The toys parents buy or make for their children form an important part of the child's immediate surroundings. All toys are educational and convey messages to children. Some toys are used for fighting, some for caring. Some encourage imitative play and the learning of existing social roles, and others encourage the child to explore new directions.

Toy shops in most locations around the world will generally have one section with toys for girls and one section with toys for boys. In the section with toys for girls, we find all sorts of objects designed to educate the small girl in her role of homemaker: pots and pans, miniature stoves and refrigerators for her role as housekeeper; dolls in all shapes for her role as mother; and for her role as the object of men's sexual interest, cosmetic kits and hair-curlers. In the section with toys for boys we find objects designed to train the small boy for jobs that carry prestige and are decisive for our way of living. Here are science kits of all kinds, buses and trucks, cars and trains. And we find big collections of war toys, from bows and arrows to rifles, guns, machine guns, revolvers, and even small uniforms.

The choice of toys is made for the child long before she or he can make any personal choice. By the time the child is able to do that, she or he is usually conditioned into "choosing" the sex-appropriate toy. Even the mobiles that are often put in the newborn baby's bedroom, frequently above the crib, are sex-typed. Mobiles for infant girls contain small dolls, angels, and flowers. Boats, cars, and cannons are for infant boys.

Elena Belotti (1973) tells from her many observations of preschool children how boys and girls are pressed into playing with sex-appropriate toys. A two-year-old boy asked his mother if she could buy him a small broom. The answer was no, that was not a toy for a boy. Boys who want to have a doll with them when they go to sleep are given a teddy bear: Boys may cuddle with doll-like figures in the shape of animals but never in the shape of a baby or a real doll! When children were left on their own and believed that they had no observers, however, Belotti found that boys were eager to play with dolls and girls with cars or anything that would move. If toys are to form a part of peace instead of war education, we must do away with war toys and also with the sex-labeling of toys. Both sexes ought to be able to play with dolls, to train themselves to take care of children and a home. Both sexes ought to be able to play with movable objects like buses and trains and, when somewhat older, to experiment with science kits.

On entering the GDR through East Berlin some years ago I was asked by the customs clearance whether I brought with me any war toys because such imports were strictly forbidden. Being so much an opposer of war toys, I was rather perplexed at this question. I thought that perhaps war toys are forbidden in the GDR. While studying in that country and deliberately visiting toy shops and day-care centers for children I noticed that this was not the case.

Though the selection of such toys in comparison to other toys seemed to be smaller than in the western world, it still existed. When I asked why I had not been allowed to bring war toys into the Republic I was given the answer that they did not want NATO war toys imported. Their boys should be taught to play with toys that copy the military equipment from the countries belonging to the Warsaw Pact!

Both in Norway and Sweden there have been successful campaigns started by women against the production and sale of war toys. And in both countries the women in the social democratic parties have been supported by youth groups within the parties and have managed to gain political acceptance for a line of severe import restrictions on such toys. Women are still working to have such toys completely prohibited.

It was mothers who organized and picketed Nabisco in 1971 to have them withdraw the kits of torture toys they had produced for boys (Holliday, 1978, p. 159). In 1971, the Aurora Toy Company introduced a new line of torture toys for boys. There were eight different kits. A typical one included a semi-nude female who was to be strapped to the platform of a guillotine with a razor-sharp blade suspended above her throat. The mothers who organized against these toys succeeded in having them withdrawn from the market. It was no accident that it was mothers, not fathers, who felt compelled to protect their children from such a glorification of violence.

Punishment and Violence

Numerous researchers have found that the more severely a child is punished, the more likely she or he is to become an aggressive juvenile delinquent. The more violence a child experiences at the hands of her or his parents, the more violent she or he is likely to be to others as an adult. The parents who beat a child provide a living example of how to use force to accomplish one's ends. Extensive research has shown that physical punishment is one of the five factors associated with the development of delinquency in young boys (Glueck and Glueck, 1950). Holliday (1978) in her book on the violent sex mentions research that show that men who have been convicted of murder were physically punished in childhood twice as often as their brothers who had not committed murder; some had almost been beaten to death.

Boys are punished more often and more severely than girls. Murray Strauss (1974) has found that boys are punished roughly twice as often as girls. Maccoby and Jacklin (1974) point out that fathers react more severely than mothers to their boys' aggressiveness and are more likely to physically punish a son for aggressive misbehavior than a daughter who does exactly the same thing. Boys are much more likely to be punished by their fathers than by their mothers. Holliday (1978) reports a survey conducted for the National Commission on the Cause and Prevention of Violence showing that almost twice as many low-education parents reported frequent spanking as high-education respondents. According to Holliday (1978) there seems to be a predictable ratio between educational and income levels and violence toward children—as income goes up physical punishment goes down. There may be several explanations for this phenomenon. One is that the lack of space and resources leads to aggression. Another may be that people with more education have learned more about the harmful effects of spanking children. This might in some instances prevent them from physically abusing their children or at least to not *report* it or be ashamed of such behavior. But it is extremely important to stress the fact that some ethnic groups, though poor, rarely or never punish children. Some American Indian tribes, for example, never use physical force on their children, while child abuse is high among American Blacks and Puerto Ricans (Gil, 1973).

In their book *Violence in the Family*, Steinmetz and Strauss (1974) state on the basis of several studies that a physically punished child is more likely to be a harsh and violent parent and so perpetuate violence down through the generations. Holliday (1978, p. 102) reports a study by Drs. Leopold Bellak and Maxine Antell (1974) demonstrating that nearly all of the Nazi criminals had been seriously mistreated in childhood. To test their hypothesis that Germans as children may be more subject to physical violence, they studied parent-child interaction on German playgrounds as compared to Danish and Italian playgrounds. Their results indicate clearly that German adults are significantly more aggressive toward German children, and German children toward other children, than either the Italians or the Danes. Holliday comments: "Though they do not claim that the parent abusiveness is *the* cause of German aggressiveness, their work strongly suggests that we take a long look at how we in this country punish children" (Holliday, 1978, p. 103). And we ought to take a look at how we socialize children to accept and participate in violence through the media, especially through what children are offered on television.

Television and Violence

Two British researchers, H. J. Eysenck and D. K. B. Nias (1978), have made a thorough analysis of the available international research data on the effects of watching violence on television. In their book, *Sex, Violence and the Media*, they conclude that it has been shown beyond a doubt that watching violence on television causes real life violence. They claim that all the many studies that show this fact have been trivialized in a most scandalous way. The data they present show that there is every reason to believe that watching violence on television will cause more than 1 percent of the population that would otherwise not be violent to resort to violence. Even if we only take 1 percent, that makes 350,000 people in Great Britain and 1.4 million people in the United States who would pass the borderline to the use of violence.

Holliday (1978) claims that of all the situational factors that are known to increase aggressiveness, it appears that the viewing of television violence is one of the most potent. Most researchers are usually reluctant to say that one thing causes another. They usually say: "There is a strong correlation between" and point out that the strong correlation does not say anything about the causal relationship. But the case is so strong on television violence that prominent and highly respected researchers like Dr. Robert M. Liebert make statements like these: "It seems to me that it has been shown beyond the reasonable shadow of a doubt that watching television produces antisocial attitudes and behavior that would not otherwise occur among entirely normal children" (Liebert, 1974, p. 99). Similarly, Leonard Eron concludes from his ten-year extensive study of television and violence that "the most plausible interpretation of these data was that early viewing of violent television caused later aggression" (Eron et al.,1974, p. 412). But this direct positive relationship between violence of preferred programs and later aggression was true only for boys! Strangely enough, television violence, which has been found to be a major contributor to boys' aggressive behavior, does not seem to influence girls. There may be several explanations for this fact. Holliday (1978) mentions some: (1) girls are socialized away from aggression, and thus prefer less violent television to begin with, (b) female characters are not as violent as male characters on television and are therefore not as potent role models for aggression and (c) females are often victims of male violence on television, and little girls identify with their pain. One explanation may also be that girls watch less television than boys because they have to do so much more unpaid housework than their brothers do.

Recent research on the question of media violence as the cause of aggression has been carried out along three main lines. One school works with the "arousal hypothesis," which holds that exciting media content (erotic, violent, humorous, etc.) can increase aggression if it is an appropriate response, as it can also increase sexual activity if that is the appropriate response. The second major school works with the "disinhibition" hypothesis. It holds that television violence, especially if it is rewarded, weakens the inhibition of the viewer to engage in similar behavior and by implication increases the viewer's readiness to engage in interpersonal aggression. The third school bases its thinking on a social learning theory. It holds that ways of behavior are learned by observation not only of real performance, but also of media-fed performance. Television violence may lead to the acquisition of aggressive responses that are imitated in appropriate situations in real life. These three schools are complementary and not exclusive.

Eyseneck and Nias (1978) belong to the second major school. They have shown that the natural inhibitions against violence are grossly reduced in children if they have a feeling that their surroundings accept violence. Children get desensitized to the use of violence. Eyseneck and Nias (1978) use this

desensitization process as their main explanation for the fact that watching
and reading about violence may lead to real life violence. It is a common
method within behavorial therapy to desensitize people who have irrational
phobias against certain things. Take a person who has an irrational phobia
against any kind of innocent spider and starts screaming when she sees one.
Behavioral therapists will try to treat this irrational fright by slowly desensitiz-
ing the patient toward spiders. They will talk to her or him in pleasant surroundings about spiders and will show the patient a small picture of a spider.
When the patient feels safe and can talk about spiders, the therapist will let
the patient see one through a window. The next time the patient will walk in a
garden and look at a spider from far off. In this manner the patient will
slowly be desensitized regarding spiders. Parents often use the same method to
help their child overcome fright about water and the sea. The parents play
with the child near the water and gradually move closer to the water. But this
method of desensitization can also be used to promote negative aims.
Eyseneck and Nias maintain that if the population of the planet Mars wanted
to find a method to brutalize the population of the earth they could not have
thought of anything better than to invent a media system that would slowly
desensitize humanity against using violence against each other. If one wants to
reduce inhibitions against the use of violence and allow for the violent person
to come forward, one should—to follow the principles of desensitization—
start by letting people watch violence in the safe and cozy atmosphere of their
own homes. Through a gradual process of becoming accustomed to and
accepting more and more violence, some of the viewers will lose their inhibitions against the use of violence in a given real life situation.

In my own country, Norway, we have at the moment only one television
channel. It is run by the state, and there are no commercials. The programs
that are produced in Norway are not normally of a violent kind. We have
especially good and valuable children's programs. But on Friday night television we have a "detective hour" with mostly American-produced detective
series that are often quite violent and usually include a murder or two. Children as young as six and seven years brag to each other about seeing the
detective hour. They maintain that the children's programs are dull; they want
action and excitement. And their fathers want to watch the detective hour, so
they watch it safely together with them, although they often experience nightmares. We are now opening up more channels with more possibilities to view
detective films, crime, and westerns. And in a country where we have had a
strict control on films shown in the movie theaters, we are now being flooded
with imported video tapes with the most grotesque and brutal violence. Children usually watch these films after they come home from school and before
their parents return from work. A schoolteacher mentioned to me that children had told her that the first time they saw these horror films where women
are raped, cut into small pieces, and sent through a meat grinder, they got sick
and had to go out and throw up. But then they gradually got used to watching

these scenes. Now they could watch all sorts of violence without becoming ill or even without having nightmares. Certainly, the desensitization process worked.

It is strange that it should be necessary to prove the effect that media violence has. We normally accept that what one reads and watches has influence. Our whole educational system takes this assumption for granted. Television is used for educational purposes in school. It would be rather strange if American children did not learn anything from the 11,000 murders they watch on television before the age of 15 (Eyseneck and Nias, 1978). Television companies, particularly in the United States, use millions of dollars to advertise their products through television. Certainly they must think that watching television influences people's behavior and actions. But the same television companies do their utmost to trivialize the effect of viewing violence on TV. This is not supposed to effect people's behavior! When it comes to having people buy their products, advertisers believe in the educational value of television and adhere to the social learning theory. They think that if people see that other people feel refreshed and happy after having a Coke, they will also want a Coke. If they watch their favorite movie star tell how good she feels after she started using a special kind of soap, then the viewer—or at least some of them—will want that soap too. It is time we realize that *all* television has an impact and "educates," even if for the wrong reason.

A few people, television producers among them, have attempted to convince the public that television violence is good since it helps people to react, thus leading to a catharsis for their personal pent-up aggression. This is the theory that was held by Aristotle regarding violence in drama. Holliday, (1978) on the other hand, refers to Plato, who argued that viewing violence increased people's aggressiveness. Plato turned out to be right, according to the numerous contemporary psychological studies from which I have quoted. It is simply not true that you can "get violence out of your system" by viewing television.

When I give lectures on peace education and on the effects of media violence there will always be some men in the audience who will claim that they do not believe that it has any harmful effects on their children. It will let out steam, they claim. They believe in the catharsis theory because they like watching detective films themselves. I often find out that the same fathers do not want their children to watch sexual acts on the television. In that case, they do not believe that watching sex films will act as a catharsis for pent-up sexual desires, but are afraid that their children will become sexually aroused and will lead a more active sex life than they would had they not seen the films. I have often pointed out this contradiction to the skeptical men in the audience to make them see how illogical their reasoning is.

In their book *Violence as Communication*, the Dutch researchers Alex P. Schmid and Janny de Graaf (1982) have a chapter on unlearning inhibitions against the use of violence. Here they remind us that an act of violence consists of two things: the act of aggression and the act of suffering from the consequences of the aggression. In violence portrayals in the media, emphasis is placed on the first aspect, while the second is largely neglected. This is done for two reasons. The first is that the aftermath of violence is long, and the act of violence is short. A shooting, stabbing, or car accident takes only seconds to depict, while the suffering of the victim and of her or his nearest family cannot be covered adequately given the time constraints that govern media programming. The second reason for this imbalance between aggression and suffering is that showing the agony of the victim is unaesthetic and upsetting to audiences. Schmid and de Graaf tell about a British commercial television station that some years ago tried to broadcast a realistic crime series (*Big Breadwinner Hog*) in which pain, wounds, and suffering were portrayed in true detail. This produced such a public outcry that the series had to be discontinued after one sequence. The viewers wanted to see people shot and killed, hanged and torn to pieces, but not how they suffered. The net effect of this imbalance seems to be that the television watcher cannot develop much sympathy for the victim. This is reinforced by the fact that in fictional crime series the people who have to suffer most are usually "bad guys" who "deserve" death and injury.

From an early age on children become accustomed to violence without simultaneously learning what its consequences are. Television comedy series, for instance, may depict how a "good guy" smashes a person with a rock, whereupon the victim reinflates like a balloon in the next scene to regain her or his original form. The humorous connotation of such scenes may ultimately not have the effect of harmlessness but facilitate the acceptance of violence as normal, inconsequential, and legitimate.

To say that much of television is fictional does not excuse it. The public's ability to distinguish between real and fictional television material is limited. Schmid and de Graaf (1982) tell about a fictional series, *Marcus Welby M.D.*, in which the leading character is a physician. The actor received, during the first five years of the program, no less than 250,000 letters from the public, mostly with requests for medical advice. Schmid and de Graaf also show that when real life violence is shown on television—for instance in the news— the same thing happens: The act of aggression is shown but not the consequences of the act. We are led to believe that violence is excitement, not primarily suffering and pain.

Kenneth Moyer (1974) who, according to Holliday (1978), has probably written more than anyone else about the physiological correlates of aggressive behavior, reports that the neural systems involved in violence are sensitized and aroused by competitive sports. Goldstein and Arms (1971) did a study to determine what effect competitive sports have on aggressive behavior. They found that hostility significantly increased in persons who had just viewed a football game. However, they found no increase in hostility in people who had observed a gymnastic exhibition. They point out that intense competition can lead to catastrophic consequences.

COOPERATION INSTEAD OF COMPETITION

One of the central values in an education for peace is the value of sharing, of cooperation. This value is the opposite of competition, of oppression, of wanting to dominate. The anthropologist Margaret Mead (1978) states that:

> In every known human society, the male's need for achievement can be recognized. Men may cook or weave or dress dolls or hunt hummingbirds, but if such activities are appropriate occupations of men, then the whole society, men and women alike, votes them as important. When the same occupations are performed by women, they are regarded as less important. In a great number of human societies, men's sureness of their sex role is tied up with their right to practise some activity that women are not allowed to practise. Their maleness, in fact, has to be underwritten by preventing women from entering some field or performing some feat.

The great tragedy of humankind is that in most societies the activities that are regarded as appropriate occupations for men are not nonviolent activities like cooking, weaving, or doll-dressing. In the western world, at least, proving to be a man usually means to become violent because our culture generally does not offer a fully accepted category for nonviolent men. I agree with García (1981) that peace education must begin to legitimize a new category of man, a nonviolent man.

Erickson (1951) in his study of 10- to 12-year-olds found that the female child was interested in including others in her world and acting in relation to them, not in competition. The competitiveness essential to aggression is clearly less strong in female children. The male child seems to be less integrated with his environment and less sensitive to external cues, like other people's faces. He acts upon rather than acting in relation to and so begins a lifelong pattern of establishing separateness and competitiveness rather than affiliation and cooperation with others. In another cross-cultural study that compared Anglo-American and Mexican children, five-through nine-year-olds were offered opportunities to make choices that would give them more rewards than their partners, equal rewards with their partners, or smaller rewards than their partners. Girls in both cultures and at all ages studied were more likely to try to equalize the rewards. Boys not only chose more for themselves but also made choices that reduced the partner's reward, even when this action did not yield more for the child himself (Knight and Kagan, 1977).

Girls' greater willingness to share resources evenly has been demonstrated in several studies. A study at the University of Tromsø found that when the boys entered the athletics hall before the girls when they were going to have physical education together, they occupied the whole hall. They would spread out and shout to each other and throw balls from one end of the hall to the other. When the girls entered, they had to form a small cluster where they were just talking quietly together until the teaching started. If the girls entered first, however, they would occupy only *half* of the athletics hall, leaving the rest to the boys (Andreassen and Mortensen, 1982).

The fights that erupt in boys' groups are often related to forming and maintaining dominance hierarchies. In a cross-cultural study, Whiting and Whiting (1973, 1975) found that in five out of six societies in different parts of the world, boys showed more egoistic dominance than girls. Edwards and Whiting (1977) also report higher male rates of such egoistic behaviors in five out of six African villages. In the same study, sex differences in the quality of the African children's social interaction were found, differences rather similar to what DiPietro (1977) found in American children: Boys more often competed, assaulted, teased, showed off to one another; girls more often offered help and affection to one another and more often used social commands, for example: "Let's do . . . ." or "you do this, I'll do that." In other words, girls appeared to be setting up an agreed-upon procedure for social activity.

The games and sports of boys are invariable more competitive than those of girls. One of my students, Nina Schjerve Pedersen (1980), recently conducted a study on the integration of the Norwegian girl scouts and boy scouts into the same troop. They had already belonged to the same scout association but to separate troops with separate leaders and also different games and sports. Nina, who was one of the top leaders of the girl scouts, favored the idea of integration and was rather instrumental in getting the two scout troops together. Afterwards she studied the effects of the integration as her thesis at my Institute. The study showed that before the integration, many women had been troop leaders and other leaders of the girl scouts. After the integration almost all troops were led by men, and the former women leaders had become assistant leaders. But even more important facts were revealed by the analysis of the types of activities that were allowed to continue and dominate the new mixed-sex organization. The analysis of the activities in the former girl scouts compared to the activities in the former boy scouts revealed that the activities of the girls were of a more cooperative nature than those of the boys. The boys had activities where they competed more against each other or against other groups of boys or other troops. Their activities were more achievement oriented. They received decorations and outward recognition when passing certain tests. Analysis of the types of activities that were allowed to continue in the mixed-sex scout movement revealed clearly that they were activities of the boys. The competitive activities of the boys became the activities for both girls and boys. The cooperative activities of the girls were lost. The integration had been on the boys' terms.

Runa Haukaa and I have shown that coeducational gymnastics as they have recently been practiced in Norway cater more to the needs of boys than girls. When boys and girls are allowed to choose between various types of physical exercises, we find that girls often choose jazz gymnastics and dance, and boys choose football or soccer. In coeducational gymnastics, the girls have to learn to play football or soccer, while boys do not have to learn to dance or do jazz gymnastics (Brock-Utne, 1982; Brock-Utne and Haukaa, 1980).

Competitive sports is a rather hot issue among Norwegian feminists and sport lovers. Should we try to have our daughters compete in sports, maybe win world championships or to take part in the Olympics? One has to start early to become a winner. Would it not make men respect women more if they could see that they are good in sports, that they even may run faster than many men? Has not the fact that Norwegian women athletes have saved Norway's honor by winning sport championships and competitions changed the attitude of men toward women's sports? Some women believe that we have to compete—and on men's terms—to gain respect in their eyes and our own. So they fight to be allowed participation in our grand national event: the Holmenkollen Ski Jumping Festival. My opinion is that if girls want to compete on men's terms, they should not be prevented from it. But I do not see that in this way we change anything in this aggressive and competitive society. In fact, I think it has the adverse effect; there will be more people competing against each other. Studies from Norway show that women are almost as physically active as men, 40 percent against 45 percent, respectively, of the total adult population (Fasting, 1982). This is when physical activity includes hiking (the most popular physical activity in Norway) and gymnastics often organized by housewives. But when we look at competitive sports, there are very few women who are organized in sport clubs and compete. Organized sports, according to the physical educational researcher Kari Fasting (1982), mean male sports. Most of the money that goes to organized sports goes to males.

The sports activities of women have always been compared to those of men, the latter being looked at as the norm, the "ideal." Fasting (1982) asks if the time has not come to question if it is possible and desirable to now develop a female sports culture different from that of males. And she quotes the American researcher Felshin (1974), who even ten years ago described the situation this way:

> . . . on one hand, the feminist position demands that the inequality of women in sport be perceived as a political issue and be confronted as sexism, without reference to evaluations of the outcome. In this view, one fights for immediate rights and for power rather than for longer-range goals that are truly received as desirable. On the other hand, the women's movement tends

to work toward feminist/humanist goals and to reject masculine standards as
the norms: on this basis, a new conception of sport for women is required.
(p. 269)

I agree that we need a new conception of sport, and not only for women.
Fasting puts it this way: "Can sports be influenced by dominating values in the
culture of women? Sports which are so dominated by achievement and competition? Personally I think this is possible. Sport for all and family sport
would be preferred to competitive sports" (Fasting, 1982, p. 52).

The value of sports should be to keep one's body in shape and have a good
time with friends. Cross-country skiing with friends from one log cabin to the
other in the mountains makes for such a good combination, as do hiking and
swimming. In the summer I normally swim long distances almost every day
with a good friend and neighbor. We never try to race the other; on the
contrary, we keep pace and talk with each other. In that way we hardly notice
how far we swim, and it is wonderful exercise.

As I write this I see my eldest son, Karsten's disappointed face when I
picked him up as a 12-year-old after a soccer match. I had driven him to the
match, and he had been so happy and excited, hoping this time he would be
able to play. He was third or fourth of the reserves, but he was always sitting
on the bench on Sundays hoping that they would let him play in the matches.
He practiced as much as he could on weekdays, but he was never allowed to
play in the match. It made my heart bleed to see his disappointed face when I
picked him up. Of course, he gradually gave up soccer all together, stopped
going to the club to practice and started using his energy to play chess and
bridge instead. He was happier, but he did not get much physical exercise. So I
started teaching him my favorite sports: diving and swimming and skiing—
both downhill and cross-country. The whole family went cross-country skiing
every Sunday in the wintertime like many Norwegian families do, enjoying the
out-of-door life, the exercise without competing against each other. In the
summertime we would go swimming and diving. He could dive exactly the
same dives as I could, and we gave each other advice. He liked having body
contact and would often tumble around in our big daybed with me, his sister
Siri, or one or two friends. I once heard him say to his best friend: "Let us
pretend that we are two lions who are exactly equally strong, but exactly." I
was so pleased to hear that comment. He had understood that it is possible in
sports to have cooperation instead of competition if one changes the rules.
When two people play badminton, for instance, they may try to see how many
times they are able to have the shuttlecock go back and forth between them
instead of trying to beat each other. If they try this cooperative way of
playing, they will try to do their utmost to play balls that their partner will be
able to catch. If they play the competitive way, they will try to fool their
partner into one corner and then smash the ball in the opposite corner. It will
be a game of hostility instead of cooperation.

If one has to compete, why not compete against one's own records? It may feel good to know that you have improved your own performance. This should be a merit in itself. You should not necessarily have to do better than someone else to feel good. You may run a distance one night and take the time and then run the same distance another night and see if you are able to run it in less time.

FATHERS AND SEX ROLES

Evidence suggests that fathers are generally more concerned than mothers that their boys and girls develop distinct sex roles. (Goodenough, 1957; Lynn, 1976; Sears, Maccoby and Levin, 1957). In a recent American experiment (referred to by Maccoby, 1980) boys were given "feminine" sets of toys to play with, while girls were given "masculine" sets of toys. The feminine set included a dollhouse with furniture, a large stove with pots and pans, and women's dress-up outfit consisting of dresses, hats, purses, shoes, and a mirror. The masculine set included an army game with soldiers and war vehicles, a highway tollbooth with cars, and cowboy outfits including hats, guns, holsters, and bandanas. The boys were asked to play with the feminine toys the way girls usually did. The girls were asked to play with the masculine toys the way boys normally did. Once each child began to play, the child's mother, father, and a same-sex playmate were ushered into the room. It was quite clear from this study that it was the fathers who were most concerned about the sex-appropriateness of their children's play. Furthermore, fathers reacted more negatively to their sons' than their daughters' sex-appropriate play. Mothers' negative reactions to sons were not affected by the type of toy the child was playing with. With daughters, mothers showed slightly more disapproval for cross-sex play. As to same-sex playmates, girls seemed to have no objection to other girls playing with boys' toys. Boys, on the other hand, did put extra negative pressure on other boys when they saw them engage in girls' activities. It seems that sex-typing pressure exerted by peers is especially strong among boys (see Maccoby, 1980).

Maccoby refers to this research without passing any judgement on the educational value of the toys per se. What do the so-called masculine toys tell the children about the world? What is their educational message? And what do the so-called feminine toys teach children? Each set of toys teaches a lesson. As I have said before, the feminine set is meant to educate girls to take care of a house and children, activities that *all* human beings should engage in. The masculine set is meant to teach boys to kill other people, activities *no* human being should be engaged in. In this perspective, the results we have referred to become really alarming. Both fathers and peers press the boys into "sex-appropriate" play, but mothers do not. Might the reason for this be that mothers find toys labeled girls-toys as more appropriate for both sexes? And when they object to their daughters' sex-inappropriate play might that be because they themselves do not like war toys?

The most striking fact about research on the role of fathers in the education of the young is the scarcity of it. Cohen and Campos (1974) point out that there exists more research on the role of toys for the child's development than on the role of the father. It has been assumed that mothers are more important for the early development of the child: accordingly, little research has been done on fathers. The scant research that was carried out prior to the last ten years dealt mostly with the father-son relationship, especially the effect of father absence on the sex role development of the son. Studies here have indicated the tendency of boys to become either more feminine or to overcompensate their masculinity when the father is absent (Jalmert, 1979).

The overwhelming part of the research conducted during the last ten years on fathers and children shows that despite the little time they actively spend with their children, fathers play a greater role in the sex-stereotyping of children than do mothers. Thygesen (1971), Jalmert (1979), and Lamb (1978) found that as boys grow older, they gradually come to prefer their father to their mother. Some girls come to prefer their fathers as they grow older, some still prefer their mother, and some like both parents equally well. A very likely interpretation of these findings is that, with growing awareness, children come to realize the higher status of males in society and wish such a status for themselves. Lamb also seeks another explanation by studying the type of contact that fathers have with children. He found that although the fathers spent much less time with their children, the time they did spend was mostly taken up with pleasure. Furthermore, mothers and fathers touched their children for different reasons. Mothers mostly touched the children in relation to ordinary caretaking: to dress or undress them, to feed them, to keep them away from objects and places. Fathers touched their children mostly to play with them. When their sons were two years old, fathers would engage in games of roughhousing with them and have friendly fights with them. They actively stimulated their sons in the direction of the typical male.

Other studies from the United States show that fathers spend much more time with their sons than with their daughters. Fathers spend twice as much time with one-year-old sons as with one-year-old daughters (Lamb and Lamb, 1976; Lamb, 1977, 1981). It is important to note that mothers do not withdraw from sons or increase their interaction with daughters in a complementary fashion (Lamb and Lamb, 1976). As the children grow older, middle-class fathers in the United States buy electrical trains for their sons and themselves to play with; they teach their sons to ski jump or play football. Even though fathers spend little time with their children, the time they spend is mostly used for play activities and mostly for their sons. And even though fathers in these studies spent very little time with their daughters, their effect on their daughters' sex-typed behavior seemed to be considerable.

In a study (Mussen and Rutherford, 1963) of actual efforts of parents to enhance sex-role behavior in first-grade children, the feminine-oriented girls had fathers who actively encouraged them to engage in sex-typical behaviors. These fathers were also more "masculine" on a questionnaire (sex role preference) than fathers of girls who were low in feminine orientation. In this study no comparable findings were obtained for fathers and sons. Bronfenbrenner (1958), reanalyzing data originally compiled by Lansky (1956), found that adolescent boys with few masculine preferences had fathers who played a traditionally feminine role in the family. It has also been found that the more aggressive a father is, the more aggressive son he will produce. Butcher (1969), for example, reports that the fathers of juvenile delinquents who were notably aggressive had high aggression scores on personality tests. Thomas Detre (1974) has found that an antisocial attitude on the part of a father is the single best predictor that a boy will become violent later in life.

Swedish researchers (referred to by Liljeström, Svensson, and Mellström, 1976) have tried to identify common characteristics of men whom they viewed as "good" fathers, in the sense that they cared for their children, respected their emerging personalities, and tried to understand the children on their own premises. These fathers had one characteristic in common: They all had spent more time with children than fathers normally do. The tragic part about this study is that the reason *why* the fathers had spent much more time with the children was not that they had volunteered to. Various circumstances, like unemployment on their own part or sickness on the part of their wives, had brought them into this situation. In some cases they had been left alone with the children, either because their wives had died or they had been divorced and the father awarded custody of the children (a practice becoming more frequent in Scandinavia). Liljeström et al. (1976) mention that no matter what the original reason for the father's greater contact with his children, the result was that he became "a good father."

While I have primarily used a social learning theory, acknowledging also that biology may play a part, in my attempt to show how aggression, competition, and oppression of women are fostered in boys, feminists who use a gynocentric psychoanalytic theory tend to locate the reproduction of male dominance and misogyny in women's mothering (Chodorow, 1978; Dinnerstein, 1977). These theorists claim that the male devaluation of everything that is looked upon as feminine rests ultimately on the fact that the male child, in breaking with his primary mother identification, must define himself as "not feminine" in order to be masculine. In this process, he develops hostilities toward and negative evaluations of women. He also develops stringent notions of what it means to be a male and what it means to be a female. The need of males to feel superior to females is an effort to reinforce their masculine identity (Johnson, 1977). Women, on the other hand, have no need to differentiate themselves from the femininity of the mother in order to achieve a sexual identity and hence do not have the psychological motive for hostility to males, for dominating males, for oppressive behavior. These gynocentric psychologists claim that if the nearly universal patterns of women being the primary nurturers of both male and female infants were altered, this dynamic might be broken. If males shared equally with females in child care, males could "identify" with a male figure in a maternal role and thus feel securely masculine, which would in turn eliminate the male motive to dominate and oppress women and look down on anything feminine.

While I certainly feel that it is important that the father shares equally in the nurturing of small children, I do not see this as a solution to male dominance in society as long as mothers and fathers are not equal to each other in marriage and in heterosexual relationships. If the father takes more care of the children but leaves all of the dishwashing, cooking, cleaning, and tidying up to mother, she will still be oppressed, and the daughter and son will learn that the mother does the dull things and the father the exciting ones. Fathers are unlikely to teach their children cooperation and sharing if they themselves compete in the workplace, want to earn more than their wives, and do not share household duties. It seems necessary that women who are living with the fathers of their children have to press the men to change their family role.

STRATEGIES FOR CHANGING MALE FAMILY ROLES— A STRUGGLE WITH MEN AT THE MICROSOCIAL LEVEL

In Norway there is a child's saying: "Father rules over mother, mother rules over me and I rule over the cat." García (1981), in her article on sex roles and peace education, states the repression exercised in the household by the husband-father creates an ideal atmosphere for authority and tyranny outside the home. Larger nations assume this *pater familias* role when they control (for their own economic benefit) the destinies of the smaller ones. When serious disagreements arise, war, repression, or blockade is always at hand—and, we may also add the beating of wives and children and economic sanctions against the wife. Unless a subordinate group—in this case, women—continually presses the majority for change and equity, then change and equity are not likely to occur. In an article on male family roles, Scanzoni (1979) also agrees that it is women who at this point in history must continually press the majority of men for change. (And probably because he is a man, he adds: "women and their male allies," whom he terms co-feminists.)

Some women have been able to press men for more equality at the microsocial level. Interesting research questions are:

• Under what conditions do some unmarried adult women actually bring about change in men's behavior, so that they are able to achieve equity and justice on their own terms throughout every phase of their paid and non-paid working lives?

- Among married women, what are the conditions under which some wives are actively seeking to change their husband's sex role patterns and privileges?

More research is needed on these questions. From studies that have been done, we may tentatively indicate three main strategies in use (Rubin and Brown, 1975; Scanzoni, 1978; Scanzoni, 1979; Strauss, 1978).

Using the self-interest strategy, women try to illustrate that men themselves would be better off if change took place. As the research literature indicates, the two areas where men would be clearly better off if roles were changed are those of *initiative* and *money*. The burden for initiating friendship, "dating," or making the first sexual advances, with the risk of being turned down, would not fall as disproportionately on males as it does now. Men may also perceive it as a benefit not to be required to bear the financial burden of being with a woman or to have to support her and their children should they start living together. He may not have to work so hard and may avoid heart attacks and other stress symptoms that affect "successful" males in such great numbers in the western world.

Women may also try to show men that they would be better off emotionally if they were allowed to cry, be weak, show their feelings. Men who have been able to transcend the barrier of traditional sex roles have found that "Women's Lib" means their own liberation, as García (1981) states it, from their own suffocating armors. She thinks that the fact that many men are now beginning to feel highly uncomfortable with their traditional aggressive roles and are refusing to define themselves as violent males should be very meaningful for the peace movement. So should the fact, noted earlier, that men who spend more time with their children become good fathers. They usually also find that being with children develops them personally and gives new meaning and quality to life.

Another strategy that is recommended is the pro-social or altruistic strategy. Scanzoni (1979) claims that some men are more willing to change the traditional pattern if they become convinced that it would not only benefit them, but that it would also be the best for women. Women living with men who hold such beliefs can appeal to their sense of fairness. It is right and fair that women should be allowed to develop their capacities fully and share the responsibility of governing the world with men. It is also fair that they should have the same amount of true leisure time as men and that they should spend longer hours in paid and unpaid work than men do. Occasionally both these strategies can be combined. They both belong to an approach where consensus is reached through appeals and discussions.

If strategies number one and two do not work, women may use a third strategy, one of negotiation (often all three strategies are used). Negotiation is a process of give and take, concessions and compromises in exchange for benefits, so that both parties concerned end up with something, although not everything they originally wanted. Women who have an education and an income of their own now have the potential to bargain with men on a relatively equal footing. Increasingly, the woman makes it quite clear that she intends to pursue her own career interests after marriage and also after childbirth. In such cases the man must negotiate with the woman as to how their mutual interests can be met, a process that his father rarely if ever experienced. Central to earlier marriage agreements was the implicit understanding that the woman would do all she could to help make the man be more successful, which would also indirectly benefit her.

If the woman is liberated and assertive enough to be frank to the man with whom she is going to enter a more permanent relationship about the division of work and power she would like to see in that relationship, this may form a good basis for an equal partnership. Scanzoni (1979) reports that in many cases, however, the couples sever their "relationship" because they are unable to negotiate and to arrive at what both perceive to be a just and equitable arrangement. Of course, it is better that the woman be explicit and that they separate than that the man should enter marriage oblivious to his wife's intentions. There is also an increasing proportion of marriages in the western world where, at the time of marriage, the woman accepts the traditional sex-typed bargain, but rejects it later on (Scanzoni, 1978). Falling in love with a man in our culture involves a strong pressure to accept traditional sex roles. The men are expected to buy gifts, the women to wait on the men, and to put in their unpaid work to the men's benefit. In Norway a frequently cited verse to young girls about to get married runs:

> Love your husband and mend his stockings
> and your life shall be a walk on roses.

I know of one well-educated married couple, both employed and earning the same amount of money, who have four children. For the first twelve years of their marriage, the wife cooked the dinner every day and usually picked up the children at daycare centers. Her husband had more leisure time. She did not question this arrangement to start with, but gradually came to do so more and more. One day she said to her husband: "Now I have made dinners for twelve years, and I do not intend to make any more dinners for the following twelve years. Now it is your turn." To begin with the husband refused with the normal excuses: He did not know how to cook, she was a much better cook, he would have to give up some extra work he was doing. The wife used here both strategy numbers two and three. She appealed to husband's sense of fairness, and she negotiated, offering to make Sunday dinners the first years. In this case it worked, and the husband has now cooked for ten years. Of course, his wife had the strength that comes from bargaining on a relatively equal footing. The alternative of leaving him would probably have been a worse alternative for him than for her, especially if they split up the children. Incidentally, he constantly receives praise for his cooking from friends and neighbors, which she never received (this was just expected from her). In this case, the husband now loves cooking and has a much closer relationship to his children than he had before the nonviolent revolution in his family. He now sees that the new arrangement also involves advantages for himself. But he did not see this before his wife in effect forced him to change his normal habits. The arrangement turned out to be better for both of them.

In the literature on negotiations in microsocial settings a distinction is made between negotiation chiefly for maximum individual profit and for maximum joint profit (Raush, Barry, Hertel, and Swain, 1974; Scanzoni, 1979). To have lasting effect, negotiations normally will have to be of the maximum joint profit kind. While some persons may question whether women should even bother to change male sex roles, Scanzoni (1979) answers by asking the nagging question: How otherwise will they change? And if they do not, won't all of us be the worse off for it?

So far I have tried to show how mothers generally are an oppressed group and how they are caught in a web of tradition when it comes to the education of their children. They generally give preferential treatment to boys and permit aggressive and dominant behavior, while they restrict their daughters and teach them to serve boys and men. Research shows that fathers and peers seem to have greater impact on the acquisition of peaceful and less peaceful behavior that is judged to be sex-appropriate. Daughters become accustomed to being oppressed like their mothers, while sons know that they are not going to become like their mothers. What implications for research, policy and child-rearing practices can be drawn from these findings?

Important areas here seem to be:

- The relationship between fathers and their children should be examined. What role do fathers play in making their sons into aggressive males? What role do fathers play in making their daughters into submissive females who willingly serve men? What about fathers who spend much time with their children, take care of them alone or in a genuine equal partnership with a woman: How does this affect their own attitude and the way children are brought up?
- Play patterns in all-boy groups and in all-girl groups ought to be studied more closely. Do we find confirmation of the research findings referred to here? Do girls in other cultures also have play patterns of less hierarchical structure than boys? Do they solve their conflicts more through the use of appeals, setting up rules (e.g., of rotation of posts) than through the use of violence?
- The nonviolent strategies used by women to press men into a more equal partnership deserve a closer look.

The implications at the policy level are numerous, but I shall mention a few:

- facilitating fathers' possibilities to take care of children and share household responsibilities by limiting the number of paid working hours each individual may work and by creating workplaces near where families live in order to avoid commuting and selective migration.
- improving women's education, salaries, and job opportunities so that women can get rid of oppression and negotiate with men on a more equal footing; this also includes improving child care facilities so that children have safe places to stay while parents are at work.
- preventing the production and sale of war toys, magazines, and films that glorify war. Supporting the production of constructive toys and literature, especially literature that indicates nonviolent conflict solutions and the work for peace.

It is difficult to see how mothers will be able to educate their children very differently from the way they do today unless they themselves can become conscious of their oppressed state and recognize how the values they have been trained to work for (like caring for others) do not stand a chance if they are only inculcated in girls, and these girls are in turn exploited and oppressed by men. Accordingly mothers will have to:

- fight their own oppression
- install the values of caring for the welfare of others in their boys as well as in their girls
- restrain the aggressive behavior of their boys as well as their girls. Children should not be allowed to commit aggressive and violent acts against each other, nor is to become self-aggressive any solution. But it is possible to take out physical aggression by sports, which do not have to be competitive ones.
- substitute boys' war toys with constructive toys. Here close cooperation is needed with the mothers or, even better, with the parents of the child's playmates.
- stop giving sons preferential treatment and create feelings of self-esteem in daughters too. Daughters may need assertiveness training.

4 Science, Higher Education and Peace Research

In the two previous chapters I have looked at peace actions and peace education from a feminist perspective. In this chapter I shall look at the responsibility of science and our universities on the question of peace and war. I shall also look at peace research from a feminist perspective.

SCIENCE AS A DESTRUCTIVE ELEMENT

Science and scientists have also made a contribution to war: The development of modern means of mass destruction would not have been possible without the 'help' of the thousands of men of science. More than 500,000 scientists are currently working to perfect instruments of death and destruction, more than half the world's scientists according to the Secretary General of UNESCO, M'Bow (1982), and the peace researcher Marek Thee (1982). This reality of scientific endeavor is far removed from the idealized version of science as the "savior of mankind" and is another example of the extent to which destructive values are embedded in all facets of society and yet generally go unquestioned. One man who has questioned the scientific enterprise, however, was the philosopher Herbert Marcuse (1964), who stated "science, by virtue of its own method and concepts, has projected and promoted a universe in which the domination of nature has remained linked to the domination of man. Were humanity to achieve a pacified world—behind science's back as it were—then the very structure of science would necessarily be changed and the 'new science' would arrive at eventually different concepts of nature and establish essentially different facts" (p. 165).

Central to the image of science is the concept of its dynamic nature: Science has gone out and conquered (we are led to believe) many of the evils that have plagued the human species and has invented all manner of solutions that make the human race the master of nature. And it is this image of dynamism, of a conquering and mastering science, that must be challenged in the context of considerations of peace. For the values of science as they are so frequently expressed are the values diametrically opposed to peace. This is one of the

111

reasons that Brian Easlea (1981), a critic of current scientific practice, has said that the call for 'a new science' looks very much like a condemnation of 'male' science and a demand for 'female' science, which is based more on fitting into an ecological framework, than on conquering it (Easlea, 1981, p. 25).

Both the feminist and ecology movements are sharply critical of the costs of competition, aggression, and domination arising from the market economy's exploitation of women and nature. Carolyn Merchant (1980), historian of science, holds that the ancient identity of nature as a nurturing mother links women's history with the history of the environment and ecological change. The female earth was central to the organic cosmology that was undermined by the scientific revolution of the sixteenth and seventeenth centuries and the rise of a market-oriented culture in early modern Europe. In her book *The Death of Nature*, Merchant (1980) shows that the mechanistic world view of modern science sanctioned the exploitation of nature, unrestrained commercial expansion, and a new socioeconomic order that subordinated women. She investigates the roots of our current environmental dilemma and its connections to science, technology, and the economy. She reexamines the formation of a world view and a science that sanctioned the domination of both nature and women. This was done by reconceptualizing reality as a machine rather than a living organism.

Merchant (1980) criticizes Francis Bacon (1561–1626), the celebrated "father of modern science," for having made a program ultimately benefiting the middle-class male entrepreneur. At this time, social transformations had already begun to reduce women to psychic and reproductive resources. Merchant shows how Bacon developed the power of language as a political instrument in reducing female nature to a resource for economic production.[1] She also shows the important part male sexism played in the seventeenth-century scientific revolution. She shows how the imagery of male sexual wooing, conquest, and penetration of a female nature is indeed very explicit in the writings of scientists and natural philosophers of the day. Isaac Barrow (1734), Newton's teacher, declared that the aim of the new philosophy was "to search Nature out of her Concealments, and unfold her dark Mysteries." Francis Bacon argued that this philosophy, the experimental philosophy, would inaugurate the "masculine birth of time," a male resurrection which would lead mankind to nature "to bind her to your service and make her your slave" (Spedding, 1962). Only such a philosophy, he claimed, would follow

---

[1]This is also well documented by Ruth Bleier (1984), who exposes the misogynist nature of sociobiology and theories of cultural evolution, and by Hubbard et al. (1980), who question the validity of traditional descriptions of women's biology.

recent mechanical inventions in not merely exerting a gentle guidance over nature's course, but would have the power to "conquer and subdue her, to shake her to her foundations." Bacon appealed to those "true sons of knowledge" who "not content to rest in and use the knowledge which has already been discovered" aspire to "penetrate further" and to overcome "nature in action" to find a way "into her inner chambers" (Spedding, 1962, p. 42).

Merchant (1980, p. 168) shows how Bacon was influenced by the witch trials of his time, of which he approved. The way he treats nature as a female to be tortured through mechanical inventions strongly suggests the interrogations of the witch trials and the mechanical devices used to torture witches. She cites Bacon from 1623 . . . "For you have but to follow and as it were hound nature in her wonderings, and you will be able when you like to lead and drive her afterwards to the same place again. . . . Neither ought a man to make scruple of entering and penetrating into these holes and corners, when the inquisition of truth is his whole object."

Nature is regarded as feminine, and the scientific quest as an essentially virile, masculine adventure with penetration as the key to manly success. The men behind the seventeenth-century scientific revolution saw nature as a woman passively awaiting the display of male virility and the subsequent birth of a series of inventions and machines that would, in Bacon's words, "conquer and subdue her and (even) shake her to her foundations." Easlea (1981) shows how experimental philosophy—that notable product of the white male mind—is a "masculine philosophy," one that by its "penetration" into the female world of matter demonstrates an impressive virility on the part of the white male. Certainly when the experimental philosophy is explicitly allied with industry and technology, the virility of science becomes indisputable. For the new scientists are not mere Aristotelian contemplators of nature, they are her penetrators and masters (Easlea, p. 126). Easlea shows how, for instance, Sir Humphry Davy, who was made President of the Royal Society in 1820, made the masculine status of the new science very clear. He quotes Davy, who maintained that there could be "no man who would not be ambitious of becoming acquainted with the most profound secrets of nature, of ascertaining her hidden operations." And he notes that the man of science is not satisfied by merely *understanding* nature, eliciting her secrets. He has to *master* her through his own instruments. "Not contented with what is found upon the surface of the earth, he [the man of science] has penetrated into her bosom, and has even searched the bottom of the ocean, for the purpose of allaying the restlessness of his desires, or of extending and increasing his power" (Easlea, 1981, p. 127). Science has become a dogma, just like Christianity. Science is looked upon as holding the secrets of the universe and is in charge. We must accept its authority. Men of science have become the new rulers both of society and nature.

Mark Oliphant (1982), a professor of physics, stated at a Pugwash[2] conference that every advance in methods of mass destruction has been made, not in
response to demands from the armed services, but from proposals put forward by men of science. All nuclear weapons originated in this way, as did all
the guidance systems for the vehicles that deliver them. Indeed, in relation to
the nuclear arms race, which feeds on the continuous input of scientific
innovation and technological skill, these factors have acquired a momentum
of their own. They have become the masters instead of the tools. There is
much truth in the statement that technology dictates policy, that new weapons
systems emerge not because of any military or security requirements, but
because of the sheer impetus of the technological process. This has been
forcefully expressed by Lord Zuckerman (1980), for many years chief scientific
adviser to the British Government.

> Here the armaments experts rule, and when it comes to nuclear weapons the
> military chiefs on both sides—who by convention are the official advisers on
> national security—usually serve only as a channel through which the men in
> the laboratories transmit their views, for it is the man in the laboratory—not
> the soldier or sailor or airman—who at the start proposes that for this or that
> arcane reason it should be useful to improve an old or to devise a new nuclear
> warhead. And if a new warhead, then a new missile; and given a new missile,
> a new system within which it has to fit. It is he, the technician not the
> commander in the field, who is at the heart of the arms race, who starts the
> process of formulating a so-called military nuclear need.

Some scientists, like Robert Oppenheimer or Andrei Sakharov, have made
weapons out of loyalty to their countries, but in the end have experienced
feelings of guilt and anxiety for the future of humankind. But most scientists
proceed with what they consider an interesting and challenging task, without
much concern for the social, political, or economic consequences of their
success. Sean MacBride, Nobel Prize winner and former Minister of Foreign
Affairs of Ireland, calls these scientists who are not concerned about the
ethical and political implications of their research for the "alienated scientists" (MacBride, 1978). In the UNESCO publication called *The Challenge of
the Year 2000*, Sean MacBride first deplores the creation of the neutron bomb
and the scientists behind that innovation. But he knows that this is only one of
the new nuclear engines intended to destroy the human race upon which
alienated scientists and militarists are working. As he states:

> In the last few weeks armament experts have told me that a new ultrasonic
> bomb has now been perfected which destabilizes the human brain and which
> can render the whole population of a city imbecile. By destroying certain cells
> in the brain, it converts human beings into raving idiots incapable of reason-
> ing or of controlling themselves; and this is an irreversible process. It also

---

[2]The Pugwash conferences are meetings of scientists from many parts of the world including
both eastern and western Europe. The first series of conferences was held in Pugwash in Canada in
July 1957. The conferences were initiated by Albert Einstein and Bertrand Russell.

does so without damaging property. It is a most desirable weapon because it does not destroy buildings nor does it spread radiation. (p. 91)

MacBride further states that the science-fiction revolution that has overtaken humanity since the last war has not been matched by the development of a counterbalancing sense of moral responsibility. Science, unaccompanied by wisdom based on moral and ethical responsibility, has in itself become a threat to human survival. Albert Einstein expressed the same thought in his well-known words: "The unleashed power of the atom has changed everything save our modes of thinking, and thus we drift toward unparalleled catastrophe" (Nathan and Nordon, 1980, p. 376).

Scientists like to think of themselves as the noble seekers for truth and a deeper understanding of the universe guided by a "pure" scientific method. In reality, however, scientists thrive on competition as much as any politician or soldier. In their relationships, scientists share many of the problems of other workers in the United States, writes the Thiman Laboratory Group of The University of California: "These problems are complex, but arise directly or indirectly from profit-seeking and competition among individuals and groups of individuals" (Mansueto, 1983, p. 114; also in Arditti et al., 1980). In their quest to make new discoveries, scientists are racing to be the *first* discoverers, the Nobel Prize winners, the heads of laboratories, the chief researchers. The ever accelerating arms race is often talked about as a competition between the two superpowers for the greatest numbers, the best and the most deadly weapons. This competition is going on in spite of the fact that both blocks already many years ago had enough bombs to destroy us all. It looks as if they are competing in having the greatest overkill capacity. Some years ago Robert McNamara headed a group of American strategic experts who were to answer the question: How many nuclear bombs would the United States require to destroy two-thirds of the industry of the Soviet Union and kill half of the Soviet population? They had found that they would need between 200 and 500 strategic nuclear warheads for such an operation. The United States did not possess 500 warheads, but between 9,000 and 10,000. The Soviet Union had 7,500.[3] Competition between the United States and the Soviet Union certainly

---

[3]This information was given by the American arms and disarmament expert Betty Goetz Lall in a lecture at Teachers College, Columbia University, July 5, 1982. Betty Goetz Lall was a member of the expert group described which was headed by Robert McNamara. A more extensive summary of her lecture may be found in Norwegian in: Brock-Utne, Birgit: Rapport fra deltakelse i FN's Andre Spesialsejon for Nedrustning, deltakelse i seminar om nedrustningsundervisning og fra møte i planleggingsgruppa for 1983-seminaret om kvinner og militarisme. (Report from the participation in the Second UN Special Session on Disarmament, participation in a seminar on disarmament education, and from the preparatory meeting planning the 1983 Seminar on Women and Militarism.) *PRIO-publikasjon X-13/82.* For further information on the priorities of our world today, see Sivard, Ruth: *World Military and Social Expenditures* 1982. Here we read that the stockpile of nuclear weapons today equals 16,000 million tons of TNT. In the second world war 3 million tons of TNT were employed, and 40–50 million people were killed.

plays a large part in the accelerating arms race, even if it is mostly used to motivate taxpayers to spend more money on the perfection of instruments for death and destruction. But it seems that the competition going on between scientists and military branches *within* each country plays an even bigger role than the competition between the superpowers. In the case of nuclear weapons, the Americans are so far ahead of the Russians in almost every aspect of the technological race that they really don't need to compete with them.

Defense observers have noted that part of the explanation for the arms race can be found in the rivalry between the various military branches helped by their scientists within each country. One of the main reasons for developing the Pershing II medium-range missile, for instance, was that the Army's Pershing I was becoming outdated, and the Army was faced with "the prospect of . . . losing the last vestiges of nuclear missile turf to the enemy: the US Air Force and US Navy," according to defense observers Alexander Cockburn, James Ridgeway, and Andrew Cockburn. Pershing II would increase the Army's status. The American Navy has been making steady progress in developing missiles that match the Air Force's in accuracy, but interservice rivalry means that even when the forces want more or less the same equipment, it is nearly always researched and developed separately. This is as true for conventional as nuclear weapons, partly because of built-in competition, partly because of sheer unwillingness to cooperate. Interservice rivalry has lent a momentum of its own to the nuclear race. In an article on competition and the nuclear arms race, Connie Mansueto (1983) concludes: "The struggle to be top dog is clearly as important to each of the armed forces as their claim to be doing their patriotic duty in deterring the Russian aggressors."

This lack of concern for the human and political consequences of research undertaken by half our research community, the lack of new modes of thinking, the competition between states, scientists, and corporations, and the interservice rivalry lead to the question whether our institutions of higher education foster attitudes like those mentioned, or whether they are able to counteract them.

The real obstacle to social responsibility in science, claims John Ziman (1982), British professor of physics, is not that scientists are peculiarly ignorant or insensitive about ethical questions, but that they acquire a set of ideas that make them part of a cult. One of the main ideas of this cult is "science for its own sake." A scientist who wants to penetrate into the inner chambers of nature and claims to be pursuing science for "its own sake" is often using this as an excuse to escape ethical questions about the use and value of what he is doing. When he (in most cases it is a man) becomes deeply involved in the pursuit of a particular bit of knowledge, he can become entirely obsessed with this inquiry, as if nothing else in the world existed. Ziman (1982) maintains that scientists lean heavily on a mystique of personal devotion to research in order to maintain high standards of performance, just as good soldiers lean heavily on the mystique of obedience to orders and personal devotion to duty. But such a mystique is essentially a myth, which ignores the social significance of whatever is done in its name. This point is forcefully driven home in some well-known poems from the Anglo-Saxon heritage. They deal with the mystique of obedience to orders and personal devotion to duty installed in soldiers.

Alfred Lord Tennyson in his famous poem, "The Charge of the Light Brigade" (1854), celebrated an actual incident of the Crimean War. Someone at the top of the military hierarchy made a mistake that resulted in 600 British soldiers being sent into a valley surrounded by Russian troops. Entering the valley could mean nothing but the sure deaths and total destruction of the whole brigade. The soldiers knew that there had to be a mistake somewhere, but according to their ethics they were not to question their superiors, they were to obey orders. The second verse reads:

> 'Forward the Light Brigade!'
> Was there a man dismay'd?
> Not 'tho the soldier knew
>   Some one had blunder'd:
> Theirs not to make reply,
> Theirs not to reason why,
> Theirs but to do and die:
> Into the valley of Death
>   Rode the six hundred.

Tennyson praises these men; they gave honor to the country. He calls them "noble six hundred." They had managed to kill hundreds of Russian soldiers before they eventually got killed themselves, and this fact added to their "nobleness." Tennyson never posed the question of what the sacrifice of the British soldiers or the killing of the Russian soldiers did to their wives, mothers, children. If he had thought about this question at all, he would have been likely to have answered in the words of one of the "Grenadiers" in Heinrich Heines famous poem on the defeat of Napoleon. When they learn that their Emperor has been taken prisoner, one says to the other (in the English translation):

> What do I care about my wife,
> what do I care about my child,
> I have more important desires.
> Let them go begging when they are hungry.
> My Kaiser, My Kaiser,
> has been taken prisoner!

As I write this, nine-year-olds are fighting in the Iranian Army, wearing plastic keys to the gate of heaven to get them in if they are gloriously killed in war. This cult of obedience, whether it is to the Emperor, to defense of one's country through military means, or to science "for its own sake" may be as individualistic as Nietzsche's cult of the superman and just as antisocial. The women who are camping at Greenham Common in England have this to say about military personnel obeying orders without thinking: "We aim to make the American personnel think. This may sound condescending, but the fact is that military training discourages independent thinking or any questioning of their individual responsibility" (Lowry, 1983, p. 75).

Scientists as well as soldiers often excuse their own behavior by claiming that they are not responsible. They are just doing their *duty* to their country, to the army, to the corporation. Others decide. This attitude seems to have characterized the German scientist Wernher von Braun. The American mathematician and song writer Tom Lehrer has written a song about him. In one of the verses, Werner von Braun, who developed large rockets both in Germany and the United States, is described this way:

> Don't say he's hypocritical,
> Say rather he's apolitical,
> "Once the rockets are,
> who cares where they fall down,"
> says Werner von Braun.

The Norwegian mathematician and peace activist, Bjørn Kirkerud, who sees how his own field, computer science and research, is being used in an escalation of the arms race, finds that there are clear dangers in letting individual researchers decide what to research (Kirkerud, 1982). He cites Samuel Cohen, the so-called "father" of the neutron bomb who, when asked if he likes to work with the development of weapons of mass destruction answers: "Honestly, yes. It is a challenge. A very fascinating job" (Kirkerud, 1982, p. 6).

How much of this apolitical attitude do we foster in our universities through our compartmentalized structure of knowledge? Virginia Woolf held that it was exactly the segmented knowledge taught at the universities together with the harsh competition that fostered attitudes that might easily lead to war. In her novel, *Three Guineas* (1938), she doubts that giving women a university education will enable them to prevent war. In her own words: ". . . if we help an educated man's daughter to go to Cambridge are we not forcing her to think not about education but about war?—not how she can learn, but how she may win the same advantages as her brother" (p. 38). If a higher education is to help women prevent war, then that education would have to be of a very different kind than the one offered by modern universities. Woolf pictures a new type of college where there would be no competition, no degrees, and the aim would not be to specialize and segregate knowledge but to combine it. Knowledge should be combined so that the consequences of any innovation for human life are not only known but also desirable.

Students of nuclear physics have told me that they may go through whole courses in nuclear physics without learning anything about the human and social consequences of the use of a nuclear bomb. Sergei Kapitza, professor of physics in Moscow, also deplores this fact. In a paper called "How to learn to think in a new way," presented at the 1982 Pugwash conference, he states: "Unfortunately, the traditional way science is taught, usually dividing every-thing into separate subjects, does not lead to a systematic approach. This lack of interdisciplinary thinking looms even larger when we consider the connec-tions between the humanities and science, the dichotomy usually designated as 'the two cultures' " (pp. 247–248). Kapitza feels that the symptoms of fear and apathy demonstrated by escapism and lack of interest shown by the younger generation in some countries may be related to this lack of an inte-grated approach in our educational system. He asks: "To what extent can the whole issue of the emergence of irrationality be traced to defects in modern education, to a lack of a more general scientific and social outlook, without which it is very difficult to start thinking in a new way not only on matters of disarmament, but on the social impact of science and technology?"

I believe that a more integrated, interdisciplinary approach is crucial for the solution of problems not only related to the arms race, but to all problems that are complex and global in nature. The modern trend of specialization, both in training and in acquiring academic recognition, does not help to encourage education in the field of interdisciplinary studies or global prob-lems. In the words of Kapitza: "Most universities, which by definition should and do have the facilities for a really universal training, are hardly in a position to encourage these studies under present conditions." He has reached exactly the same conclusion that Virginia Woolf reached 40 years before. I fear that they are both right. I also fear that at a time when interdisciplinary studies are more needed than ever, they are more difficult to have. At a time when new thinking is required, when we should restructure knowledge and break out of our compartmentalized academic training, there is no money, no time, no encouragement to do so. The economic decline, which has also hit universities and students, makes most people more cautious, less brave and daring. The catchwords: "Keine Experimente" (no experiments) can be heard. Students have to take paid work to make ends meet and do not have the time and incentive of the sixties revolutionaries to demand the breaking up of the hierarchical relationships in the universities and the restructuring of knowl-edge. Their most important concern is to get a job, and being stamped as a radical does not help. This fact may also explain why campus opposition in the United States against contracts with the Department of Defense, which was very strong in the late sixties and the early seventies, has largely vanished by now. In fact, with the current trend, the Department of Defense is wel-comed back to the campus, because it can help alleviate the financial strain of the universities and because there is little vocal criticism of military-funded projects in American colleges and universities (Gleditsch, Hagelin, and Kristoffersen, 1982). We have to watch out for such a development in European colleges and universities. What we already notice is that more recent, critical and interdisciplinary studies like women's studies, ecological studies, and peace studies are experiencing the financial constraint of the universities to a higher degree than the more conventional subjects. When one regularly visits university book stores in major cities of the United States and western Europe one is struck by the decline in critical sociological literature and the increase in literature on data processing and computer science without political and social reflections.

Difficulties experienced in introducing women's studies or peace studies into institutions of higher learning, while new studies like computer science and oil technology expand, tell little about the knowledge we need to cope with societal problems but quite a bit about current power constellations. Those who have the power also have the authority to dictate what knowledge is desirable. They have the power to define concepts and to stamp their own thinking as rational and objective. They stamp the thinking and the studies of their adversaries as political and irrational. Militarists have, for instance, almost succeeded in stamping as rational the completely illogical creed that we must rearm to disarm. As Basil Bernstein (1971) has pointed out, the way a society selects, classifies, distributes, transmits, and evaluates knowledge it considers to be public "reflects both the distribution of power and the principles of social control" (p. 67). The myth of "apolitical objective knowledge" has served the establishment well; those with resources have often been able to use them to protect their existing resources, and to gain more, without their activities being too closely scrutinized.

In recent years feminist criticism of the academic disciplines has made a most significant contribution to the debate on the politics of knowledge by disputing the validity of objectivity. Adrienne Rich (1979) when criticizing men's studies also argues that in a patriarchal society, objectivity is the name we give to male subjectivity. In the introduction to a book on the impact of feminism on the academic disciplines, the Australian feminist researcher Dale Spender (1981b) states: "Rather than separate the personal and political from the production of knowledge, feminists are attempting to bring them together and in this synthesis they are striving to construct more accurate, adequate and comprehensive explanations than those which emerged under the reign of so-called objectivity and male supremacy" (p. 7). John Ziman (1982) in his article on the false ideology of science likewise unveils the principles that "science is rational and objective" and "science is neutral" as myths serving the powerful. He points out that "to give their discoveries the best chance of preliminary acceptance, scientists adopt a style of formal rationality, insisting that the conclusions they arrive at are logically compelling. This theoretical device is assisted by an impersonal stance. Scientific papers are written 'objectively' as if the author had no hand in the matter, but were simply reporting events and arguments in which he or she had no personal interest" (p. 168). He finds that much of the so-called rationality of science is superficial, little better than special pleading for an interpretation that is far from proven by the evidence.

Much of the so-called objectivity is spurious, little more than a depersonalized abstract formulation of the prejudices and interests unconsciously shared by a particular group of scientists working in a particular field. Innumerable "crackpot" theories of health and disease have been rationalized by medical science on the slenderest evidence. Deplorable nineteenth-century theories of racial superiority, strongly influenced by the doctrines of social Darwinism and highly advantageous to the politics of imperialism, were supposed to be scientifically rational and objective. I certainly agree with Ziman when he states: "Rather than proclaiming such doctrines, it is the responsibility of the scientists to show that they grossly misuse the authority of science to rationalize particular social positions" (p. 169). The doctrine that scientific knowledge is "objective" and "neutral," like the parallel doctrine that science can be separated from politics, can be used to conceal the intimate connection between research and policy, between thought and action. These doctrines also inhibit the exercise of collective social responsibility by formal scientific organizations such as professional societies. But it must also be mentioned that quite recently the world has witnessed a great concern for the growing prospects of a nuclear holocaust from groups of professionals and intellectuals, if not directly from the professional organizations and learned societies themselves, for example, such groups as physicians for social responsibility and teachers, lawyers, and psychologists for peace.

Though the disarmament question as such is not one of the issues tackled frontally in the UNESCO Recommendation of 1974 on the status of scientific researchers, there are important principles bearing on this question that can be found in the recommendation. In paragraph 12 of the chapter on the education and training of scientific researchers, it is stated that member states should lend their support to all educational initiatives to incorporate or develop elements of social and environmental sciences in the curricula and courses concerning the natural sciences and technology. Likewise, educational techniques should be developed and used to awaken and stimulate such personal qualities and habits of mind as: intellectual integrity; ability to review a problem in light of all its human implications; skill in seeing the ethical implications in issues involving the search for new knowledge, which may seem at first to be of a technical nature only; vigilance as to the probable and possible social and ecological consequences of scientific research and experimental development activities; willingness to communicate with others, not only in scientific and technological circles, but also outside those circles, which implies willingness to work in a team in a multioccupational context.

NO MORE STUDIES OF WAR

Most conflicts in the daily personal lives of all of us and between states are solved through nonviolent means. Yet when we look at the picture given us by the mass media and also in our history books it is difficult to believe this fact. Our history books are an endless account of men's wars, of kings, conquests, and exploitation. Both women and nonviolent solutions of conflicts are made invisible. We know that there have been many conflicts in history that have had the same ingredients of those conflicts that have led to war, but that have been somehow solved through peaceful and nonviolent means. These conflicts receive little attention in the mass media or in history books. They even attract little attention from the peace research community. As an example of such a conflict we could mention the 1905 conflicts between Norway and Sweden, which had all the ingredients to escalate into full-scale war, even troops lined up on both sides of the frontier. But the war was avoided. People who worked to avoid it on both sides and went on missions back and forth were at that time stamped as traitors to their country and said to be lacking patriotism. But the friendly relations between Norway and Sweden since that time certainly benefit from the fact that the war was avoided. If universities were to train for peace instead of war, we would have to do something about the teaching of history as well as furthering research on nonviolent conflict solutions. We would also need to be trained in conflict resolution skills. This, as well as a better integration of human and social sciences with the natural sciences and the introduction of problem-centered and interdisciplinary studies like peace studies, would be a significant contribution the universities could make to sensitize students to the growing dangers surrounding us.

Elise Boulding, professor of sociology in the United States and member of the governing board of the United Nations University,[4] finds that our whole educational system should be geared toward creating more confidence and competence in conflict resolution by means other than violence (Boulding, 1982). In an article in *The Bulletin of the Atomic Scientists* she states: "The declining civilian competence in conflict resolution and a too-small cadre of mediation professionals tend to push conflict intensities up towards the top of the pyramid" (p. 60). She has drawn the following conflict pyramid, with everyday conflict management at the bottom, then formal negotiation, arbitration as the next step, law enforcement as a third resort, and military force as the technique of last resort.

Boulding makes a strong case for the contention that there has been a dangerous move up the pyramid. For instance, law enforcement personnel are

[4]United Nations University is a network of cooperating research institutions around the world with headquarters in Tokyo, Japan, established by the United Nations and founded by voluntary contributions from UN member states.

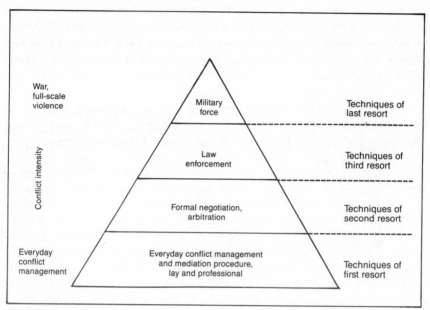

Fig. 4.1. The Violent Conflict Pyramid.

more apt to be called in than are mediators. People who feel afraid and defenseless, whether they are in the military, in government, or the private sector, will not pursue arms reduction. Capabilities for problem-solving must be strengthened at lower levels. The same thought is advocated by the peace researcher Johan Galtung (1981) when he talks about the need for the development of conflict imagination. According to him we need a much larger reservoir of people around the world who are capable of handling conflict constructively. Boulding suggests that the United States ought to establish a federal academy for research and training in peace and conflict resolution as well as having these skills taught in schools and universities.

These ideas correspond largely to thinking that was expressed in the World Congress on Disarmament Education organized by UNESCO in Paris in June 1980. At the opening of this Congress, Jan Mortenson, the Secretary-General of the United Nations Centre for Disarmament in New York, said that the primary program of disarmament education should be to explain to the largest number of people that in the nuclear age, security was not to be found in an ever-expanding accumulation of arms, but in the development of international cooperation. The congress stated that the world needs more disarmament education both in the sense of education *about* disarmament and education *for* disarmament. Education for disarmament would mean an education for caring, tolerance, solidarity, and cooperation. The constitution of UNESCO starts with the well-known words: "Since wars begin in the minds of men [sic.; no feminist would like to change that wording], it is in the minds of men that the defences of peace must be constructed." And I must agree: Wars do not usually start with men throwing bombs at each other, but with war propaganda, with the creation of enemies, distrust, fear, and hostility. Do we foster such attitudes in the universities?

Virginia Woolf (1938) argued convincingly that our universities educate for war. Later the same thoughts were expressed by the Brazilian educator Paulo Freire, when he coined the phrase: "All education is education for war." He was then thinking of the attitudes that are created within a hierarchical and highly competitive system, like most of our educational institutions. He was also referring to what he calls the banking concept of education. He uses this concept to define a type of education in which the teacher "makes deposits," which the students patiently receive, memorize, and repeat. When elaborating on this concept he describes common authoritarian teaching practices in which the teacher talks and the students listen, the teacher chooses the program content, and the students adapt to it (Freire, 1972). When we look at our own preschool children or at first graders on entering school we see lively and curious small human beings who constantly ask questions: Why doesn't the sun fall down? Why has a dog no feathers? Why does it rain? They ask questions for which they do not know the answers, and they ask an older person whom they think might know the answer. After some years in school we end up with a situation where the teacher is the one who asks questions, but questions for which he or she knows the answer. And the teacher asks the students not because he or she is genuinely interested in the answers, but because he or she wants to control whether they know them. The students do not ask any more. In the widely read Swedish children's book *Pippi Long-stocking* by Astrid Lindgren, the nature child Pippi, who normally does not attend school, exclaims with all her natural surprise when she learns that the mathematics teacher knew the answer to the question she had just posed: "But, that is unfair. You knew the answer all the time. Why on earth did you ask *us* for it?" (Some educational and sociological analysts may try to explain to Pippi that the content in school is not as important as the acquiring of certain attitudes like listening, obeying, taking orders, learning one's place in a pecking order!)

I have earlier stated how the arms race is motivated by competition not only between military blocs and so-called superpowers, but also between countries within the same block and between military branches within the same country. Our academic institutions also nourish and thrive on competition. As university teachers, we are continuously rated against each other. Our institutions are hierarchies where we compete for academic glory, promotions, better pay, bigger offices, and publication in high-ranking journals. Cooperation between university teachers within institutes and across institutes and faculties is actively discouraged. There is little true sharing, since everyone is competing against everyone else and guarding insights and ideas lest they be stolen. Such an atmosphere breeds distrust.

The students are also taught to compete against each other. It is not enough to be good, one has to be better than one's fellow students. In the cases where a relative grading system is used, this structural violence is built into the system. As a student one also learns that the professors like to see references to their own work and like the students to be able to repeat from their lectures. Certainly the banking concept of education is also at work at universities. The banking concept of education, characterized by attempts to control thinking and action and to lead students to adjust to the world as it is, according to Freire (1972, p. 51), is necrophilic. That is, it is nourished by love of death, not life.

When discussing the role of the universities in disarmament education I have been dealing with the topic both in the broad sense of education *for* disarmament and in the narrower sense, education *about* disarmament. When disarmament experts talk about disarmament education they often talk about it in the narrower sense. It is easier to create interdisciplinary courses in disarmament education at the university level than to change the whole university system and many of the values entrenched in it. Such courses should deal with nonviolent conflict solutions, disarmament proposals, and the role of mass media and public opinion in creating a climate conducive to the halting of the arms race. In April 1982 the conference of the International Association of Universities, which was held in Munich (FRG) and represented more than 800 institutions of higher education in 119 countries, unanimously adopted an appeal to those working in higher education and to the student youth of all continents:

> The arms race is transforming the most remarkable achievements of the human genius into evil creations. This situation fills us with anxiety for the future of mankind, whose sacred right to life no one dares challenge. This is why we are launching an appeal to workers in institutions of higher education, students and all men of honour on Earth. Let us fight side by side, always and everywhere, against the dangers of thermonuclear war.

Similar thoughts were expressed in a greeting message to the Standing Conference of Rectors, Presidents and Vice-Chancellors of the European Universities held in Hamburg (FRG), November 18 and 19, 1982. The greeting message was signed by several well-known Nobel Prize winners, by famous scientists, physicians, health-politicians and students:

> . . . the universities carry a particular responsibility to spread the knowledge about the consequences of nuclear war and to educate students as well as young scientists in the spirit of peace and international understanding. . . .
> We think that common efforts are essential so that strong cooperation of the

universities in Europe and in the world could also help to make peace safer
and prevent a nuclear war.

But the introduction of peace studies, of courses packed with factual
knowledge about the arms race and the dangers of nuclear war, important as
they are, may not *change* our modes of thinking. In a Swedish UNESCO
report in 1976, no connection was found between the information level of the
students and their attitudes to important social questions. The study concludes that factual information may not change attitudes and modes of thinking if the conditions surrounding the learning situation do not change
simultaneously (Samhällskunnskap och samhällssyn, 1976) (Knowledge of
and Attitudes to Social Questions)

The group of educationalists in the World Assembly for Peace and Life,
against Nuclear War, which was held in Prague, Czechoslovakia in June 1983
expressed in their final report "the need for group work in schools and to
work against competition in educational systems"[5] Another section of this
final report reads: "The participants expressed demand for basing our life on
the values of caring and cooperation instead of competition, and urged that
peace education be integrated in all subjects instead of on brief separate
occasions."

In many ways peace education and studies should be the kind of education
that would meet with the approval of Virginia Woolf. In peace education one
tries to work against competition and build on the values of caring and
cooperation. And peace studies are interdisciplinary, not segmented. But there
is a danger that peace education will be education *about* peace instead of
education *for* peace. And there is a danger that peace research will be narrow
instead of broad and deal more with the *instruments* of collective murder,
with technicalities, rather than with the human and social consequences of the
arms race.

Do women peace researchers have other priorities within peace research
than men? Could the steadily growing knowledge base in women's studies
inspire peace studies?

---

[5]The World Assembly for Peace and Life, against Nuclear War gathered more than 3,000
participants from all over the world. Among these were also invited experts on health, law,
education, art, science, religion, journalism. There was a special "women's center" all through the
Assembly. Dialogues on various topics were organized the first several days. Later in the week time
was set aside for work in special interest groups. The group of educationalists was organized under
the auspices of UNESCO. Liselotta Waldheim-Natural from the Center for Disarmament in
Geneva informed participants about the World Disarmament Campaign and the work of the UN
and UNESCO in the field of disarmament education and information. The World Assembly for
Peace and Life, against Nuclear War was organized by the World Peace Council and the Women's
International League for Peace and Freedom.

THE ROLE OF WOMEN IN PEACE RESEARCH

The systematic study of peace and the establishment of separate peace research institutes are of recent origin. Almost all of the approximately 400 peace research institutes mentioned in the *World Directory of Peace Research Institutes* (UNESCO, 1981, 4th rev. ed.) have been created after the Second World War, most of them since 1960. (And most of the peace research institutes of the world have been concentrated in northwestern Europe and the U.S.) In an article on the development of peace research, the well-known Norwegian peace researcher Johan Galtung (1979) points to the fact that the field of peace research has undergone the same development as the peace concept itself. One started concentrating on direct violence in a rather narrow sense, then added the study of structural violence as it affected the body (starvation), and finally added structural violence affecting the mind (oppression, alienation). Peace research institutes in the Third World often concentrate on structural violence, because for them this is the most important type of violence. These institutes are often called institutes for development studies.

The International Peace Research Association was founded in 1964. It was 17 years after that, in a meeting in Orilla, Canada in 1981, that we organized a women's network within IPRA. We decided that it was vital to the fields of peace research that feminist issues and analysis form part of the research. Certainly the field of women's studies would have much to offer the field of peace studies and vice versa. There can be no peace as long as women are oppressed, starved, battered, and beaten. We started relating the work in the various commissions to the lives of our sisters. How much did human rights also include women's rights—the right not to be beaten or sexually exploited? And could peace education be studied as if girls and boys were given the same education? We also asked if there was any reason why women who adhere to the new feminist ideology should think differently about defense questions than men.

Elise Boulding (1980, 1981) has conducted a survey to elicit the views of women scholars working in disarmament-related fields on the further development of peace research. The results of the survey were presented by UNESCO to the World Conference of the United Nations Decade for Women. A more extensive account of the results can be found in the international journal *Women's Studies International Quarterly* (Boulding, 1981). Forty-one scholars from 17 countries all over the world responded to the survey. Boulding tried to divide the work of the women scholars who responded to the survey into several groups. At the end she came up with two categories, which she called new conceptual frameworks and new social order. While the average age of the respondents in each group was 32–35, she found more older women in the new framework than in the new order category. Boulding states that the youth of many of the women researchers is surprising until one considers that women are probably now entering the field of peace research in larger numbers than before. Several of the women in the survey, especially those from the new social order group, move back and forth between the roles of journalist, community organizer, and research associate in a research institute.

Topics for the current and planned research of the respondents can be grouped under four themes: (a) studies of the military, (b) development studies, (c) arms control and disarmament, and (d) disarmament strategies, nonviolent alternatives. One-half of the topics involves studies of the military, arms control, and disarmament processes. If we lump these two categories together with development studies which are closely linked with both military studies and disarmament processes, we can say that five-eighths of the topics are centered on arms, arms control, and development. This fits the general pattern of what peace researchers do. What is of special interest is that nearly 40 percent of the topics represented research on strategies for a disarmed world and on nonviolent alternatives. Eleven scholars are looking at grass-roots movements, localism and organized nonviolence. Seven are looking at alternative cultures and value systems. Five researchers are looking at behavioral skills of conflict management and nonviolence, while five others are working with disarmament education and curriculum development. While these topics are traditional for peace researchers, they do not receive the same attention proportionally by male researchers. This great interest on the part of women scholars in disarmament strategies and the fact that quite a number of women are working academically with research on skills of conflict management show that there is a pool of qualified women to draw from when committees on disarmament questions are set up. Yet these women are seldom used. Boulding (1980) states: "It is frequently said that there are 'no qualified women available' in the disarmament and security field. This study explodes that myth" (p. 46). Perhaps the best internationally known women experts are Alva Myrdal, who served as Cabinet Minister for Disarmament in Sweden in the 1960s, Mary Kaldor, who serves on the Minister of State's Advisory Panel on Disarmament for the United Kingdom, and Betty Goetz Lall, who is currently the United States representative on the United Nations Panel of Experts on the Relationship between Disarmament and International Security. These women tend to be the ones most frequently called upon. But there are many more women who are well qualified on disarmament issues, and Boulding asks why they are not used.

Betty Goetz Lall (1979) writes regarding the U.S. scene:

> Women are largely excluded from the SALT negotiating process. No women are members of the negotiation teams of the two sides. They do not constitute part of the back-up team in the United States which helps to prepare the rationale for policy-formulations. We do not know the composition of the Soviet teams. There are no women on the Senate Committees which will vote

or participate in the hearings on SALT II and only one woman on the staffs of the Committees who will have any major role on preparing for Senate consideration. Furthermore, among the public groups to present congressional testimony, few women are likely to be representatives of their organizations.

Eleanor Smeal, who is the Director of the Gender Gap Campaign Project in the United States and on the advisory board of the first National Women's Conference to prevent Nuclear War, is also concerned about the fact that nowhere have women been more excluded from decision making than in the military and foreign affairs. In a leaflet distributed by the National Women's Conference to Prevent Nuclear War, she says: "When it comes to the military and questions of nuclear disarmament, the gender gap becomes the gender gulf."

Elise Boulding reports that there is a general feeling among the new framework scholars that there has been too much mindless data gathering, particularly in arms trade research and research on the technicalities of curbing the arms race. "In general," Boulding summarizes, "there is a call to move away from the pseudo-scientific, pseudo-technical approach to arms control and concentrate on the issues that affect each of us." And she goes on quoting a couple of the researchers: "It's not the response time of radar or the trajectory of ballistic missiles, but the economic and social cost of military expenditures and the consequences of military solutions to political problems that matter." Boulding also finds that there is, in general, a fairly complete rejection of current research approaches, even the most "liberal" ones, and that the group of women peace researchers are attempting to formulate new research priorities in order to make visible the real issues. They are more interested in the social and human consequences of the arms race than in the more technical matters, in weapons-counting.

This result reminds me of what happened to a friend of mine, a teacher, when her class studied the Second World War. Her class of 16-year-olds wanted to study various aspects of this war. She received suggestions for topics to study from her class and wrote the topics down on the blackboard. The pupils in the class were to form groups around the various topics and study them for a week. Among the topics they suggested were: Which battles were fought during the war? What types of weapons were used? What type of uniforms did the various nations have? How did people live during the war? What did it feel like to have a father or mother who was in prison? Guess what happened when the pupils in the class were allowed to form groups around the topics suggested? The groups formed were single-sexed! Just like women peace researchers, the girls in the class had chosen to look at the human and social consequences of war. They interviewed parents and other adults about the scarcity of food during the war, about what it felt like when the sirens blew. They interviewed people who'd had someone in their nearest family in prison. What did they do? How did it feel? The boys went to the military museum and studied the weapons and the uniforms used in the war. They found statistics about the battles and interviewed military men. It is easy to see that the boys and girls learned different lessons from their study. War was excitement according to the boys. The girls thought of war as fright, lack of food, and immense suffering. They had learned that war had to be avoided, that disarmament was urgently needed.

According to Boulding's study, some women peace researchers are trying to build up images of a disarmed world, of a new culture free from patriarchy and the techniques of dominance associated with the male cultures of East and West, North and South. Women with experience in teaching and training in education come to their later research roles with a focus on the conscious-ness of children and how a new nonmilitary order can be built with the knowledge that comes from research on children's attitudes. The women want to explore structures and social roles that will make a disarmed world possi-ble. Boulding cites some of the researchers in her study who have harsh words for peace researchers "who write in journals read by likeminded academics . . . and have had little or no impact on world arms or military policy" (Boulding, 1980, p. 48). But researchers who work closely with the peace movement and with the starving people receive praise. They are researchers having a role much like the barefoot doctor in community health in China. One may call them "barefoot researchers." These researchers seek to make visible at the grass-roots level the ingredients of a self-sufficient demilitarized social order for the communities of Asia.

Research on value systems and morality that provides legitimation for the military-industrial complex is also a major concern for women scholars. There is too little of this research going on. It ought to be given high priority. Boulding cites one scholar, a specialist in nonviolence, who puts it this way:

> The main issues in disarmament are not the technical ones to which so much attention is given, nor even political ones (in the usual sense of that term), but social and psychological. Yet practically nobody pays attention to these latter topics. Moreover, I think research on non-violent *alternatives* is crucial. When we have seriously explored some non-violent alternatives, we may get some measures of disarmament. I don't think it will happen the other way around. By non-violent alternatives I mean such things as non-violent conflict resolu-tion, non-violent civilian defence, unarmed peace-keeping, etc. but also eco-nomic structures that do not destroy, new kinds of social relationships, etc. I also am not sure how much research we need in the conventional sense of that term. I think we need to *think*. I think we need to act creatively—which includes experimenting with alternatives. I think we need to understand bet-ter the ultimate source of our anxieties and fears (which may involve some research). But I do not happen to think that we will be saved by social science as that is ordinarily construed. We suffer mainly from a paralysis of will. Most people do not think we are capable of creating a relatively non-violent world (Boulding, 1980, p. 50).

From Boulding's study it is clear that women researchers want to change the existing priorities of peace research. We do not know how many of the researchers in her study had any training at all in women's studies. Women's studies and peace studies ought to enrich each other and be involved in a mutual learning process. As there are links between the feminist movement and the work for peace, there are also similarities between women's studies and peace studies. Researchers trained in women's studies should be able to broaden the field to include direct and personal violence and to bring with them some very fruitful insights that would enrich peace research. There are also concepts and insights developed within peace research that may inspire thoughts and analysis within women's studies.

THE LINK BETWEEN THE FEMINIST MOVEMENT AND THE WORK OF PEACE

Throughout the history of the women's movements we can detect two parallel trends.:

1. Women fighting for their own rights become more politically concerned and see that most institutions around them have been built by men and have to be changed. They see that they have to fight against the institution of war to be able to continue the struggle for liberation.
2. Women fighting for the rights of others, for "greater" causes than their own liberation, discover that they themselves enjoy few rights and that they have to fight against their own oppression in order to help others.

As an illustration of the fact that women's fight for their own rights often becomes more widely political and frequently leads to a fight against violence and war we do well to remember the work of early feminist writers, such as Swedish authors Fredrika Bremer and Ellen Key and the Norwegian author, Camilla Collett. The strong women's peace movement in Europe and subsequently in the United States prior to World War I was initiated and run by feminists who had been fighting for women's right to vote and hold political office. At the outburst of the First World War, the women's peace movement in the United States was greatly inspired by two militant suffragists and pacifists, the British Emmeline Pethick-Lawrence and the Hungarian Rosika Schwimmer (Costin, 1982). They both toured the country lecturing, talking with political leaders about peace, and arousing American women to join European women in a general protest against war. Emmeline Pethick-Lawrence was known to American women for her militant efforts on behalf of extending the suffrage to British women. For her actions in demanding the vote, she endured repeated imprisonments and, on at least one occasion, the dreaded and cruel forced feeding used in the prisons to break the hunger strike of suffragists. The shock of the reality of European war prompted Pethick-

Lawrence to try to apply to the cause of peace the strategies that had inspired the struggle for women's emancipation (Pethick-Lawrence, 1938). She was an eloquent orator, and upon her arrival in America spoke out against the passive established peace societies, stating that the peace movement must learn from the women's movement: It was time for women to be active, angry, and militant. The Hungarian feminist Rosika Schwimmer had become prominent in the international suffrage movement in 1904 during the formation of the International Woman Suffrage Alliance. There she became acquainted with Carrie Chapman Catt, president of the Alliance, who later supported Schwimmer's efforts to organize women in the United States into a women's peace movement. Schwimmer was also known as an eloquent and persuasive speaker. She is said to have been deeply moving in her descriptions of the devastations of war (Costin, 1982, p. 306). She showed brilliant insights into the causes of war. Degen (1939, pp. 28–29) documented an incidence in which Schwimmer warned Lloyd George at a breakfast with him in July 1914 that the Sarajevo incident would certainly result in war between Austria-Hungary and Serbia with incalculable consequences throughout Europe unless mediation was instigated promptly. Lloyd George later recorded in his war memoirs that Schwimmer was the only individual at that time who suggested to him the imminence of war. Schwimmer was also convinced that a war ended by militarists, with peace terms dictated by militarism, could only mean that the seeds of another war were planted for the next generation.

Costin (1982) tells that in order to take advantage of the interest in peace aroused by Rosika Schwimmer and Emmeline Pethick-Lawrence, the American feminists Carrie Chapman Catt and Jane Addams jointly called a national conference to which women's groups from all over the country were invited. Several thousand women came to Washington in January 1915 to consider the great tragedy the world war represented to them and to try to unify their efforts for peace. The delegates were nearly all suffragists, but the organizations they represented were diverse.

Women are again taking a very active part in peace movements. All-women peace groups have been initiators of large and successful peace marches and festivals. Many of the women in the all-women peace groups are feminists and are realistic about much of the male chauvinism that is common in mixed sex political groups. They find that feminists have something to teach other women and men when it comes to security and defense questions, when it comes to fighting against the oppressive structures of patriarchy and creating a new and peaceful society. They also feel that their experiences from the organizational and practical work in the women's liberation movement should be drawn upon in the peace movement. They know that they have to fight against war. They are not so naive as to believe that we shall have a peaceful society in the sense that women are no longer oppressed if a nuclear or other war is avoided.

I have already given several examples illustrating the fact that women fighting for greater causes than their own liberation discover that they have to fight against their own oppression in order to help others. I have mentioned the campaign against slavery and the civil rights movement. Women have discovered over and over again that even though they have been fighting side by side with men during wars and revolutions, their brave fight has been "forgotten" and they are sent back to the kitchen sink when the war is over. In chapter 2 I mentioned the radical feminists in London, who warn the Greenham Common Women that the fight for women's liberation and an alternative society might be forgotten in the antinuclear campaigns. It is necessary to combine this work with a study of the oppressive structures of the patriarchal state, of the value system beneath military research and development, the military-industrial complex. It is my experience from Norwegian Women for Peace groups that many women who have joined them have not been part of the feminist movement earlier but have become feminists through their study of the war system and work in the peace movement.

While the new feminist movement has not been particularly concerned about military policy until rather recently, it has done much ideological work that is of great importance when a new concept of defense and security is being formed. As feminists we are more concerned with the concept of liberation than with the concept of equality. We do not want equality on men's premises; we do not want to become like men. Rather than asking how many women we find in various male institutions, we ask what chances women have or have had to influence these institutions with their values, their culture. Numerical equality is not enough. Women constitute about half of the population of the earth, yet, according to United Nations statistics [*Report of the World Conference of the United Nations Decade for Women: Equality, Development and Peace* (DOC. A/CONF. 94/35), 1980] although we are responsible for 66 percent of all work produced in the world (paid and unpaid) we receive only 10 percent of the salaries. The same statistics show that men own 99 percent of all the property in the world, women 1 percent. The fact that there are so many of us has not meant that we have had any power to change patriarchy or the male institutions that our societies are built upon. This fact has not prevented us from being oppressed like a deviant minority group all over the world. It is important that women in great numbers enter male institutions, but that in itself is not necessarily going to change society. Women in these institutions constitute a potential force that can change the institution in a more humane direction. But women in male institutions are usually not able to make changes because the existing structures are so strong and the women are often too few, have lower positions, sometimes do not unite, and frequently are working a double shift. Furthermore, if they want to get promoted and to reach power within a patriarchal institution, they will have to play the game on the premises of the patriarchy. Their own way of thinking will easily be invaded by a patriarchal mind set.

In the new feminist movement, we have been concerned with liberation from oppressive structures. These structures are caused as much by capitalism (both private and state capitalism) as by patriarchy. Many of us were trained in Marxist thought, but we have come to see that Marxist theory does not suffice when it comes to analyzing the oppression of women. Instead of starting an analysis in the sphere of production, maybe we should start it in the sphere of reproduction (and why, by the way, should the act of producing a baby be called reproduction?). The concept of work used by Marx rules out the unpaid housework done by women all over the world; it makes this work invisible. We are not concerned with mere ownership of male institutions, with getting power, becoming equal and getting into leading positions. We want to change male institutions, change male society. Unfortunately, in order to change society, we need power.

In what direction do we want to change society? First of all, we want a society based on the fact that children have to be well taken care of and should be the responsibility of women and men alike. We want a society where human beings matter, where children, old, and sick people are taken care of. Therefore, we are demanding six-hour working days for all adults and enough child-care centers for all children. The right to paid work is a human right that must be granted to all. Therefore the paid work has to be shared among all adults. Since children, old people, and disabled people are as much the responsibility of men as women, men should also have enough time to take part in the caring aspects of life. Such a participation would have to have an effect on their upbringing and their thinking. We are also concerned with the breaking down of hierarchical structures and the creation of egalitarian structures. The new feminist movement itself is organized in small self-governed cells, a "flat" structure without a strong centralized leadership. It has been fighting against the private violence committed by men, violence that takes the form of rape or wife battering.

Women who adhere to the new feminist ideology will naturally think differently about defense questions than most men. They will be skeptical of military institutions, which are mainly created by men and in many ways are the incarnation of masculinism. They will not accept such concepts as "security" and "defense." Women have a long tradition of nonintegration into the military machinery. This tradition should make us able to look at so-called defense questions with fresh eyes. We have a long tradition of fighting for our rights through nonviolent means. If we bring our way of thinking not only into the peace movement, but also into peace studies, we should be able to bring some new and valuable insights into those studies. Our own insights have often been formed through a process of action and research carried on within the field of women's studies.

Both women's studies and peace research are recent areas of study on the academic scene. They do not enjoy high academic prestige. By their very nature they are controversial and deal with what are seen as "political matters." The accusation that research and politics are mixed and too interwoven is often heard. Peace research and women's studies resemble each other in the fact that they are looked upon as more controversial and threatening the nearer they get "to home." Research on military installations in one's own country is considered more threatening than research on other military matters, such as the strategic doctrines of other countries. Feminist research looking into the distribution of money *within* the family encounters difficulties and is not easy to undertake.

There are many overlapping areas between peace studies and women's studies. Indeed it is difficult to think of any part of women's studies that could not be included in peace studies when peace is defined as broadly as by the UN and UNESCO, referred to in the first chapter. It would seem necessary to add the research results gained within women's studies to the knowledge base of peace studies. Likewise there is research within peace studies of great interest to feminist research, for instance, research on alternative futures and alternative development. Research comparing military and social expenditures is also of importance for work within women's studies. Both fields of study draw on knowledge from various established academic disciplines. They are both problem oriented and naturally cross academic boundaries. This means that scholars working in these fields come from many different academic backgrounds and frequently have some knowledge of other academic fields than their own. They have to try to work together across academic boundaries and understand that their different backgrounds may be an asset as well as a hindrance for cooperation.

For instance, within women's studies in Norway we have had a rather difficult discussion about the concept of "women's culture." Here the difficulties stemmed from the fact that some of the researchers had a sociological training and thought of the concept "culture" in sociological terms, while other scholars had an anthropological training and therefore had a different understanding of the same concept. An interdisciplinary approach is a difficult one, yet there is no other way to work with problems of such magnitude and complexity as those dealt with within peace research and within women's studies.

In a study, 63 peace research institutes were asked which academic subjects they were interested in having represented among their research staff. They had to choose from a list of 19 subjects. More than half of the institutes chose at least ten of the named subjects. Seven of the institutes had named 17 or more of the subjects (Ruge, 1967).

Women's studies, as we know them today, can in many ways be said to owe their existence to the new feminist movement of the sixties and seventies. Sex roles had certainly been a research topic before, but the consciousness-raising groups of the feminist movement led women to see that many of their problems were not personal or psychological ones, but were rooted in social and economic structures. The analysis of these structures, how they are built, developed and can be changed, became an important research topic. Many of the women who have fought for women's studies have also been involved in the feminist movement. Ideally their research should not merely make women able to understand the nature and extent of their oppression, but also aid them in changing oppressive structures. Women's studies have been created on the basis of women's concrete experiences with sexual oppression and exploitation (Leira, 1980). This connection to the women's liberation movement is very clear. It is possible to show that the same topics that have been debated in the women's liberation movement have also been researched within women's studies (Haukaa, 1979, 1982). Much of the research within women's studies has been action oriented.

There is also a clear connection between the peace movement and peace studies. Peace research as we have known it the last 25 to 30 years can in many ways be said to have been born from the new peace movements after the Second World War. The perspective has been slowly widened as the awareness of the structural violence within states and between so-called developed and developing countries has grown. The peace researcher Johan Galtung (1979) sees the widening of the peace concept and the field of peace research as fruitful. Peace studies should draw on insight from various fields and be action oriented. Peace research is met with some of the same expectations from the peace movement as women's studies are met with from the women's liberation movement. Peace groups want the peace research community to serve them, give them information, help them to act. They are disappointed when the researchers do not have time to attend their meetings or if they do come, talk in academic jargon or research language, which is difficult to grasp. The discrepancy between the academic research language and the daily language of ordinary people is a topic of concern both for peace researchers and feminist researchers. It seems to be more so for female researchers either in women's studies or in peace research than for men.

Elise Boulding's study showed that women scholars working in peace research often went back and forth between the jobs of community organizer, peace researcher, journalist, and peace activist. This has also frequently been the case for feminist researchers. Although this shifting of work from research to journalism and activism may often stem from the fact that few women have tenured positions within feminist research or peace research, it has the beneficial effect of preventing researchers from building ivory towers. Both feminist researchers and peace researchers seem to be concerned with practicing what they preach. Feminist researchers try to support each other, cooperating instead of competing, to organize across academic boundaries. When they are working within the universities they are trying to build new and cooperative structures cutting across disciplines. And they are often punished for this by the existing patriarchal and competitive structures of the universities. The way to get promoted in a university system is normally to have one's academic work evaluated by a committee of superiors. These committees are seldom interdisciplinary. In universities in Norway, and I would think in many other countries as well, there exists a rule that one can never sit on an evaluation committee to judge the qualifications of someone with whom one has been a coauthor. Since so many feminist researchers have cooperated, it makes it extremely hard for them to find qualified committees to judge their work. Single authored studies are also given more credit within the traditional university system than coproductions. But this does not deter feminist researchers from working and publishing together. Some peace research institutes also try to promote a flat and cooperative structure where everybody shares in the decision making. The peace research institute where I was working a couple of years ago, the International Peace Research Institute of Oslo, is known for practicing an equal pay scale for everyone employed at the Institute. This means that the typists, receptionists, librarians, and other administrative personnel receive the same salary as the researchers and the research director. The position of research director rotates between the researchers. The idea behind this was that a peace structure should be created within a peace research institute. Likewise, everybody is supposed to take his or her turn in tea making, dishwashing, and cleaning the house. But it is not easy to make such practices work within a patriarchal and competitive society.

Both women's studies and peace studies are value oriented. In women's studies, one discusses how women are oppressed and exploited in many different ways all over the world. There is a basic assumption that this is wrong and must be changed. We are exposing existing structures and trying to envisage not yet existing structures. Some researchers are putting together women's thoughts for an alternative way of organizing society, working with visionary thought. In peace studies some of the work should analyze conditions for a lasting peace. The basic assumption here is that war and violent conflict solutions are undesirable and ought to be done away with. Both disarmament and lasting peace are nonexisting experiences.

Obviously there are differences between women's studies and peace studies. One of them is the proportion of women in these research fields. While there are very few male researchers in the field of women's studies, women are in the minority among peace researchers. Since men do not have any experience with feminist research, those who build a bridge between these two research areas will have to be women. Yet at the Peace Research Institute of Oslo, for instance, hardly any of the women have a background in women's studies. Being a female peace researcher is not the same as being trained in women's studies. Yet the interest for such studies and personal friendships with researchers in this field is much greater among the female than the male research community. While peace research (though under constant scrutiny, in my country at least) has *some* permanent research positions connected to it, women's studies are not that established. This means that it is more difficult to get jobs and promotions with qualifications solely in feminist research than within peace research.

WOULD THE INCLUSION OF MORE WOMEN IN PEACE RESEARCH CHANGE THE EXISTING PRIORITIES IN THE FIELD AND IF SO, IN WHAT DIRECTION?

It is likely that more women working in peace research would indeed change the field significantly. Such a statement can be backed up by Elise Boulding's study as well as looking at research done by women scholars at the International Peace Research Institute of Oslo, Norway. The ability of women scholars to bring in new perspectives varies with their own training and earlier commitment to feminist ideas. Several studies within the field of feminist research (Brock-Utne and Haukaa, 1980; Spender, 1981; Spender and Sarah, 1980) have shown that our educational system fosters male values. Our coeducational schools are not truly coeducational. They are boys' schools with girls in them. The longer a woman is subjected to such a system without having an alternative group to strengthen the female culture, the more she will resemble a man in her thinking and outlook. (For clarification and discussion of the term "female culture" see Ås, 1975.)

Peace is often described as a state characterized by a high degree of power-sharing, by egalitarian structures and freedom from as well direct as indirect or structural violence. It is a state where women are not oppressed. Both feminists and peace researchers should be interested in conducting research on questions like: What conditions must be met if peace is to be achieved? How is a lasting peace secured? How are egalitarian structures built up in a hierarchical society? How does one counteract hierarchies and competition? Creative and imaginative work to outline the ingredients and do research on the conditions for such a state should be of great interest for feminists as it should be for peace researchers. When countries are "developing" or new technology is introduced, feminist researchers are likely to look into the consequences of the development from the viewpoint of women and children in the area. (A recent example of this approach is Burns, 1981.) An extension of this topic of study might lead us into the study of the connection between militarism and sexism. The connection is rather clear, as has been pointed out by several researchers. (Brock-Utne, 1981a,b; Daly, 1979; García, 1981; Reardon, 1981, as well as in chapter 2 dealing with "the ideal mother" and "the ideal soldier").

Women's work for peace has been characterized by the use of a variety of nonviolent strategies. Women are taught from their early childhood not to be physically violent. In Boulding's study, women researchers found that negotiation processes were studied far too little. There was also too little attention paid to the development of models of peaceful settlement of conflict. If female researchers were allowed to do research on what they found most lacking and especially important in peace research, models for nonviolent conflict solutions would have high priority. Here women's role in peace movements should be made visible.

Adding a feminist perspective to peace research would also mean reducing the value and use of traditional economic indicators such as average household income, per capita income, and per capita food consumption. As mentioned in the first part of this paper it is necessary to look into:

1. how economic resources are distributed within the family and with what consequences
2. which family members have acquired greater decision-making powers over others
3. who within the family makes how much contribution to family income
4. what the labor contribution of each family member is
5. whether the labor contribution of each family member is commensurate with the benefits he or she derives from membership in it

Such an analysis would make the actual labor of family members visible, including the daily drudgery and unpaid work that are mostly done by women. Results would certainly vary from one country to another, from one class to another, from one caste to another. Yet analysis along the suggested lines might reveal many facts about the universal oppression of women, which are impossible to find by using traditional economic indicators. The type of analysis that is suggested here is, of course, much more time consuming from a research point of view than just making a survey based on traditional economic indicators. In order to analyze the labor contribution and decision-making power of each family member it may be necessary to use labor intensive research techniques like participant observation and time studies.

One of the results of Boulding's study, as already mentioned, was that female peace researchers wanted more research on the social and economic consequences of the arms race. As mentioned in Chapter 2, the Swedish Undersecretary of State, Inga Thorsson, has become well-known for her speech to the first UN Special Session for Disarmament in 1978 where she showed how the redistribution of 5 percent of the world military expenditures to social benefits for children in developing countries would lead to astonishing improvements in the health conditions of these children. We need other studies of the same kind.

The relationship between the arms race and the increased unemployment in the western world also needs further study. A feminist perspective here would add to the analysis of which sex gets jobs in the military sector and which sex loses jobs in the civilian sector due to increased military spending. From which sector is money taken when military spending is increased? What would this money otherwise have been spent for? Who would have benefited from this spending and who is losing now? Is the money taken more from women and children than from men? The Marion Anderson study reported in the first chapter of this book is posing questions like these and attempting answers for the U.S. scene. But it is only a first and promising beginning and lacks the thoroughness and scope that such a study needs leaving many questions unanswered. More research along these lines is needed. Conducting such research would be to add a feminist perspective to research already regarded as peace research. Including research on personal violence against women as a part of peace research would however broaden the field. I find that such a widening of the field to include personal and direct violence against women would be fruitful and necessary. I am thinking of wife battering, genital mutilation, dowry torture and deaths, rape of women both in civilian life, as refugees, in the military, and as political prisoners. These data are hard to get because the women involved feel ashamed and find it hard to reveal the fact that they have been raped and/or sexually abused. There has also been an unwillingness on the part of male society to deal with these matters. If the abuses and rapes are committed by the husband, there has been a tendency to regard this direct violence not as a violation of basic human rights, but as something belonging to the privacy of the home. One of the great accomplishments of the new feminist movement and of feminist research is to make the personal political and official. Wife-beating is certainly not a private matter. It is a violation of human rights and should be treated as such.

Most respondents in Boulding's study agreed that the ambivalences of public opinion on disarmament versus defense and defense versus aggression needed to be studied. As mentioned before, public opinion polls on disarmament, defense, and military questions show clear differences between opinions held by men and by women. These differences between the attitudes of women and men would be interesting to explore further.

Within the International Peace Research Association a commission that has a relatively large number of women is the Peace Education Commission. This is not surprising, since there are many women in the academic field of education. These women bring with them knowledge from research on children's attitudes and on the way children are socialized and learn. Some of these women scholars have also been working within the field of women's studies and have knowledge about the ways girls learn to be passive, oppressed, and to be the "other." An interesting area for study would be to look more at the socialization we give boys, how boys learn the role of oppressor, and how their socialization is more war-like than what their sisters receive. Not only boys' toys and trivial literature ought to be studied, but also the way small boys are taught or allowed to solve conflicts between themselves. A comparable study of the way small girls solve conflicts could be of interest. Likewise a study of cooperation versus competition in games and sports would be of interest.

RECOMMENDATIONS CONCERNING THE STRENGTHENING OF RESEARCH ON WOMEN AND PEACE

I have argued for the inclusion of a feminist perspective in peace research. I have also made the point that topics that are now studied under the women's studies or feminist research (like wife abuse) should also belong to peace research. So-called private violence also needs to be studied in the same context as official violence and made visible and official. If peace research were broadened to include more of the points I have mentioned, the field would naturally attract more female researchers. At the same time the inclusion of more women, especially those with a background in feminist research, would also shift the emphasis of the field of peace research.

Presently we have far too little peace research of any kind. If we put as much time, energy, and money into peace research as we do into research on weapons of destruction, there is no doubt that we'll find new solutions. I am not suggesting here that the few mostly male researchers in the field be substituted by female researchers; rather I am arguing for a great increase of researchers devoted to peace studies all over the world. This increase should comprise researchers with a feminist perspective. A great problem within the field of peace studies when broadened to include a feminist perspective is the difficulty of gaining access to research done in the Third World. These studies tend to become centered on Europe and North America because of the greater availability of studies done in the western and northern hemispheres. More research in the Third World and from women Third World scholars is needed. There is also a great need to have this research distributed to all the developing countries and the so-called developed world. It is also of the greatest importance that scholars within peace studies working from a feminist perspective are provided with the infrastructure that makes it possible for them to write papers and meet at regular intervals. This is necessary both at the national, the regional, and the international levels.

The international peace research community is organized through the International Peace Research Association (IPRA). IPRA, like most research organizations, is dominated by men. But, as already mentioned, in 1981 a network of feminist scholars within the organization was founded (see also Chapter 3). Thanks to economic support from UNESCO, it was possible to arrange an international seminar on women, militarism, and disarmament in Gyor, Hungary in August 1983. The seminar lasted for three days and took place right before the biannual conference of IPRA. There were 24 participants from

Asia, Latin America, Africa, Australia, the United States, and both eastern and western Europe.

A report from the seminar is available at the Oslo International Peace Research Institute (PRIO/INFORM 14/83). The need for more national and regional meetings was felt by several of the scholars participating at Gyor. Having such an international forum to report to as the IPRA women's network stimulates collection of studies and research from one's own region.

The participants in the consultation on women, militarism, and disarmament held in Gyor, Hungary, August 25–28, 1983, submitted a list of research priorities within the field we were discussing. This list of priorities was presented to the 10th General Conference of IPRA, which was held after the women's seminar. In the list of research priorities we emphasized that research was needed on:

1. sexism and sex role socialization
2. the connections between sexism and other forms of discrimination and violence and between militarism and development
3. the common characteristics of feminist and peace movements
4. the connections between action and research
5. core concepts, root causes, and strategies for a change of values and consciousness, in order to understand better the effects of militarization as well as direct violence on women and the role of women in promoting new understanding of war and peace and for ensuring that these issues are in the forefront of peace research

Research on the first points listed will certainly broaden the field of peace research. To bring such insights into peace research would be to acknowledge that there shall be no "private violence." All violence should be studied and be part of peace research. We find that the role of women in promoting new understanding of war and peace ought to be an important topic in peace research. In Chapter 3 I tried to show how small girls solve conflicts in a different manner than boys. In Chapter 2 I tried to show how women work for peace. Certainly women may promote new insights into peace and help to make a better world.

5 Feminism as the Starting Point for Effective Disarmament

Like the Australian Minister for Education, Susan Ryan, who was cited in the beginning of the book, I believe that it is the relationship between feminism and disarmament that provides hope for change. If women are to create a more peaceful world and do away with the male institution of war we must get more power before men have destroyed our earth. I believe that we can create a world of peace, with equality instead of hierarchy, leadership instead of domination, self-mastery instead of mastery over others, cooperation instead of competition, skills and talents used to draw people together rather than to wedge them apart and with caring for other human beings, animals, and plants. But in order to do all this, certain requirements must be fulfilled.

WOMEN MUST HAVE THE OPPORTUNITY AND THE TIME TO FORMULATE A DEFENSE POLICY FOR THE MODERN FEMINIST MOVEMENT

The older women who, until recently, have made up the majority of members in Women's International League for Peace and Freedom must have felt disappointed when younger women in the modern feminist movement did not join them some years ago in their fight against the male institution of war and militarism. It seemed that the younger women were too preoccupied with their own immediate problems: women's rights to paid jobs, equal pay, nurseries and kindergartens for all children, safe school roads, self-determined abortion, and encouraging men to share the housework and care of children. Today, as shown in Chapter 2, women from the new feminist movement are also fighting war and the threat of a nuclear holocaust. But the ideological work that was going on in the new feminist movement some years ago has a great bearing on the questions of peace and war. It is important that it continue. If they are able to succeed, all liberation movements need a more or less formal and informal network in which the interests and ideology of the liberation movement can be worked out and formulated. Most radical feminists of today agree that what we want is not equality on mens' terms. We do not want to copy men's ways, because we do not see them as worth copying. We do not want to build hierarchies in our organizations or create winners and losers. We want a sharing of responsibility and power. Just as we do not want to create winners and losers in our immediate surroundings, we also want to do away with exploitation on a global level. We must share what there is and become accustomed to the fact that some of us may have to lower our standard of living so that others can also have a decent life. We want to continue to practice the caring rationality that has come to us as the result of a female upbringing and extend this rationality to men. As we are against the exploitation of living beings, we are also against the exploitation of the earth. We want to see pollution and exploitation stopped.

In recent years feminist scholars have done admirable work in posing feminist questions in various academic fields, in political life, and in various other institutions of male society. Often we can build on the work of our foremothers to make this work visible and bring it out of oblivion. Good examples of such work to make our foremothers visible are two recent books. The one by Dale Spender (1982) is entitled *Women of Ideas and What Men Have Done to Them*. The other book is a German book edited by Gisela Brinker-Gabler (1980) called *Frauen gegen den Kreig* [*Women against War*], which presents short novels, speeches, and conference and action reports written by German-speaking women between 1896 and 1941. Here we find early feminist studies on war. We have much to learn from many of them. Many of these women also warned their sisters against copying men's ways. Many of them were actively opposing men within their own political parties.

Feminist scholars ask questions like: What have we gained by having access to men's education? (Brock-Utne and Haukaa, 1980; Spender and Sarah, 1980). By being trained to compete and to compartmentalize knowledge? Studies within physics show that girls are interested in physics if they learn about the human and social consequences of scientific discoveries and inventions (Sjöberg, 1982); otherwise they become disappointed and drop out of physics. They do not think it satisfying to learn only about the splitting of atoms. They want to know about the use of nuclear energy, the effects of an atomic bomb on the lives of human beings and the environment. Boys feel satisfied with what they are offered at school: compartmentalized knowledge. There is no reason to maintain that boys want better science than girls want. But some male researchers working on this topic maintain that when girls drop out of physics in school there is more reason to ask: what is wrong with the teaching of physics instead of what is wrong with girls? (Sjöberg, 1982; Sjöberg and Lie, 1984).

As already mentioned in Chapter 3 feminist scholars working with the teaching of sports and athletics are asking what the relationship of feminism to sports should be (Fasting, 1982, Felshin, 1974). Are we to accept the male institution of sports? Are we going to compete against each other like men do? Are we to copy men's sports in the name of equality? Are we going to compete against men, maybe beat them on their own premises? Are they going to respect us if we run faster than they do? We have to ask whether we want to become better to compete, to take over men's sports and men's rules, to accept that it is fun to beat others, or to make men lose? Feminist scholars working with women in sports have coined the concept "feminist sports," which are sports without competition. Sports where families and groups of people experience the fun of doing physical exercise together without anyone being the winner or loser. One could arrange mountain hikes, skiing week-ends, outdoor camping tours where old and young from various nations meet and have a good time together, a time to build up body and spirit. Would not this create a better climate of understanding than having young men compete against each other for chauvinistic and nationalistic reasons?

We have to look at the values embedded in our man-made institutions, in our way of living. We have to ask the question:

Do we want to defend territories? Why should we help men defend their territories? Are we perhaps defending a way of living? Are we giving our lives for the continued existence of the patriarchal state? Naturally men have more reason to defend the continued existence of male society than women have. If we help men to conquer some oppressor, do we have any guarantee that we and our daughters will be less oppressed in the years to come than we are now?

Of course, we want to defend our lives and the lives of our children, we want to defend life on this earth, which men are about to destroy. But do we want to defend territories? Property? As the Norwegian feminist, Berit Ås (1982) argues, women have a very different relationship to territories than men. "It is not women who have owned and exploited countries on a large scale. They have neither been landlords nor feudal masters." I have already quoted UN statistics showing that women now only own 1 percent of all private property in the world, and this percentage is diminishing. Is it this 1 percent we are asked to defend or the 99 percent owned by males? If we are helping men to defend their 99 percent of the property, are we going to get any of it afterwards or will we be allowed to decide how it is going to be used?

Berit Ås (1982) finds that the weak connection of women to property in our part of the world is partly due to the fact that, through marriage, women are supposed to leave their families and their local community and follow the man to his community or to wherever he finds employment. She sees women's weak connection to territory as one of the main reasons why women are disposed to feel and believe differently toward war than men. Men are accustomed to conquer territory; they see it as their right to own space. This can often be seen in the way men use the space around them when they talk (Spender, 1980). It can further be seen in the ways boys use corridors and playgrounds in coeducational schools, as if they owned them. Girls often have to sneak along the walls, while boys make use of most of the space available (Spender and Sarah, 1980). An interesting study about the use of space was recently conducted at the University of Tromsø, Norway (Andreassen and Mortensen, 1982). The researchers looked at what happened when the boys and the girls in coeducational physical education classes arrived in the same athletics hall from two separate wardrobes. They looked at the informal activities going on before the real teaching had started, before the teacher intervened and organized activities. After some observations the researchers found a fixed pattern that kept repeating itself: when the boys arrived first, they always occupied the whole hall. They would start throwing balls to each other at great length and shouting to each other from a long distance. When the girls arrived later there was no space left for them, so they formed a small group, taking as little space as possible. There they stood talking or jumping up and down until the teacher started instruction. When on the other hand, the girls arrived at the hall first, they occupied only half of the hall, leaving the other half for the boys. They did so without making any notice of it, without drawing a chalk line or anything of the sort. They seemed to be doing it rather naturally. They would start throwing balls to each other but within their own territory, and their shouts would not be dominating the whole hall.

To women it seems logical that the means one decides to use should be in congruence with the aims one wants to achieve. So if you want peace, you try to achieve this by peaceful means, you start preparing for peace. I see the correspondence between Bertha von Suttner and Alfred Nobel as an excellent illustration of what I would call feminist peace policy versus masculine peace policy. They both claimed that they were working for peace, they both even declared themselves as pacifists. But the means he wanted to use to achieve peace were to get more and more armaments. He believed in the saying: "If you want peace, prepare for war." He claimed that he was doing more for the maintenance of peace with his dynamite and cannons than she was doing through all her pacifist writings and organization of peace conferences. She worked to mobilize opinion against the institution of war, against the manufacturing and use of deadly weapons. She wanted to do away with all arms, with all instruments of murder.

The day Alfred Nobel wrote about has arrived, but the troops have not been dismissed. On the contrary, the great overkill capacity of modern nation states has not stopped the world from rearming as never before in history. Nobel's tactics have not worked, although they are the ones that have been given priority and taxpayers' money in all the patriarchal nations. Feminists believe that if the aim is complete disarmament, one must first stop further rearmament and start disarming. There is no other way to disarmament than to disarm. This should seem logical; maybe it is feminist logic. Male logic seems to dictate that in order to achieve disarmament one must first rearm. But rearmament is not disarmament!

One of the leaders of the Norwegian Women for Peace, Bett Romstad (1982), said about women's and men's logic concerning peace and war:

> We find it logical that without weapons there will be no war. We consequently want to do away with weapons. We want disarmament. Without nuclear weapons, there will be no nuclear war. Consequently we want nuclear disarmament. When a child feels threatened and becomes aggressive, we find it logical to take away the threat. We find it logical that when one wants disarmament, one must stop rearming. But men maintain that women are not rational beings, we are not logical. They talk with contempt about "women's logic." To men it seems logical to "defend" peace by the accumulation of weapons. To men it seems logical to prevent a nuclear war by acquiring *more* nuclear arms. To threaten the aggressive child even more. They even claim that one must rearm to disarm. Men claim that Norway had its 9th of April [the date of the German occupation in 1940] because we were not armed *well* enough. Women find that a better explanation is that we had let Germany rearm. But at least our military "defense" was so weak few Norwegians were killed and we had a population that fought its way through the war through self-reliance and the use of non-violent civilian resistance. (p. 2).

Romstad voices ideas that are clearly related to our early foremothers in the fight for peace, women like Bertha von Suttner, Ellen Key, Selma Lagerlöf, Fredrika Bremer, Clara Zetkin, and Rosa Luxemburg. We have to ask ourselves: Why didn't the logical thinking of women win the day? How was it possible that the highly illogical and irrational thinking of men was stamped as rational by those in power? The answer is rather simple: Those in power also have the power to define the world. They have the power to define concepts, to allocate prestigious words to their own thinking, and to stamp out the thinking of others through words that have a negative connotation. Those in power also have the power to define concepts like defense, security, and justice. They have the power to stamp their own thinking as rational—a word of honor in a world where emotions are looked down upon and reason is highly valued—even though, according to most criteria, it is highly irrational. Those in power are men. In the patriarchal societies of our time men stamp their own mainstream thinking as rational and manly. "You think and you act like a man" to them is a compliment (to feminists it is not). To think and act like a woman is no compliment in a patriarchal society (except to feminists).

WOMEN SHOULD NOT INTEGRATE INTO THE MILITARY INSTITUTION

If women are going to work as a peace force, we should remain outsiders to male institutions such as the military. One of the reasons why women in all of the countries I know of where polls according to sex have been taken are more hostile to the arms race and deployment of nuclear weapons is because women have been and still largely are outsiders to the military. Women are able to think new thoughts, to formulate other solutions.

Instead of becoming like men, killing the woman in us like the military requires men to do, we should help men reject the military institution. We should help men to think and feel like women. Instead of copying the ways of our oppressors, we should join the work of our pacifist foremothers, start reading their thoughts, and build upon their thinking. We should become acquainted with the works of women from the socialist, social-democratic, and communist parties in Germany at the turn of the century, women like Rosa Luxemburg (1870–1919) and Clara Zetkin (1857–1933), who organized protest meetings against the war-supporting policy of the Socialist Party (Brinker-Gabler, 1980). Besides these socialist-pacifist women, we should also know the women from the conservative women's movement like Helene Stöcker (1869–1943), who worked for pacifism during the fascist period up to 1938 in Switzerland and died in exile in New York. In addition to socialists and conservatives, there were also radical feminists who were committed to pacifism. Gisela Brinker-Gabler (1980) mentions many of these women in her book and presents speeches and action-reports they have made. Reviewing this book, Hanne Birckenbach (1982), a younger feminist and peace activist, states:

> Reading *Women Against War* I felt somewhat ashamed of the fact that I and my generation have not been aware of the intensive work earlier women had undertaken in opposing war and the issues they had raised about how war affects us as women. . . . I am convinced that we should resume the thread of the early feminists' studies on war and do hope that women in other countries follow the work of the German editor by attempting to recover the first steps which women made in the beginning of the twentieth century, the century of weapons of mass destruction. (p. 383)

We certainly have much to learn from these women who were fighting the male institution of war.

WOMEN MUST GET POWER

If we keep working with feminist peace policies, do not join the military, develop our "women's logic," continue to care for others, feel compassion, share power, and become more assertive, will we then be able to change the world? I think we might have a chance provided we do not copy men.

Women constitute the most active members of the peace movement at the grass-roots level and also the greatest potential peace force according to opinion polls. We know that several of the major military decisions that have been made by western governments and parliaments the last years, despite demonstrations and protests from peace movements, would not have been taken if women had been governing the countries. Men who really want other solutions to security problems should vote for women in the next elections and see to it that these women are able to act and think like women, not as men in skirts. As women we have to believe in ourselves and other women to have the strength, endurance, compassion, and passion to continue our struggle for a better, more humane, and truly peaceful future.

REFERENCES

Abzug, Bella. 1984. *Gender Gap. A Guide to Political Power for American Women.* Boston: Houghton Mifflin Company.

Aguilar-San Juan, Delia. 1982. Feminism and the National Liberation Struggle in the Philippines. *Women's Studies International Forum*, 5: 3/4: 253–261.

Alderson, Lynn. 1983. "Greenham Common and All That." in *Breaching the Peace. 'A Collection of Radical Feminist Papers.'* London: Only Women Press Ltd.

Anderson, Marion. 1982a. *The Empty Pork Barrel: Unemployment and the Pentagon Budget.* 2d ed. Lansing, MI: Employment Research Associates.

Anderson, Marion. 1982b. *Neither Jobs, nor Security: Women's Unemployment and the Pentagon Budget.* Lansing, MI: Employment Research Associates.

Andreassen, Geir og Elin Mortensen. En studie av sammenhengen mellom kjønn, atferd og dominans i fellesundervisning av jenter og gutter i kroppsøvingsfaget. Universitetet i Tromsø. *Grunnfagsoppgave.* Vår 1982. (A Study of the interrelationship between sex, behavior and dominance in the co-education of girls and boys in athletics. Reported 1982).

Anker, Nini Roll. 1945. *Kvinnen og den svarte fuglen* [The woman and the black bird].

Arcana, Judith. 1983. *Every Mother's Son. The role of mothers in the making of men.* London: The Women's Press.

Arditti, Rita; Brennan, Pat; and Cavrak, Steve. 1980. *Science and Liberation.* Boston: South End Press.

Arditti, Rita; Duelli Klein, Renate; and Minden, Shelley. eds. 1984. *Test-tube Women. What Future for Motherhood?* London: Pandora Press.

Ås, Berit. 1975. On Female Culture. An attempt to formulate a theory of women's solidarity and action. *Acta Sociologica.* Copenhagen, Denmark. 18: 2/3.

Ås, Berit. 1981. A five-dimensional model for change: contradictions and feminist consciousness. *Women's Studies International Quarterly.* 4: 1: 101–115.

Ås, Berit. 1982. A materialistic view of men's and women's attitudes towards war. *Women's Studies International Forum.* 5: 3/4: 355–365.

Baker, Robert; and Ball, Sandra. 1969. *Violence and the Media.* A staff Report to the National Commission on the Causes and Prevention of Violence. Washington, DC: U.S. Government Printing Office.

Bard, Merton. 1974. "The Study and Modification of Intra-familial Violence." In *Violence in the Family* edited by Suzanne Steinmetz and Murray Strauss. New York: Dodd, Mead and Company.

Barrow, Isaac. 1970. *The Usefulness of Mathematical Learning Explained and Demonstrated.* 1734. Frank Cass.

151

Bellak, Leopold; and Antell, Maxine. 1974. "An Intercultural Study of Aggressive Behavior on Children's Playgrounds." *American Journal of Orthopsychiatry* (Cited in Holliday, 1978). **44**: 503.

Bellow, Linda; Berry, Carolle; Cunningham, Joyce; Jackson, Margaret; Jeffreys, Sheila; and Jones, Carol. 1983. *Breaching the Peace. A collection of radical feminist papers.* Only Women Press, Ltd., pp. 18–22.

Belotti, Elena Gianini. 1976. *Dalla parte delle bambine.* Milano: Gianiacomo Feltrinelli Editore, 1973. Norwegian edition: *Slik former vi jentene.* (The making of girls) Oslo: Gyldendal Norsk Forlag.

Bergom Larsson, Maria. 1979. "Women and Technology in Industrialized Countries." pp. 47–69. In *Knowledge and Control*, edited by Michael Young. London: Collier MacMillan.

Bernstein, Basil. 1971. "On the Classification and Framing of Knowledge." pp. 47–69. In *Knowledge and Control*, edited by Michael Young. London: Collier MacMillan.

Birckenbach, Hanne. "Book Review of *Women against War* by Gisella Brinker-Gabler." 1982. *Women's Studies International Forum* **5**: 3/4: 383–385.

Bleier, Ruth. 1984. *Science and Gender—A Critique of Biology and its Theories on Women.* New York: Pergamon Press.

Bose, Anima. 1977. *Mahatma Gandhi. A Contemporary Perspective.* New Delhi: B.R. Publishing Corporation.

Boulding, Elise. "Education for Peace." 1982. *The Bulletin of the Atomic Scientists* **38**: 6: 60.

Boulding, Elise. 1978. "Las mujeres y la violencia social [Women and Social Violence]. In *Revista Internacional de Ciencias Sociales* [International Social Science Journal] Paris: UNESCO. **30**: 4.

Boulding, Elise. "The Role of Women in the Development of Peace Research." In *The role of women in peace movements, in the development of peace research and in the promotion of friendly relations between nations.* Paper presented by UNESCO to the World Conference for the United Nations Decade for Women, Copenhagen, July 14–30, 1980. 45–54.

Boulding, Elise. 1981. Perspectives of Women Researchers on Disarmament, National Security and World Order." *Women's Studies International Quarterly* IV **1**: 27–41.

Breaching the Peace. 1983. *A Collection of Radical Feminist Papers.* London: Only Women Press, Ltd.

Brekke, Liv. 1982. *Kvinner, krig og fred.* [Women, war and peace] A publication from the International Peace Research Institute of Oslo. Oslo. *PRIO publikasjon P-17/82.*

Brinker-Gabler, Gisela. 1980. *Frauen gegen den Krieg* [Women against war]. Frankfurt am Main: Fischer Taschenbuch Verlag.

Brock-Utne, Birgit. 1981a. *The Role of Women as Mothers and Members of Society in the Education of Young People for Peace, Mutual Understanding and Respect for Human Rights.* Commissioned paper for a UNESCO expert meeting on the role of women in peace education. New Delhi, India, December 7–11, 1981. *ED—81/ CON. 609/2.* A more extensive version can be identified as PRIO publication S-12/ 81.

Brock-Utne, Birgit. 1981b. *Disarmament Education as a Distinct Field of Study.* Paper presented at the 9th IPRA General Conference, Toronto, Canada, session on Peace Education, June 21–26.

REFERENCES 153

Brock-Utne, Birgit. 1981c. Kvinner i fredsarbeid. Sivertsen, Stockholm, Vislie (eds.). (Women in work for peace). In: *Kvinner viser vei*. (A woman leads the way) Oslo. Aschehoug, Festschrift to Eva Nordland.

Brock-Utne, Birgit. 1982a. "What are the Effects of Curricular Options?" In *Sex Stereotyping in Schools*, edited by Council of Europe. Swets & Zeitlinger-Lisse.

Brock-Utne, Birgit. 1982b. "Girls and the Hidden Curriculum of the Compulsory School." *Tidskrift för Nordisk Förening för Pedagogisk Forskning*. (Journal for the Nordic Society for Educational Research, no. 1–2, 1982. Special issue on women and education).

Brock-Utne, Birgit. 1982c. "Ett kvinneperspektiv på norsk forsvarspolitikk." (A feminist perspective on Norwegian defense policy.) PRIO publikasjon P-6/82.

Brock-Utne, Birgit. 1982d. "Gewaltfrei Denken. Zur rolle der Frauen in der Friedensforschung." (Non-violent thinking. On the role of women in peace research.) In Ranzio-Plath, Crista (ed.): *Was Geht uns Frauen der Krieg an?* Rowohlt Verlag.

Brock-Utne, Birgit. 1982e. *Rauhan Kasvatus. "Rauke Saa alkunsa naisten mielissa."* (Women and Peace. "Peace starts in the minds of women.") Naiser Raukan Puolesta.

Brock-Utne, Birgit. 1983a. Likestilt til å drepe. (Equal to kill). *Ny Tids kronikk. 13. April.*

Brock-Utne, Birgit. 1983b. "Are Universities Educating for War?" Key note lecture held at Johann Wolfgang Goethe-University, Frankfurt am Main, Federal Republic of Germany, September, 1983 in connection with the IV International Congress of the European Association for research and development in higher education, Oslo.

Brock-Utne, Birgit. 1983c. *Education as the Key to Equal Participation of Women in the Development Process.* Commissioned paper prepared on request for the Nordic seminar on WOMEN IN DEVELOPMENT held near Helsinki November 9–11, 1983.

Brock-Utne, Birgit. 1983d. *Research on Women and Peace*, prepared on request for the expert group meeting on the participation of women in promoting international peace and cooperation held in Vienna 5–9 December, 1983.

Brock-Utne, Birgit. 1984. "The Relationship of Feminism to Peace and Peace Education." *Bulletin of Peace Proposals.* **15**: 2: 149–154.

Brock-Utne, Birgit; and Haukaa, Runa. *Kunnskap uten makt* [Knowledge without power]. Oslo/Bergen/Tromsø: Norwegian Universities Press, 1980. Reprinted 1981 and 1984.

Bronfenbrenner, Urie. 1958. "The Study of Identification through Inter-Personal Perception." In *Person Perception and Interpersonal Behavior.* Stanford: Stanford University Press.

Brown, Wilmette. 1983. *Black Women and the Peace Movement.* International Women's Day Convention. Copies of the pamphlet are available from: King's Cross Women's Centre, 71 Tonbridge Street, London WX, 1, England.

Brownmiller, Susan. 1975. *Against Our Will: Men, Women and Rape.* New York: Simon and Schuster.

Brunet, Odette, and Lezine, Irene. 1966. *I primi anni del bambino.* Roma: Armando. (Cited in Belotti, 1973).

Burns, Robin. 1981. Continuity and Change in Peace Education. *Bulletin of Peace Proposals,* **2**: 115–123.

Burns, Robin. *Development, Disarmament and Women: Some New Connections.* Paper delivered at Victorian Association for Peace Studies, March 1982.

Burton, Eve. 1983. "Surviving the Flight of Horror: The Story of Refugee Women." *Indochina Issues.* A publication of the Center for International Policy. February, no. 4.

Buss, Arnold. 1971. "Aggression Pays." In *The Control of Aggression and Violence*, edited by Jerome Singer. New York: Academic Press.

Bussey, Gertrude, and Time, Margaret. 1980. *Pioneers for Peace. Women's International League for Peace and Freedom 1915-1965.* Oxford: Alden Press.

Butcher, N. 1969. "MMPI Characteristics of Externalizing and Internalizing Boys and their Parents." In *MMPI Research Developments and Clinical Applications,* edited by James Butcher. New York: McGraw-Hill. (Cited in Holliday, 1978.)

Buvinic, Mayra. 1981. Introduction to "Women and Development: Indicators of their Changing Role." *Socio-economic studies*, Paris. UNESCO. No. 3.

Buvinic, Mayra, and Youssef, Nadia H. 1978. *Woman-headed Households: The Ignored Factor in Development Planning.* Washington, DC: International Center for Research on Women.

Caldecott, Leonie. 1983. "At the Foot of the Mountain: The Shibokusa Women of Kita Fuji." In *Keeping the Peace.* Edited by Lynne Jones. London: The Women's Press.

Cambridge Women's Peace Collective. 1984. *My Country is the Whole World. An Anthology of Women's Work on Peace and War.* London: Pandora Press.

Camp, Kay. 1977. *Listen to the Women for a Change.*

Carloni, Alice Stewart. 1981. "Sex Disparities in the Distribution of Food within Rural Households." *Food and Nutrition* 7: 1.

Chapkis, Wendy, and Wings, Mary. 1981. "The Private Benjamin Syndrome." In *Loaded Questions. Women in the Military*, edited by Wendy Chapkis. Amsterdam, Washington DC: Transnational Institute.

Chodorow, Nancy. 1978. *The Reproduction of Mothering.* Berkeley: University of California Press.

Cisse, Jeanne Martin. 1975. "Woman, the first teacher." *Prospects* V 3: 347-352.

Cohen, L.J., and Campos, J.J. 1974. "Father, Mother and Stranger as Elicitors of Attachment Behaviors in Infancy." *Developmental Psychology* X. 146-154.

Costin, Lela B. 1982. "Feminism, Pacifism, Internationalism and the 1915 International Congress of Women." *Women's Studies International Forum.* 5: 3/4: 301-315.

Daly, Mary. 1979. *Gyn/Ecology.* London: The Women's Press.

D'Andrade, Roy. 1966. "Sex Differences and Cultural Institutions." In *The Development of Sex Differences*, edited by E.E. Maccoby. Stanford: Stanford University Press.

Davis, Elisabeth Gould. 1971. *The First Sex.* New York: Putnam's Sons. Later reprinted by Penguin Books.

Degen, Marie Louise. 1939. *The History of the Woman's Peace Party. John Hopkins University Studies in Historical and Political Science*, Series LVII, no. 3.

Detre, Thomas et al. 1974. "The Nosology of Violence." In *Neural Basis for Violence and Aggression*, edited by Fields and Sweet. (Cited in Holliday, 1978).

Dinnerstein, Dorothy. 1977. *The Mermaid and the Minotaur.* Harper Colophon Books.

DiPietro, J. 1977. *Rough and tumble play: A function of gender.* Unpublished manuscript. Stanford University, Psychology Department. (Cited in Maccoby 1980.)

Dumas, L.J. 1981. "Disarmament and economy in advanced industrialized countries—the US and the USSR." *Bulletin of Peace Proposals.* **12**: 1: 1–100.

Easlea, Brian. 1981. *Science and sexual oppression. Patriarchy's confrontation with woman and nature.* London: Weidenfeld and Nicholson.

Edwards, C.P. and B. Whiting. 1977. *Sex differences in children's social interaction.* Unpublished report to the Ford Foundation. (Cited in Maccoby, 1980).

Eglin, Josephine. 1982. Cited in *Feminism and the Peace Movement: The Universalistic Nature of the Struggle against Injustice and Violence.* Paper. University of Bradford. England.

Eichler, Margrit. 1980. *The Double Standard.* New York: St. Martin's Press.

Eisler, Riane. Women and Peace. Editorial in: *Women's International Network News.* (WIN NEWS) June 1982. (Lexington, MA)

Ellefsen, Sven. 1981. Mishandling av kone og barn blir lovlig i USA? (Violence against wife and children becomes legal in the US?) *Dagbladet,* 17 June.

Elster, Ellen. *Kvinner i det militære* [Women in the Military]. Paper delivered at a seminar on "Women and militarism" held at Sundvollen near Oslo, November 11–12, 1982, sponsored by International Peace Research Institute of Oslo.

Enloe, Cynthia. 1979. Women—the Reserve Army of Army Labor. Paper delivered at the department of government. Clark University, Worcester, MA.

Enloe, Cynthia. 1981. "NATO: What is it and why should women care?" In *Loaded questions. Women in the military.* Amsterdam, Washington, DC: Transnational Institute.

Enloe, Cynthia. 1983. *Does Khaki become You? The Militarisation of Women's Lives.* London: Pluto Press.

Erickson, Eric. 1951. "Sex Differences in the Play Configurations of Preadolescents." *American Journal of Orthopsychiatry.* **21**: 667. (Cited in Holliday, 1978.)

Eron, Leonard et al. 1974. "How Learning Conditions in Early Childhood—including Mass Media—Relate to Aggression in Late Adolescence." *American Journal of Orthopsychiatry.* **44**: 412. (Cited in Holliday, 1978.)

Eysenck, H.J. and Nias, D.K.B. 1978. *Sex, Violence and the Media.* London: Maurice Temple Smith.

Fasteau, Marc Feigen. 1975. *The Male Machine.* New York: Delta Books.

Fasting, Kari. "Female sports—Equal but Different." *Tidsskrift for Nordisk Forening for Pedagogisk Forskning.* 1–2/1982. Special issue on sexism and education. pp. 46–56. (Journal of the Nordic Society for Educational Research) Sweden.

Felshin, J. 1974. Social Commentary. Chapter 7. In Gerber, E.W. et. al, *The American Women in Sport.* Boston: Addison Wesley.

Freire, Paulo. 1972. *Pedagogy of the Oppressed.* New York: Penguin Books.

Galsworthy, John. 1933. *The Forsyte Saga.* New York: Scribner.

Galtung, Johan. 1967. In: *Alternativer—5 års fredsdebatt.* (Alternatives: Five Years of Peace Debate). Oslo: Pax forlag. p. 209.

Galtung, Johan. 1981. "Disarmament education: a partial answer." *Approaching Disarmament Education*, edited by Magnus Haavelsrud. Guildford: Westbury House. In association with the Peace Education Commission of the International Peace Research Association.

Galtung, Johan. 1979. "Fredsforskning." (Peace Research). In *Pax Leksikon*. **2**: 439–440. Oslo: Pax Forlag.

Galtung, Johan. 1975. "Peace Education: Problems and Conflicts." In *Education for Peace—Reflection and Action*. Guildford. IPC Science and Technology Press.

Gandhi, Mahatma. 1927. "Women and Ornaments." *Young India* 8.

Gandhi, Mahatma. "Swaraj through Women." *Harijan* 2 (December, 1939).

Gandhi, Mahatma. What is Woman's Role? *Harijan* 24 (February, 1940).

Garbo, Gunnar. 1975. *"Opprustet og forsvarslós."* (Armed and Defenseless) Oslo: Gyldendal Norsk Forlag.

García, Celina. 1981. Androgyny and Peace Education. *Bulletin of Peace Proposals* 2: 163–178.

Giele, J.Z., and Smock, A.C. 1977. *Women: Roles and Status in Eight Countries*. New York: John Wiley & Sons.

Gil, David. 1973. *Violence against Children*. Cambridge: Harvard University Press.

Gilder, George. 1973. *Sexual suicide*. New York: Quadrangle Books.

Gilligan, Carole. 1981. *In a Different Voice*. Cambridge: Harvard University Press.

Gleditsch, Nils Petter; Hagelin, Bjórn; and Kristoffersen, Ragnar. 1982. "Some Transitional Patterns of Military R & D." *PRIO-publication S-6/82. p. 47*. Oslo: International Peace Research Institute.

Glueck, Eleanor and Sheldon. 1950. *Unravelling Juvenile Delinquency*. Cambridge: Harvard University Press.

Goldstein, Jeffrey, and Arms, Robert. 1971. "Effects of Observing Athletic Contests on Hostility." *Sociometry* **34**: 83. (Cited in Holliday, 1978.)

Goodenough, E.W. 1957. "Interest in Persons as an Aspect of Sex Differences in the Early Years." *Genetic Psychology Monographs*. **55**: 287–323.

Green, Frankie. 1983. "Not Weaving but Frowning." In *Breaching The Peace. A collection of radical feminist papers*. London: Only Women Press.

Green, Richard. 1974. "The Behaviorally Feminine Male Child." In *Sex Differences in Behavior*, edited by Richard Friedman. (Cited in Holliday, 1978.)

Green, R. 1976. "One Hundred Ten Feminine and Masculine Boys: Behavioral Contrasts and Demographic Similarities." *Archives of Sexual Behavior.* 5: 425–446.

Haavelsrud, Magnus (ed.). 1981. *Approaching disarmament education*. Guildford: Westbury House.

Haavelsrud, Magnus (ed.) 1975. *Education for Peace Reflection and Action*. Guilford: IPC Science and Technology Press.

Halberstam, David. 1972. *The Best and the Brightest*. New York: Random House.

Haukaa, Runa. 1982. *Bak slagordene. Den nye kvinnebevegelsen i Norge*. (Behind the Slogans. The New Feminist Movement in Norway). Oslo: Pax forlag.

Haukaa, Runa. 1979. Sosial bevegelse og sosial teori. (Social Movements and Social Theories). *Sosiologi i dag* nr. 2.

Hawke, C.C. 1950. Castration and Sex Crimes. *American Journal of Mental Deficiency*. **55**: 220. (Cited in Holliday, 1978).

Heikens, Carolein: 1981. "Freedom Fighters." In *Loaded questions. Women in the military.* Amsterdam and Washington DC: Transnational Institute.

Holliday, Laurel. 1978. *The Violent Sex. Male Psychobiology and the Evolution of Consciousness.* Guerneville, CA: Bluestocking Books.

Horowitz, B., and Kishwar, Madhu. "Family life—the unequal deal." *Manushi*, no. 11, 1982.

Hoskins, Betty and Holmes, Helen Bequaert. 1984. "Technology and prenatal femicide." In *Test-tube women. What future for motherhood?* edited by Rita Arditti, Renate Duelli Klein, and Shelley Minden. London: Pandora Press.

House of Commons. 1976. *Report on Violence in Marriage.* Vol. 1, London.

Hubbard, Ruth; Herifin, Mary Sue; and Fried, Barbara (eds.). 1980. *Biological Woman—The Convenient Myth.* Cambridge: Schenkman.

Hutt, Corinne. 1972. *Males and Females.* Harmondsworth. Penguin Books.

Indochina Project. 120 Maryland Ave. N.E., Washington, DC 20002.

Jacklin, C.N. and Maccoby, E.E. 1978. Social behavior at 33 months in same-sex and mixed sex dyads, *Child Development* 49: 557–69.

Jalmert, Lars. 1979. *Små barns sociale utveckling* (The social development of small children). Stockholm. Norwegian edition: *Små barns sociale utvikling.* Oslo: Pax Forlag, 1980.

Janssen-Jurreit. 1976. *Seximus. Über die Abtreibung der Frauenfrage* [Sexism: The male monopoly of thought]. München/Wien: Carl Hanser Verlag. An abbreviated version has been translated into Swedish: *Sexism: Manssamhälletts ideologi och historia.* Stockholm: Norstedt Trykkeri, 1979; *Sexism—The Monopoly of Male Thought.* London: Pluto Press, 1982.

John, Helen. Engelske kvinder har belejret militærbaser [British women have laid seige to military bases]. In an interview by Maria Cuculiza in the Danish newspaper *Information*, March 15, 1982.

Johnson, Miriam. 1977. "Androgyny and the Maternal Principle." *School Review,* 1: 50–69.

Jones, Lynne (ed.) 1983. *Keeping the Peace. Women's Peace Handbook.* London: The Women's Press.

Jones, Lynne. 1983. "On Common Ground: The Women's Peace Camp at Greenham Common." *Keeping the Peace.* London: The Women's Press.

Jorfald, Ursula. 1962.*Bertha von Suttner.* Oslo, Forum Boktrykkeri.

Juan, Delia Aguilar-San. 1982. "Feminism and the national liberation struggle in the Philippines." *Women's Studies International Forum.* 5: 3/4.

Kapitza, Sergei. 1982. "Social Consciousness and Education for Disarmament. In *Scientists—The Arms Race and Disarmament.* Edited by Joseph Rotblat. London: Taylor and Francis Ltd.

Kelkar, Govind. 1983. *Women and structural violence in India.* Paper presented at the UNESCO/IPRA consultation on women, militarism and disarmament in Gyor, Hungary, 25–28 August, 1983.

Kempf, Beatrix. 1964. *Bertha von Suttner.* Wien: Österreichischer Bundesverlag.

King, Ynestra. 1983. "All is Connectedness: Scenes from the Women's Pentagon Action USA." In Jones, Lynne (ed.): *Keeping the Peace.* London: The Women's Press Ltd.

Kirkerud, Bjørn. 1982. Forskerens ansvar. (The responsibility of the scientist). *Samtiden* **4**: 2-7. (Oslo.)

Knight, G.P., and Kagan, S. 1977. Development of Prosocial and Competitive Behaviors in Anglo-American and Mexican-American Children. *Child Development.* **48**: 1394-95.

Koen, Susan, and Swaim, Nina. 1980. *Handbook for Women on the nuclear mentality.* Norwich, VT: Wand. For additional copies of the handbook write to: Wand, Box 421, Norwich, VT 05055.

Kronsberg, Sandora. 1981. "An Investigation of Parent Intervention Behavior with Toddler Boys and Girls." *Doctoral Dissertation,* University of Oregon.

Lall, Betty Goetz. 1979. "SALT and the coming public debate." *Women Lawyers' Journal.* **65**: 2.

Lamb, M.E. 1978. "The Father's Role in the Infant's Social World." *Mother/Child Father/Child Relationship,* edited by J.H. Stevens and M. Mathews. New York: National Association for the Education of Young Children.

Lamb, Michael. 1977. "The Development of Parental Preferences in the First Two Years of Life." *Sex Roles* **3**: 495-497.

Lamb, Michael, 1981. *The Role of the Father in Child Development.* New York: Wiley.

Lamb, Michael, and Lamb, Jamie. 1976. "The Nature and Importance of the Father-Infant Relationship. *The Family Coordinator* **25**: 379-387.

Lansky, L.M. 1956. *Patterns of Defense Against Conflict.* Unpublished Doctoral Dissertation, University of Michigan. (Cited in Lynn, 1976.)

Lasch, Christopher. 1980. *The Culture of Narcissism.* London: Abacus.

Leira, Arnlaug. 1980. Kvinneforskning. (Women Studies) In *Pax leksikon.* (The Pax Encyclopedia). **4**: 67-68.

LeMaire, L. 1956. "Danish Experience Regarding the Castration of Sexual Offenders." *Journal of Criminal Law and Criminology* **47**: 294. (Cited in Holliday, 1978.)

León, Magdalena. 1983. *Consultation on Women, Militarism and Disarmament.* Paper presented to the UNESCO/IPRA consultation on women, militarism and disarmament in Gyor, Hungary, August 25-28, 1983.

Liebert, Robert. 1974. "Television and Children's Aggressive Behavior: Another Look." *American Journal of Psychoanalysis* **34**: 99. (Cited in Holliday, 1978.)

Liljeström, Rita; Svensson, G.; Liljeström, G.; Mellström; Furst, G. 1976. *Roller i omvandling.* (Sex roles in transition) (sou 1976:71). Stockholm: Liber.

Longdon, Trisha. 1983. Essay. In *Breaching the Peace.* London: Only Women Press. pp. 16-18.

Lowry, Maggie. 1983. "A Voice from the Peace Camps. Greenham Common and Upper Heyford." In *Over our Dead Bodies. Women against the Bomb,* edited by Dorothy Thompson. London: Virago Press. p. 75.

Lynn, D.B. 1974. *The Father: His Role in Child Development.* Belmont, CA: Brooks/Cole.

Lynn, D.B. 1976. "Fathers and Sex-role Development." *The Family Coordinator XXV.* No. 4, October.

MacBride, Sean. 1978. "Brainwashing with a Good Clean Bomb." In *Suicide or Survival? The Challenge of the Year 2000*. Paris: UNESCO.

Maccoby, E.E., and Jacklin, C.N. 1974. *The Psychology of Sex Differences*. Stanford: Stanford University Press.

Maccoby, Eleanor. 1980. *Social Development. Psychology Growth and the Parent-child Relationship*. New York/London/Toronto: Harcourt Brace Jovanovich.

Maksimova, Margarita. Statement at the Amsterdam Conference, November 27–29, 1981, sponsored by WILPF. Published in the report *Women of Europe in Action for Peace*, 1982.

Mansueto, Connie. 1983. "Take the Toys from the Boys. Competition and the Nuclear Arms Race." In *Over our Dead Bodies*, p. 114. London: Virago Press.

Marcuse, Herbert. 1964. *One Dimensional Man*. London: Routledge and Kegan Paul.

Marcuse, Herbert. 1969. *An Essay on Liberation*. Allen Lane.

Marcuse, Herbert. 1972. *Counterrevolution and Revolt*. Allen Lane.

M'Bow, Amadou-Mahtar. 1982. "Arms for Peace? Arms or Peace," in J. Rotblat, ed., *Scientists—The arms race and disarmament*. London: Taylor & Francis Ltd.

McAllister, Pam (ed.) 1982. *Reweaving the Web of Life. Feminism and Non-violence*. Philadelphia: New Society Publishers.

McLean, Scilla. 1982. Report on UNESCO's Report: The Role of Women in Peace Movements. *Women's Studies International Forum*. 5: 3/4: 317–329.

Mead, Margaret. 1978. *Male and Female*. New York: Penguin Books.

Megens, Ine, and Wings, Mary. 1981. "The Recruitment of Women." In *Loaded questions. Women in the military*. Amsterdam and Washington, DC: Transnational Institute.

Merchant, Carolyn. 1980. *The Death of Nature*. San Francisco: Harper & Row.

Moyer, Kenneth. 1974. "A Physiological Model of Aggression." In *Neural Bases for Violence and Aggression*. Warren H. Green. Cited in Holliday, 1978.

Mussen, P., and Rutherford, E. 1963. "Parent-child Relations and Parental Personality in Relation to Young Children's Sexrole Preferences. *Child Development* 34: 589–607.

Myrdal, Alva. 1976. *The Game of Disarmament*. New York: Pantheon.

Nathan, O., and Nordon, H. 1980. *Einstein on Peace*. New York: Simon and Schuster.

Newland, Kathleen, 1979. *The Sisterhood of Man*. New York/London: Worldwatch Institute.

Nietzsche, Friedrich, 1968. *Also Sprach Zarathustra. Ein Buch für Alle und Keinen*. (1883–1885) Berlin: Walter de Gruyter & Co.

Nietzsche, Friedrich. 1969. 1885, English edition. *Thus spoke Zarathustra*. New York: Penguin Books.

Nordland, Eva. 1968. *Mors egen gutt*. (Mother's own boy.) Bergen: J.W. Eide A/S Offset-trykkeri.

Oliphant, Mark. 1982. "Comment on the social responsibilities of scientists." In Rotblat, Joseph (ed): *Scientists, the Arms Race and Disarmament*. London: Taylor and Francis Ltd.

Pedersen, Nina. 1980. Integrering av pike og guttespeiderne av Norges Speiderforbund. (The integration of the girls scouts and the boy scouts of the Norwegian Scout

Association) *Hovedoppgave.* Det sosialpedagogiske studiet [Institute for Educational Research]. The University of Oslo.

Pethick-Lawrence, Emmeline. 1938. *My Part in a Changing World.* London: Victor Gollancz.

Pines, Susan. 1984. "Women's Pentagon Action." In Cambridge Women's Peace Collective: *My Countries in the Whole World. An Anthology of Women's Work on Peace and War.* London, Boston, Melbourne: Pandora Press.

Pizzey, Erin. 1974. *Scream Quietly or the Neighbors Will Hear.* Harmondsworth: Penguin.

Pope, C. and Whiting, B. 1973. "A Cross-Cultural Analysis of Sex Differences in the Behavior of Children Aged Three to Eleven." *Journal of Social Psychology* **91**: 171. (Cited in Holliday, 1978.)

Randzio-Plath, Christa (ed.). 1981. *Was geht uns Frauen der Krieg an?* (Does War Concern Women?) Hamburg: Rowohlt Verlag.

Rausch, H.L.; Barry, W.A.; Hertel, R.K.; and Swain, M.A. 1974. *Communication, Conflict and Marriage.* San Francisco: Jossey-Bass.

Reardon, Betty. *Militarism and Sexism. UME Connexion.* Vol. IX. No. 3. Fall 1981. UME Connexion c/o Educational Ministries/ABC. Valley Forge, PA.

Reardon, Betty. 1982. *Sexism and the War System.* Paper written for the Institute for World Order.

Records of the General Conference Resolutions. 1980. Twenty-first session. Belgrade, Vol. 1. Paris. UNESCO.

Reithaug, Tone. 1983. Kjønnsforskjeller i språkbruk ved overgang fra barnehage til skole. (Sex differences in language usage on the transition from kindergarden to school). *Tidsskrift for Nordisk Forening for Pedagogisk Forskning. no. 3-4.*

Report of the committee on the Status of Women in India: *Towards Equality.* Government of India. Department of Social Welfare, Ministry of Education and Social Welfare, December 1974.

Report of the World Conference of the United Nations Decade for Women: Equality, Development and Peace. Copenhagen. 14–30 July, 1981. A/Conf. 94/35. New York. United Nations. 1980. Sales No. E. 80. IV. 3.

Rheingold, H.L. and Cook, K.V. 1975. The Content of Boys and Girls Rooms as an Index of Parents' Behavior. *Child Development.* **46**: 459–563.

Rich, Adrienne. 1979. *On Lies, Secrets and Silences.* New York: Norton.

Roggencamp, Viola. 1984. Abortion of a special kind: male sex selection in India. In Arditti, Rita Renate Duelli Klein and Shelley Minden (eds.), *Test-tube Women. What future for motherhood?* London: Pandora Press.

Röhrs, Hermann. 1983. *Frieden—eine pädagogische Aufgabe. Idee und Realität der Friedenspädagogik.* (Peace—an educational task. Ideas and reality in peace education.) Agenter Pedersen: Westermann.

Romstad, Bett. 1982. *Hvorfor egen kvinneorganisering for fred?* [Why have a separate women's movement for peace?] Paper delivered at a seminar on "Women and Militarism" held at Sundvollen, November 11–12, sponsored by the International Peace Research Institute of Oslo. A summary of the paper is given in *PRIO Report 13/83. pp. 20–29.*

Rotblat, Joseph (Ed.). 1982. *Scientists—The Arms Race and Disarmament.* London: Taylor and Francis, Ltd.

Rubin, J.A., and Brown, B.R. 1975. *The Social Psychology of Bargaining and Negotiation.* New York: Academic.

Ruge, Marie Holmboe. 1967. Fredsforskning. [Peace research]. In *Alternativer—5 års fredsdebatt.* (Alternatives—Five years of peace debate) Pax Forlag.

Ryland, Shane. 1977. "The Theory and Impact of Gandhi's Feminism." *Journal of South Asian Literature.* 3/4.

Samhällskunnskap och samhällssyn. 1976. (Knowledge about and attitudes towards society) En internationell studie. Stockholm. Utbildningsförlaget. Skolöverstyrelsen 1976. This Swedish study is part of a bigger project undertaken by the UNESCO Institue in Hamburg. Here the attitudes of youngsters from various countries to important social and global questions were measured.

Scanzoni, John. 1978. *Sex Roles, Women's Work and Marital Conflict: A Study of Family Change.* Lexington, MA: Hearth/Lexington.

Scanzoni, John. 1979. Strategies for Changing Male Family Roles: Research and Practice Implication. *The Family Coordinator.* 27: 4: 435–45.

Schmid, Alex and de Graaf, Janny. 1982. *Violence as Communication. Insurgent Terrorism and the Western News Media.* London and Beverly Hills: Sage Publications.

Scholten-Van Iterson, Gonie. 1982. Women's Work for Peace—Some Aspects. In *Women of Europe in action for Peace.* A report on a conference for action to end the arms race, for disarmament and for peace called by Women's International League for Peace and Freedom. Nov. 1981.

Sears, R.R.; Maccoby, E.E.; and Levin, H. 1957. *Patterns of Child Rearing.* New York: Row, Peterson.

Second Medium-Term Plan. (1984–1989) 1983. 4 XC/4 Approved. Paris: UNESCO.

Sharara, Yolla Polity. Women and the Politics in Lebanon. Khamsin: *Journal of Revolutionary Socialists of the Middle East. No. 6. 1978.*

Sharma, Arvind. 1981. Gandhi as a Feminist Emancipator and Kasturba as a Martyr. *Gandhi Marg.* 28: 214–221.

Sivard, Ruth Leger. 1981. *World Military and Social Expenditures.* Leesburg, Virginia: World Priorities.

Sjöberg, Svein. 1982. "Soft Girls and Hard Science." *Tidsskrift for Nordisk forening for Pedagogisk Forskning. The Journal of the Nordic Society for Educational Research.* No. 1-2. Published at the University of Lund.

Sjöberg, Svein and Lie, Svein. 1984. Myke jenter: harde tag (Soft girls and hard science). Oslo: Universitetsforlaget.

Skinningsrud, Tone. 1982. Education for Equality—The Similarity in Strategies for Eliminating Class, Gender and Ethnic Differences in Education. *Tidsskrift för Nordisk Förening för Pedagogisk Forskning* [Journal of the Nordic Society for Educational Research] 1-2: 14–20. Special issue on women and education.

Southard, Barbara. 1981. "The Feminism of Mahatma Gandhi." *Gandhi Marg* 31 October.

Spedding, J.; Ellis, R.L.; and Heath, D.N. (eds.) 1962. *The works of Francis Bacon.* Facsimile, Stuttgart-Bad Cannstate. Vol. IV.

Spender, Dale. 1980. *Man-made Language.* London: Routledge and Kegan Paul.

Spender, Dale. 1981a. *Men's Education—Women's View.* Writers and Readers. London: Publishing Cooperative.

Spender, Dale. (ed.) 1981b. *Men's Studies Modified. The Impact of Feminism on the Academic Disciplines.* Oxford: Pergamon Press.

Spender, Dale. 1982. *Women of Ideas and What Men Have Done to Them.* London: Routledge and Kegan Paul.

Spender, Dale, and Sarah, Elizabeth. (eds.) 1980. *Learning to Lose. Sexism and Education.* London: The Women's Press.

Stark, Rodney, and McEvoy, James. 1970. "Middle-Class Violence." *Psychology Today.*

Steinem, Gloria. 1980. "Authoritarianism begins at home—the Nazi Connection." *Ms,* nos. 4 and 5, October and November.

Steinmetz, Suzanne K., and Strauss, Murray A. (eds.) 1974. *Violence in the Family.* New York: Dodd, Mead and Company.

Stene, Helga. 1982. *Norske kvinners motstandsarbeid under andre verdenkrig.* [The civilian resistance by Norwegian women during the Second World War). Paper delivered at a seminar on "Women and Militarism" held at Sundvollen, near Oslo, November 1–12, sponsored by the International Peace Research Institute of Oslo.

Strauss, Murray. 1974. "Some Social Antecedents of Physical Punishment." In Steinmetz, Suzanne and Murray Strauss, *Violence in the Family.* New York: Dodd, Mead, and Co.

Strauss, A. 1978. *Negotiations: Varieties, Contexts, Processes and Social Order.* San Francisco: Jossey-Bass.

Thee, Marek. 1982. "The Race in Military Technology." In Roblat, Joseph (Ed.), *Scientists—The Arms Race and Disarmament.* London: Taylor & Francis Ltd. p. 51.

Thee, Marek. 1983. "Swords into Ploughshares: The Quest for Peace and Human Development." *International Labour Review.* **122**: 5. September–October.

Thinking Ahead. 1977. *UNESCO and the Challenges of Today and Tomorrow.* Paris: UNESCO.

Thomas, P. 1964. *Indian Women through the Ages.* London: Asia Publishing House.

Thompson, Dorothy (ed.) 1983. *Over our dead bodies. Women against the bomb.* London: Virago Press.

Thorsson, Inga. 1978. *Nedrustning—utvikling.* Fra FN's spesialsesjon 1 1978. *FN— Sambandet Oslo. (Disarmament—development. From the UN Special Session in 1978.)*

Thygesen, B. 1971. *Faderens betydning for kønsrolleudviklingen.* (The importance of the father for sex role development) *Nordisk Psykologi XXIII* pp. 275–89.

Tiffany, Jennifer. 1981. Equal Opportunity Trap. In Chapkis (ed.): *Loaded Questions. Women in the military.* Amsterdam and Washington, DC: Transnational Institute.

Tiger, Lionel. 1969. *Men in Groups.* New York: Random House.

Tiger, Lionel, and Fox, Robin. 1971. *The Imperial Animal.* New York: Holt, Rinehart and Winston.

United Nations. *The Relationship Between Disarmament and Development.* Study Series 5, New York, 1982. Can also be identified as document A/36/356, 5 October 1981 to the United Nations General Assembly thirty-sixth session, agenda items 51 (d) and 69. Also called "the Thorsson report" after its chairwoman.

U.N. High Commissioner for Refugees. The Situation of Women Refugees the World Over. *Document No. A/CONF.94/24* presented to the World Conference of the United Nations Decade for Women.

Van der Gaast, Sonja. 1981. "Women Against Nuclear Weapons." In *Women of Europe in Action for Peace.* Conference report from a conference held in the Netherlands, November 27–29, 1981, sponsored by Women's International League for Peace and Freedom. pp. 40–45.

Vargas, Ines. 1983. *Women and Violence. PRIO Working paper 17/83.* Oslo: International Peace Research Institute of Oslo.

von Suttner, Bertha. 1883. *Inventarium einer Seele.* (Inventory of a soul) Leipzig. W. Friedrich.

von Suttner, Bertha. *Es Löwos.* 1883. Dresden, E. Pierson, 1894.

von Suttner, Bertha. 1885. *Ein schlecter Mensch.* (A bad person) München O. Heinricks.

von Suttner, Bertha. 1886. *High Life.* München. O. Heinricks.

von Suttner, Bertha. 1888. *Das Maschinenzeitalter.* (The Age of Machines) Zurich. Verlags-Magazin.

von Suttner, Bertha. 1889. *Die Waffen nieder.* (Down with arms.) Dresden, E. Pierson.

von Suttner, Bertha. 1901. *Die Waffen nieder. Eine Lebensgeschichte.* (Down with Arms. A Life Story.) Dresden, E. Pierson.

von Suttner, Bertha. 1902. *Martha's Kinder. Eine Fortsetzung zu "die Waffen nieder."* (Martha's Children. A Continuation of Down with Arms.) Dresden, E. Pierson.

von Suttner, Bertha. 1904. *Briefe an einen Toten.* [Letters to a deceased] Dresden, E. Pierson.

von Suttner, Bertha. 1906. Gesammelte Schriften. 12 Bd. (Collected Works. 12 Volumes).

von Suttner, Bertha. 1909. Memoiren. (Memoirs) Stuttgart. Deutsche Verlags-Anstalt.

von Suttner, Bertha. 1912. Die Barbarisierung der Luft. (The Barbarization of the Air.) Berlin: Verlag der "Friedens-Warte."

Wernersson, Inga. 1977. *Köndifferentiering i grundskolan;* (Sex differentiation in the elementary school) Göteborg Studies in Educational Sciences. 22. Göteborg: Göteborg Universitet.

Whiting, B.B.; and Whiting, J.W.M. 1973. "Altruistic and Egoistic Behavior in Six cultures." In L. Nader and T.W. Maretzki (eds.), *Cultural Illness and Health: Essays in Human Adaptation.* Washington, D.C.: American Anthropological Association. (Cited in Maccoby, 1980).

Whiting, B.B.; and Whiting, J.W.M. 1975. *Children of Six Cultures.* Cambridge: Harvard University Press.

Williamson, Nancy. 1978. *Boys or Girls? Parents Preference and Sex Control.* Washington, D.C.: Population Reference Bureau. (Cited in Newland, 1979.)

Willis, David. 1978. "Divorce Rate—A Concern in USSR." *Christian Science Monitor.* January 9. (Cited in Newland, 1979).

Wolfgang, M. and Strohm, R.B. 1956. The Relationship Between Alcohol and Criminal Homicide. *Quarterly Journal of Studies of Alcohol.* No. 17.

Woolf, Virginia. 1938. *Three Guineas.* London: The Hogarth Press. Reprinted in Penguin Books, New York, 1977.

"World nuclear stockpiles." 1983. In *World Arms and Disarmament.* SIPRI Yearbook. London: Taylor and Francis.

Wormdahl, Cecilie. 1979. *Kvinner i strid.* (Women in Strife) Gyldendal.

Ynestra, King. 1983. "All is Connectedness: Scenes from the Women's Pentagon Action." USA. In Jones, Lynne (ed.) *Keeping the Peace.* London: The Women's Press.

Yuval-Davis, Nira. 1981. "The Israeli Example." In Chapkis (ed.). *Loaded Questions. Women in the Military.* Amsterdam and Washington, DC: Transnational Institute.

Zetkin, Clara: *Ausgewählte Reden und Schriften.* (Selected speeches and works.) Berlin. Institut t. Marxismus-Leninismus. Dietz Verlag. 1957–1960. Vol. I. Auswahl aus de Fahren. 1889–1917.

Ziman, John. 1982. "Basic Principles." In *Scientists—The Arms Race and Disarmament.* London: Taylor and Francis Ltd.

Zuckerman, Lord. 1980. *Science Advisers and Nuclear Weapons.* London: The Menard Press.

Index

About the Author

Birgit Brock-Utne is a social scientist, who holds the position of Associate Professor at the Institute for Educational Research at the University of Oslo, Norway. She has studied in the United States—at Stanford University, California and the University of Illinois, where she received her Masters in Education. Her main academic interests are peace education, peace research, feminist studies and educational innovation and action research. She has written several books and a number of articles on these issues, predominantly in her native Norwegian. She has been a guest researcher at the International Institute of Peace Research, Oslo and is widely known as a peace educator and peace activist in her own country. In addition, Professor Brock-Utne has served the international community as a consultant to UNESCO, OECD, the European Council, the Nordic Council and the United Nations. Currently, she is a member of the board of the Nordic Society for Educational Research and of the International Peace Research Association.

\ I \